Lord,
I Give You
This Day

366 Appointments with God

Lord, I Give You *This Day*

KAY ARTHUR

WATERBROOK
PRESS

LORD, I GIVE YOU THIS DAY
PUBLISHED BY WATERBROOK PRESS
12265 Oracle Boulevard, Suite 200
Colorado Springs, Colorado 80921
A division of Random House Inc.

Italics in Scripture quotations indicate the author's added emphasis.

Material adapted from *Lord, Give Me a Heart for You; Lord, I Need Grace to Make It Today; Lord, I Want to Know You; Lord, Only You Can Change Me; Lord, Heal My Hurts; Lord, Is It Warfare? Teach Me to Stand; Lord, I'm Torn Between Two Masters; Lord, Where Are You When Bad Things Happen?*

10-Digit ISBN: 1-4000-7160-7
13-Digit ISBN: 978-1-4000-7160-9

Library of Congress Cataloging-in-Publication Data
Arthur, Kay, 1933-
Lord, I give you this day : 366 appointments with God / by Kay Arthur. — 1st ed.
p. cm.
ISBN-13: 978-1-4000-7160-9
I. Title.
BV4811.A7735 2006
242'.2—dc22

2006028052

Printed in the United States of America
2006—First Edition

10 9 8 7 6 5 4 3 2 1

To Mark and Leslie
for the days ahead

All to Jesus I surrender;
All to Him I freely give;
I will ever love and trust Him,
In His presence daily live.

All to Jesus I surrender;
Humbly at His feet I bow,
Worldly pleasures all forsaken;
Take me, Jesus, take me now.

All to Jesus I surrender;
Make me, Savior, wholly Thine;
Let me feel the Holy Spirit,
Truly know that Thou art mine.

All to Jesus I surrender;
Lord, I give myself to Thee;
Fill me with Thy love and power;
Let Thy blessing fall on me.

All to Jesus I surrender;
Now I feel the sacred flame.
Oh, the joy of full salvation!
Glory, glory, to His Name!

—Judson W. Van DeVenter

Introduction

Do you long for intimate communion with the Father? Are you eager to experience God's grace in all its glorious aspects?

Do you desire to truly walk by the Spirit, not giving in to the pull of the world and the flesh?

Do you yearn for God's balm to heal the wounds of the past?

Would you like to face each day with quiet confidence and bold faith, fully prepared to cope with whatever it brings?

All this and more—all the abundance of life promised by Christ—comes with surrender, my friend.

For believers, surrendering to God is not a one-time occurrence; it's a matter of continually bowing our hearts before the Lord, laying our desire for control at His feet, and rising again to do whatever He asks us to do, through the power of the Holy Spirit. Surrender means inviting the Potter to reshape us and transform us, moment by moment, into the image of His Son, Jesus Christ. It means taking God at His word, trusting that He can and will use even our most painful circumstances for our good and His glory.

When you make a consistent practice of surrendering, inviting God to complete His good work in you no matter what it takes, you'll find your life and your relationships transformed. As you stop trying to control the direction of your life and instead allow God's Word and wisdom to guide your footsteps, you'll realize that His grace is sufficient for every encounter along the way. When you stop struggling against the frustrations of the day, choosing rather to dwell in the everlasting arms of the eternal God, you'll gain a deeper understanding of the character of your Lord and of His unfailing, unshakable love.

While your circumstances may be difficult, even painful, through the discipline of surrender you will find God's strength perfected in your weakness. And you will be able to face each day, each moment, each opportunity and challenge with a hope that does not falter.

That's what this devotional is all about, beloved. Each brief, one-page reading addresses the challenges and joys of surrendered living and points you to unchangeable, eternal truths about your God, His Word, and His love for you. Within each devotional, you'll find a verse or two set in boldface; these scriptures provide key thoughts on which you'll want to meditate throughout your day. You may even want to memorize these verses so you can bring them to mind and draw on their insights for encouragement and guidance.

I pray that God will use this book to strengthen and deepen your relationship with Him. May the verses from Scripture whet your appetite for His Word that it may become more precious to you than your necessary food. And in the days ahead, may you commit your way to the Lord, fully trusting Him to give you the desires of your heart.

~

Thank You, heavenly Father, for the privilege of knowing and being sanctified by Your Word, which is truth (John 17:17). May Your truths divinely minister to the precious readers of this book.

January 1

Oh, beloved of God, wouldn't you like to know that at the end of your life—not to mention the end of this day, the end of this year—you could declare, as the apostle Paul did, **"I have fought the good fight, I have finished the course, I have kept the faith"** (2 Timothy 4:7)?

Wouldn't you like to be assured that you could experience all the difficult situations Paul faced and say in total sincerity and truth, without one drop of egotism, "Follow me. Be an imitator of me, even as I am of Christ Jesus" (1 Corinthians 11:1; Philippians 3:17)?

Can you imagine having such confidence? Confidence, not brashness. Confidence in the midst of cross fire. Confidence even if the government threatened to take your life for what you believed and lived. Confidence that you could stand alone, even though others deserted you because they loved this present life more than the next.

This is the heart I long for, and I trust you do too, my friend. And because Paul, a human like us, had it, we can have hearts that beat with bold faith and passion for God if we'll follow his example.

When your heart belongs to God and you will to do His will, you can walk in the confidence that God will lead you by His Spirit, step by step. Our responsibility is simply to commit our way unto Him in faith's trust, and He will bring it to pass. (See Proverbs 3:5–6.)

Lord, thank You for holding my hand, for leading me in Your paths. Establish my steps today that I may walk in a way that is pleasing to You.

January 2

May I ask, dear one, what is on your calendar for today, for this week? In the midst of all of life's demands, have you scheduled some time to be alone with your heavenly Father, to hear His words to you?

I believe it's absolutely crucial that you and I slow our pace and discipline our time in order to be in the Word of God on a daily basis. Why? Because when we're not in the Word—reading it through consistently—we forget who our God is and what He expects and requires. We have a tendency to rationalize our humanity and forget His holiness.

We lose our perspective of eternity and become ensnared in the temporal. We lose the burning, overriding passion fueled by truth that brings our flesh into subjection. We lose the heart-desire to be holy, to please God, to be perfect even as our heavenly Father is perfect. We lose that driving inner hunger for righteousness, which comes in those quiet moments of meditation as we sit at the feet of the Most High God in prayer and adoration.

Solomon eloquently expressed the importance of our spending time in God's Word: "**My son, give attention to my words.... Keep them in the midst of your heart. For they are life to those who find them, and health to all their body**" (Proverbs 4:20–22).

How can you be sure to keep God and His Word in the midst of your heart today?

Father, give me a hunger and passion not only to read Your life-giving words but also to use them as my guide for every decision, opportunity, or challenge I face today.

January 3

Are you wrestling today with the uncertainties of life, struggling to find a solid footing for your faith?

Oh, friend, let me assure you that no matter what changes are occurring in your life, in your job, in your family, in your nation, there is always one stabilizing factor upon which you can rest: your God. He is the immovable Rock. You can hide in Him.

God is from everlasting to everlasting—the beginning and the end (Revelation 21:6). He always has been, and He always will be. The prophet Habakkuk prayed, **"Are You not from everlasting, O LORD, my God, my Holy One?"** (1:12).

If He is eternal, then all things find their beginning and end in Him. "All things came into being through Him, and apart from Him nothing came into being that has come into being" (John 1:3). "For from Him and through Him and to Him are all things" (Romans 11:36).

One thing will always remain: God. And because He is immutable—unchanging—He will always be the same, and He will never leave you nor forsake you (Hebrews 13:5).

He is always there with arms opened wide, your everlasting Father God.

May I suggest you take a few minutes to meditate on the fact that no matter what else in your life may change, God will not. He can bring stability to your life. Claim that in faith.

Everlasting, unchanging God, I praise You for Your eternal faithfulness, and I claim Your promise to never leave nor forsake me.

January 4

Oh, friend, is your heart troubled? Is fear lurking in the shadows of your consciousness? Do you feel insecure about anything at all? If the answer to any of these questions is yes, will you turn to your protector, the One who stands waiting for you to come and bury yourself in the security of all He is?

Remember, "**The name of the LORD is a strong tower; the righteous runs into it and is safe**" (Proverbs 18:10).

The Father longs for us to know more of who He is that we might more fully "trust in the name of the LORD and rely on [our] God" (Isaiah 50:10). Just before He went to Calvary, Jesus prayed on our behalf "that they may know You, the only true God, and Jesus Christ whom You have sent" (John 17:3).

Beloved, where do you run in time of need? When the hounds of trouble, worry, and fear pursue you; when the dogs of temptation, corruption, and evil seek to overtake you; when your energy is spent; when weakness saps you; when you feel you cannot run any longer, where do you turn? Who is your refuge?

The goal of Paul's life was "that I may know Him" (Philippians 3:10). How I pray it will become the goal of your life!

~

I want to know more of You, dear Lord, so that I can in full confidence and faith throw the weight of my life on You at every moment of the day. "On God my salvation and my glory rest; the rock of my strength, my refuge is in God" (Psalm 62:7).

January 5

Do you ever wonder why God created you? What is the purpose for your life? And how can this purpose direct your choices today?

In Isaiah 43 we read, "**You are precious in My sight.... Everyone who is called by My name, and whom I have created for My glory, whom I have formed, even whom I have made**" (verses 4, 7).

So God has created you for His glory. What does that mean to you, oh, child of God, called by His name? Think about it. How will you live today if you're living for His glory?

Let's look at one other scripture that describes God's purpose for you: "For You created all things, and because of Your will they existed, and were created" (Revelation 4:11). According to this verse, you were created for His will. The King James Version says "pleasure." In essence, they are the same. If we live for His will, that is His pleasure, or if we bring Him pleasure, it is because we have done His will.

You and I have been created for God's glory, for His pleasure. Our lives are to be lived in such a way as to reflect Him, to show the world the character of God—His love, His peace, His mercy, His gentleness. We are to live for Him, to accomplish His will. To miss this purpose is to miss fulfillment. It is to have existed rather than to have lived.

How I pray we'll be guided by these truths today.

Creator God, how wonderful to know that I am precious in Your sight. Help me to live every moment of this day for Your glorious purposes.

January 6

Precious one, are you living in the awesome reality of your freedom from sin and death?

When Christ died on the cross, all our sins were forgiven. We are fully reconciled to God through Christ's death. This truth is critical because it's through sin that Satan gains power over us.

The writer of Hebrews, in referring to Jesus, says:

> **Therefore, since the children share in flesh and blood, He Himself likewise also partook of the same, that through death He might render powerless him who had the power of death, that is, the devil, and might free those who through fear of death were subject to slavery all their lives.** (2:14–15)

Until Calvary, Satan had the power of death, the authority to hold us in sin's consequence, which is eternal punishment and separation from God. But Jesus became flesh and blood in order to die for us and render him powerless.

Our Kinsman Redeemer took care of that which gave Satan control over us—sin! At the moment Jesus cried, "My God, My God, why hast Thou forsaken Me?" all the sins of mankind were transferred to the head of the sinless Lamb of God. Through His sacrifice, our sins were covered once for all time (Hebrews 10:8–12).

Sin, Satan, and death no longer have any power over us. Hallelujah!

~

Almighty God, what peace there is in knowing that You reign sovereign in the world and in my life. Thank You that I can walk in righteousness because Jesus has broken the chains of sin and death.

Whatever circumstances you face today, I have great news: **"But we have this treasure in earthen vessels, so that the surpassing greatness of the power will be of God and not from ourselves"** (2 Corinthians 4:7).

You are a vessel, precious one, made by God to contain God. Who could ask for any higher privilege? You—you, a human being—indwelt by God! That is the height of glory. Yet how is that height of glory manifested to others?

It is manifested in the difficulties of life that all humanity faces and deals with on one level or another. It is manifested when we experience "death"—death to a dream, a hope, an ambition. Death when we are despised, rejected, scorned. But because of the presence of God within us, because of the power of God, it's a death that brings life to others.

Jesus told His disciples, "Unless a grain of wheat falls into the earth and dies, it remains alone; but if it dies, it bears much fruit" (John 12:24). Fruit is born out of death; death produces life. As we face difficulties, others can see that something—some power, some knowledge—enables us to handle them in a way that they could not, in a way that isn't natural.

And when they ask, they find out that the difference is God. They see in us His grace, and this brings glory to the One who fills the vessel.

Will you walk through this day with the truth of your calling stamped on your heart?

~

Father God, help me to remember that I am a vessel filled with Your presence. When trouble and frustration come my way, let my response reflect Your power and grace.

January 8

May I ask, what does your life today reveal about where you will spend eternity?

Jesus told a parable in which he contrasted weeds, or tares, with wheat—righteous individuals who will inherit the kingdom of heaven:

> The kingdom of heaven may be compared to a man who sowed good seed in his field. But while his men were sleeping, his enemy came and sowed tares among the wheat, and went away. **But when the wheat sprouted and bore grain, then the tares became evident also.** (Matthew 13:24–26)

It's difficult to distinguish weeds from wheat. Only by their fruit can you really tell which is which. Are you wheat or tares? What does the fruit of your life bear witness to?

As you consider these questions, let me give you two cautions. First, don't allow yourself to be unjustly condemned by the accuser of the brethren, who would have you doubt a salvation you genuinely possess. On the other hand, don't allow the enemy to deceive you into thinking you have salvation when you don't! Walking down an aisle, being baptized, being born into a Christian family, joining a church, or making a public "profession" of faith is no guarantee of salvation.

God knows who are His. His Spirit will not only bear witness with your spirit, but He has also given you the short epistle of 1 John that you might inspect your own fruit and see if it gives evidence of true salvation.

~

Ask God to speak to your spirit through His Spirit and make evident to you the state of your heart.

January 9

Beloved, has the great liberating reality of your resurrection to new life in Christ gripped your heart?

Salvation brings us a whole new life because of our identification with Jesus Christ. For this reason Paul wrote in 2 Corinthians 5:17: "**Therefore if anyone is in Christ, he is a new creature; the old things passed away; behold, new things have come.**" Old things have passed because you died with Christ. New things have come because you were raised with Christ.

Romans 6:6 says that our old self, or old man, was crucified with Jesus "in order that our body of sin might be done away with, so that we would no longer be slaves to sin." This means that everything you were before you were saved died with Jesus Christ. You are now a new creature and are able to walk in newness of life because the death of the old man set you free. You are no longer a slave to sin.

When you receive Jesus Christ as your Savior, you become a participant in the New Covenant, the covenant of grace, which gives you the indwelling Holy Spirit. You are no longer under the Law.

And because you are no longer under the Law, sin cannot be master over you.

Oh, won't you rejoice in this truth and let it guide your life today as you serve God faithfully in the power of the Holy Spirit?

I thank You, God, that You have made me a new creature in Christ Jesus. Thank You for freeing me from slavery to sin so that I can serve You this day in righteousness.

January 10

Are you starting your day with the confidence that, in Christ, you have absolutely everything you need to live victoriously in every circumstance you encounter? All you have to do is lay hold of it.

The writer of Hebrews admonishes us to "**see to it that no one comes short of the grace of God; that no root of bitterness springing up causes trouble, and by it many be defiled**" (12:15). What does it mean to come short of the grace of God? First, let's define *grace.* You have often heard the definition that grace is "unmerited favor," and that's exactly right. Grace is God's favor to those of us who did not merit, earn, or deserve it in any way.

But I've fallen in love with another definition of grace: "Grace is all that Christ is, made available to me." Therefore, for you to fall short of the grace of God is for you to fail to appropriate all that God has for you!

Romans 5:2 says that when you were saved, you obtained an introduction by faith into the grace of God in which you stand. There it is! Everything that you will ever need, made available to you! You are standing in God's adequacy for every situation of life. To fall short then of the grace of God is to fail to appropriate that in which you stand. It's just a matter of stooping down and in faith scooping it up, because you stand with all the grace of God surrounding you.

So stoop and scoop!

Loving Father, You have given me all that I need to live sensibly and righteously in this present age. Let me never fall short of Your grace by forgetting all that You've made available to me.

January 11

Do you realize, beloved, that God's grace isn't just something that has redeemed us from past sin but that His grace is active in our lives today?

And because it is, you and I are able to live productive lives that have eternal significance. Consider Paul's encouragement to the Thessalonians: "**Now may our Lord Jesus Christ Himself and God our Father, who has loved us and given us eternal comfort and good hope by grace, comfort and strengthen your hearts in every good work and word**" (2 Thessalonians 2:16–17).

Often we think of grace as merely doctrine that explains our salvation, something that occurred in the past. But grace is power in action. Oh, if we could only get this truth into our heads and then into our daily lives, what passion it would bring to our service to Him and for Him!

Remember, grace is all of God. Man just becomes the vessel to contain the grace of God. Consequently, when it comes to a life of obedience and service, even the desire and the power to obey and to serve God come from Him.

God not only has given us comfort and hope by His grace, but He is the One who strengthens our "hearts in every good work and word." Our motivation to live for Him comes from Him. And our ability to do what He desires comes from Him. It is all of grace!

Gracious Father, help me to keep my eyes always on You, remembering that any work I do is to be accomplished for Your glory and by Your strength and grace.

As you set priorities for the days ahead, what role does God's will play in your planning and decision making? Are you motivated by a desire to please Him in all that you do?

Philippians 2:12–13 assures us that God not only gives us the desire to do His good pleasure but that He gives us the ability to do it: "So then, my beloved, just as you have always obeyed, not as in my presence only, but now much more in my absence, **work out your salvation with fear and trembling; for it is God who is at work in you, both to will and to work for His good pleasure.**"

God doesn't tell us to work *for* our salvation; He tells us to work *out* our salvation. We are to carry out to completion that which God works in us.

In light of that truth, won't you take a few minutes and search out where you are? Have you felt God urging you to a certain course of action? Have you felt there was something you should do but you resisted either because you felt inadequate or because you simply didn't want to do it? How does your reasoning stack up against the truths of God's Word?

Go to God in prayer and ask Him to help you carry out to completion whatever He wants to do in you or through you. You will be amazed by the change in your life when you pull out the stops and let God be God in all of His power!

~

Please show me, dear God, what You'd have me do today. I surrender myself to will and to work for Your pleasure.

January 13

Precious one, do you ever find yourself battling a sense of inadequacy? So many people do, and I'm among them when I forget the awesome truths laid out in the Bible, the truths of what God says about every child of His.

Consider, for example, Paul's powerful reminder: **"Not that we are adequate in ourselves to consider anything as coming from ourselves, but our adequacy is from God"** (2 Corinthians 3:5).

I've been on my knees before the Lord, in tears asking Him to forgive me for forgetting these truths, for failing to live in the light of them, for looking to man rather than to Him, for allowing what I see, feel, and think is necessary or strategic to overtake what I know is truth.

I am adequate because I am a child of God—and so are you. Nothing, absolutely nothing else matters but to walk in the knowledge of that adequacy. To live accordingly in total dependence upon Him alone. If we do that—and if that alone is our passion, our single goal—then we'll have succeeded in the eyes of the only One who really counts, Almighty God. And we will not be found inadequate.

He alone is the One to whom we answer, dear friend.

~

O Father, help me to lay hold of the truth of my adequacy in You. Show me how to stand against all the wiles and schemes of the evil one and to detect his lies, to bring every thought captive to the obedience of Jesus Christ. I thank You that You have made me adequate and called me to this task, and therefore I am not alone. You are my adequacy. How I thank You for hearing and answering me.

January 14

Have you found yourself seeking the approval of others, worried that you'll never be "good enough," no matter how hard you strive? Take a moment to meditate on Paul's words of truth: "You are our letter, written in our hearts, known and read by all men; being manifested that **you are a letter of Christ, cared for by us, written not with ink but with the Spirit of the living God, not on tablets of stone but on tablets of human hearts**" (2 Corinthians 3:2–3).

One of the main reasons we tend to focus on our inadequacy, even though we're truly born of God, is because we forget what it means to be a letter of Christ, written by the Spirit of God. We slip into our old, performance-based ways of thinking. Or we come under the influence of those who would seek to make sure we stay on that straight and narrow path and therefore give us their list of the dos and don'ts of holiness.

The truth, as revealed in God's Word, is that we're made adequate only one way: through the New Covenant and the ministry of the Spirit. Our adequacy will never come from ourselves. Did you see that, precious one? Let me say it again: your adequacy will never come from anything you can do or be apart from Christ. Your adequacy will come only from God.

Forgive me, God, for trying to live in my own strength, for pursuing the good opinion of others rather than seeking Your heart. Thank You for Your Holy Spirit, who makes me adequate for Your service.

January 15

Do you realize how many people are disappointed with their Christianity? It just does not seem to satisfy, so they give themselves to temporal things, chasing material possessions, financial security, a beautiful body. Could it be that they have never experienced true Christianity?

Look at those who claim to be children of God. How many individuals do you see whose earnest expectation and hope is "that I will not be put to shame in anything, but that with all boldness, Christ will even now, as always, be exalted in my body, whether by life or by death" (Philippians 1:20)? How many do you know who live a life that says, "For to me, to live is Christ and to die is gain" (Philippians 1:21)?

Now don't write off those who live this way as the fanatics, the supersaints, the ones whose duty it is to live that life because they are called to full-time service of some sort. Commitment to the will of God ought to be the norm for every one of His children!

What about you, beloved? Are you ready to make the psalmist's words your own, to pray with all sincerity, "**With all my heart I have sought You; do not let me wander from Your commandments**" (Psalm 119:10)?

~

Lord, I long to see You glorified in everything I do. Give me the strength and courage to remain faithful to Your will today, that every word and action may exalt You.

January 16

Are you considering compromise in some area of your life? Perhaps you've already lowered your standards just a little when it comes to where you surf on the Internet, the movies you choose, or the conversations you have with friends. Does what we do really matter as long as you and I acknowledge Jesus as Lord and tell Him we want His free gift of eternal life?

Yes, it does!

Remember the question Jesus posed to those who claimed to be His disciples: **"Why do you call Me, 'Lord, Lord,' and do not do what I say?"** (Luke 6:46).

Lord is more than a word; it indicates a relationship. The lordship of God means His total possession of us and our submission to Him as Lord and Master. We will never know His sufficiency apart from knowing Him as Lord, as Master. Only a servant can be totally dependent upon his master to meet all of his needs.

Keep these questions before you today: Can a person really be saved and deny God's right to rule over his life? Can you call Him "Lord," refuse to do the things He tells you to do, and still go to heaven? Read Matthew 7:21–27 and meditate on Jesus' words.

Grasping the reality of His lordship could make all the difference in your understanding of true Christianity and in how you choose to live day by day.

My life holds true meaning only as I do Your will, dear Lord. Help me to hear Your voice today and to obey without hesitation. I want to serve You with a whole heart, submitting to Your wise and gracious instruction.

January 17

You may know many people who call themselves "spiritual seekers" yet who never seem to truly see God. Others call themselves agnostics or even atheists, citing lack of evidence for God's existence. And sadly, even many who call themselves Christians confess they rarely hear from God or see His hand at work in their lives.

So what's the problem? The reason so many people can't really see God and don't have an intimate relationship with Him is because their hearts are so defiled. They are so filled with the filth and muck of this world that they have no spiritual sensitivity.

That is why it is vital for you to spend time being made clean every single day. Stand in the holy shower of God's Word, and scrub yourself from head to toe. Be made clean by the washing of the water of His Word (Ephesians 5:25–26). Let it convict you of any sin that clings to you, then seek God's forgiveness through confession. Get rid of the stench of this world. Then you can pray with a pure heart, "**As for me, I shall behold Your face in righteousness; I will be satisfied with Your likeness when I awake**" (Psalm 17:15).

When you allow the Word of God to purify your heart and mind, when you consistently spend time in confession and repentance, you will be transformed. Your life will be a sweet fragrance in the nostrils of God.

~

Think about these things and talk to God about them. If you have neglected His Word, then confess that and get into the habit of spending time in the Scriptures. Bible studies and other books can help you, but you must also make sure that you read through God's Word consistently.

January 18

Do you find yourself caught up in the busyness of life, so concerned about what you feel you need to accomplish that you aren't taking care of yourself?

Consider Paul's words to believers who felt pressured to conform to certain dietary restrictions or physical demonstrations of righteousness: "**These are matters which have, to be sure, the appearance of wisdom in self-made religion and self-abasement and severe treatment of the body, but are of no value against fleshly indulgence**" (Colossians 2:23).

For years I thought it wasn't spiritual to sleep, and I sometimes drove my body mercilessly. However, over time God has made me aware of the fact that we cannot abuse our bodies without paying a price. There are natural laws; we live in bodies of flesh that have God-ordained limitations, that need a minimum of eight hours of sleep and the proper nourishment of wholesome foods in order to operate at their maximum.

I believe God would have us balance our lives. When I watch Jesus in the Gospels, I see that He spent nights in prayer, but I also know that there wasn't a frenzy about His life. I love what He said in John 17:4, as He talked with His Father on behalf of His disciples and on behalf of those who would later believe on His name: "I glorified You on the earth, having accomplished the work which You have given Me to do." This is my prayer—to finish the work He gives me, not the labors I myself take on for whatever reason.

Father, help me to listen only to Your voice rather than pursuing self-imposed goals or giving in to the demands of others. Let me accomplish the work You have given me and then leave the rest in Your capable hands.

January 19

Beloved, do you consistently approach the throne of God to present your petitions and seek His ways? In Colossians 4:2 we are urged, "**Devote yourselves to prayer, keeping alert in it with an attitude of thanksgiving.**"

Oh, that you and I would remember the power of watching and praying "with all prayer and supplication in the Spirit" (Ephesians 6:18, KJV).

Such prayer is desperately needed in our own homes. Many parents are experiencing traumatic and disconcerting trials with their children and are so frustrated because there seems to be no solution in sight. They don't know what's happening, but it's disrupting their family life.

I wonder how much of it is warfare? Our children live in an environment increasingly permeated by the powers of darkness. Notice the popular items in a toy store. Take a look at mesmerizing images flashing across television, the computer, and movie screens. All those things and more are enforced and sealed in full color on moldable minds. When you consider these influences along with the things being promoted in schools and universities, it's obvious that someone is out to destroy not only our children's values but their relationship with their families.

Evil is blatant. Satan is gaining fast. Oh, Christian soldier, pray defensively for your children, grandchildren, and the children of this nation. Pray they don't enter into temptation but that they will be protected against the devil and his snares.

~

Ask the Lord to show you how to pray for your child or, if you don't have children at home, for the children in your family, church, and community.

January 20

Whose approval are you seeking today? And what effect will that have on the things you read, the words you speak, or how you spend your time?

Jesus warns, "**Beware of practicing your righteousness before men to be noticed by them; otherwise you have no reward with your Father who is in heaven**" (Matthew 6:1).

It's hard, isn't it, not to want or seek the approval of others? I know. I've been there, and this is an area I must watch very carefully.

Approbation is something we all love and, in a sense, need. Yet as disciples of Christ, Jesus moves us to a new plane, the higher plane of living for one ultimate purpose: to bring Him pleasure. How we need to "have as our ambition, whether at home or absent, to be pleasing to Him" (2 Corinthians 5:9).

To maintain this, we need to ask the same question Paul asked—and come to the same conclusion: "For am I now seeking the favor of men, or of God? Or am I striving to please men? If I were still trying to please men, I would not be a bond-servant of Christ" (Galatians 1:10).

Our approval is to come from God. And if that is so, then we must do what we do for Him, not for the reward of praise from others.

~

Let my words and actions be pleasing to You, Lord, regardless of what others may think or say. I hunger only for Your approval, and I will wait patiently for Your reward.

January 21

Is a lifestyle of righteousness making you a target of ridicule or persecution? Remember the words of Jesus: **"Blessed are you when people insult you and persecute you, and falsely say all kinds of evil against you because of Me. Rejoice and be glad, for your reward in heaven is great; for in the same way they persecuted the prophets who were before you"** (Matthew 5:11–12).

Whenever we're persecuted for the sake of righteousness, we can rejoice. Why? Because our reward in heaven is great, and because we've joined the ranks of those who counted it a privilege to lay down their lives and reputations for God.

Notice that 1 Peter 4:13 suggests there are degrees of persecution: "But to the degree that you share the sufferings of Christ, keep on rejoicing." I think God is saying: the greater the obedience, the greater the righteousness. The greater the righteousness, the greater the suffering. The greater the suffering, the greater the rejoicing.

Are you suffering at all for the gospel? If not, could it be that you've compromised God's standard of righteousness, becoming so like the world that your life does not expose their sin and, therefore, they feel comfortable with you? Or are you insulated in your own little Christian atmosphere, having forgotten that you're an ambassador for Jesus Christ, commissioned to witness to the lost?

Life speeds by so quickly! Examine yourself now so you can make any necessary changes while you still have the opportunity to live boldly for the One who died for you.

~

Help me, O God, to live unashamedly, unfalteringly for You, rejoicing in any and every opportunity to share in Christ's suffering.

January 22

How can you and I deliberately give each day to God, in complete surrender to His will and His ways?

I think it would be so good if every morning, before we ever put our feet on the floor or rise from bed, we would make the conscious decision that this day, no matter what the discipline, the cost, we are going to live for Christ. It would be the first commitment of the day, spoken aloud—a confession with our mouths from our hearts.

I say that because habits like this help us keep our focus. In 2 Corinthians 5:15, Paul says of Jesus, "**He died for all, so that they who live might no longer live for themselves, but for Him who died and rose again on their behalf.**" As we rise, we rise to live a resurrected life as new creatures for the resurrected One.

What a difference it should make to know that we're no longer to live for ourselves but for God. May it be the governing ambition of our lives to fulfill the purpose for which we were created: to be pleasing to God in life and in death.

Lord, I give You this day. No matter the cost, I choose to live for You and for Your glory. Guide my steps that I may please You in every way. Guide my thoughts so that I might have Your wisdom on the issues of the day.

January 23

Have you ever wondered how some individuals can get so messed up? Why do people ruin their lives and the lives of others? Maybe you're wondering today how in the world you or someone you love has gotten into such a mess.

I realize that the answer goes back to the problem of inherent sin. And I know that Jesus is the only person ever born who wasn't born in sin. However, I also believe that many of our problems can be traced back to someone's failure to listen to God and obey Him.

Consider God's words through the prophet Jeremiah: "**I commanded them, saying, 'Obey My voice…that it may be well with you.' Yet they did not obey or incline their ear, but walked in their own counsels and in the stubbornness of their evil heart**" (7:23–24).

When people do not listen to the Word of the Lord, it affects families, which in turn affect societies, which in turn affect nations, which in turn can affect the world. Now that may seem simplistic to you, but if you will carefully read the Word of God, you will see that it is true. Sin originally entered into the world because Adam and Eve did not listen to God. Eve listened, instead, to Satan and believed a lie. And what they did affected all future generations.

Stop for a few minutes and think about the effect your choice—to obey or disobey the instructions of the Bible—will have on those around you. What impact will this knowledge have on your actions today?

~

Your Word is a lamp to my feet and a light to my path (Psalm 119:105). Help me to listen carefully to Your wisdom and counsel and thereby avoid wounding myself or others.

January 24

Whether you're struggling with disappointment, discouragement, fear, or heartache—whatever your circumstances today, beloved—I pray you will choose to trust in the truth of this promise: "**And we know that God causes all things to work together for good to those who love God, to those who are called according to His purpose**" (Romans 8:28).

This truth is reality because God is the Great Redeemer. He redeems all your past and uses it to conform you to the image of His Son. He is for you, not against you. And if He is for you, who can be against you? Neither death, nor life, nor angels, nor principalities, nor things present, nor things to come, nor powers, nor height, nor depth, nor any other created thing shall be able to separate you from the love of God, which is in Christ Jesus our Lord (Romans 8:29–39, selected verses).

God's love is unconditional, everlasting, transforming. A love demonstrated and received at Calvary. And it is at Calvary that you, beloved of God, will find your city of refuge, your place of healing.

Won't you lay the worries and cares of your day at His feet and let Him take care of the rest?

What a comfort there is, dear Father, in knowing that You are using my present and my past to work together something good—to transform me into the image of Your Son. O Father, by Your Spirit keep the knowledge of this truth ever before me.

January 25

My friend, where do you go to satisfy your deepest longings?

In his role as a prophet, Jeremiah tried to awaken his people to the knowledge that God was the only One who could satisfy all their longings, heal all their wounds, and provide them with everything they needed for life and godliness.

God pointed out exactly where they'd gone wrong: "**For My people have committed two evils: They have forsaken Me, the fountain of living waters, to hew for themselves cisterns, broken cisterns that can hold no water**" (Jeremiah 2:13). In other words, they had turned from God and His ways to the flesh and its ways. They did not draw from Him that which is essential for life—living water.

A cistern is simply a place to store something, usually water. What you put into a cistern is what you get out of it. In contrast, a wellspring has an unseen source from which you draw. The people of Jeremiah's day had forsaken the Fountain of Living Waters for broken cisterns that couldn't even hold water! We do the same thing when we turn from the Word of God to the counsel and wisdom of man.

Oh, beloved, our loving, all-sufficient God wants to satisfy our every longing. In Him is found the wellspring of life (John 4:14). Where will you seek spiritual refreshment today?

Forgive me, Lord, for trying to find spiritual strength apart from You. Thank You that You have provided all that is essential for a godly life through Your Son, Jesus, and through the Holy Spirit, who lives in me.

January 26

Beloved of God, is your heart aching today because of a broken relationship? Are you angry with someone—or is someone, perhaps, angry with you?

All wounds ultimately have their root in sin. We have wounded others, or they us. Either way, we (or others) chose to walk independently of God and His Word. We chose not to listen, to believe, or to obey Him.

Sin wounds. Sin mars. Sin disfigures. Sin destroys. And were it not for the cross of Calvary, sin's destruction would be permanent, irreversible. But according to the Bible, the cross is God's means of healing: "**He was pierced through for our transgressions, He was crushed for our iniquities; the chastening for our well-being fell upon Him, and by His scourging we are healed**" (Isaiah 53:5).

Sin wounds; the cross heals. Through the healing power of Calvary, no matter what has happened to you, you can live without bitterness or hatred. You can live a life free from that which would otherwise distort, disfigure, or destroy you.

At the cross of Calvary, we receive all God wrought for us through our Lord's death and resurrection. Because of the cross, you and I have a representative in heaven who can intercede on our behalf. At the cross Jesus fully experienced the ravages of sin, pain, and suffering. You haven't lived through anything that Jesus has not also endured. He was made sin for you. That is Calvary love—and there is no wound that Calvary cannot heal.

I thank You, God, that Calvary's love holds healing for every wound, for every sorrow I have endured or have caused others to endure. Let Your healing love and grace flow into and through my life today.

January 27

How would those around you characterize your words and behavior? Is the love of Christ evident in how you treat other people? Or is your conversation marked by a judgmental attitude? So many Christians violate the principle of love—and it tears the heart out of their Christian testimony. Didn't Jesus say, **"By this all men will know that you are My disciples, if you have love for one another"** (John 13:35)?

Judging without love is often a symptom of patching together our own code or standard for righteousness. We develop a set of dos and don'ts that determine a person's spiritual status—and then we seek to impose these upon others. I think this is what Jesus warns against in Matthew 7 when He tells us to be careful how we judge others. He knows the weakness of our flesh. He knows that as He calls us to a high standard of living, it is apt to make us judgmental. How right He is!

How can you and I tell if we are judging with righteous judgment rather than according to appearance?

We will know by our attitude.

What is our motivation? Is love of God missing? Is love of our neighbor missing? Are we concerned about that speck in a brother's eye in a condemning way? If any of these things are true, we can know that we are breaking Jesus' commandment not to judge.

~

Forgive me, righteous God, for replacing Your standards with my own, for judging others who don't live or act as I think they should. Remove my judgmental attitude and help me walk in love.

January 28

Have you ever felt it was hopeless, that you could never really be right with God? Are some people destined to be helpless victims of their own sinful natures?

God spoke through the prophet Jeremiah, saying, "The heart is more deceitful than all else and is desperately sick; who can understand it? I, the LORD, search the heart, I test the mind, even to give to each man according to his ways, according to the results of his deeds" (Jeremiah 17:9–10).

Then there is no hope, is there? Yes, there is! **"I will put My law within them and on their heart I will write it"** (Jeremiah 31:33).

Man can be right with God! Righteousness is more than goodness; it is a right standing with God. To be righteous means to do what God says is right, to live according to His standards. But righteousness in man requires a new heart, which God has promised to those who belong to Him: "I will give you a new heart and put a new spirit within you.... I will put My Spirit within you and cause you to walk in My statutes, and you will be careful to observe My ordinances" (Ezekiel 36:26–27).

All this—a new heart and a new spirit—can be yours. You can be right with God! You can be righteous. You need not live in an endless cycle of sin and failure. You can have a new heart.

Have you already embraced God's offer of a new heart through faith in Jesus Christ? Then praise Him for this incredible gift! If not, now is the acceptable time. Now is the day of salvation (2 Corinthians 6:2). Ask God to give you a new heart and a new spirit.

January 29

Ever since Satan's triumph in the Garden of Eden, he's sought to deceive us, to blind our eyes to the light of the one truth that can free us from his dominion—the gospel of Jesus Christ. But his reign will one day come to an end.

> **The great dragon was thrown down, the serpent of old who is called the devil and Satan, who deceives the whole world; he was thrown down to the earth, and his angels were thrown down with him.** (Revelation 12:9)

Meanwhile, Satan storms heaven as the accuser of the brethren and roams the earth, seeking to devour all he can. As the ruler of this world and of the power of the air, Satan has legions of angelic beings who serve under him in various administrative capacities as rulers and authorities. Powers and dominions are his, as are the world forces of this darkness and spiritual forces of evil in the heavenly places.

He appears in the Gospels, Acts, and the Epistles. Satan plays a major role in the prophetic book of Revelation, where we learn how his wrath builds as his time grows shorter, because he is aware that soon the King of kings will come and make all His enemies His footstool! We learn that Satan will be bound for a thousand years, released for a short time, and then cast into the lake of fire.

Although that time is probably closer than we realize, it is not quite upon us. Satan still continues to be the adversary of every child of God. Therefore, we must be on the alert.

~

Keep my eyes, my heart, my mind sharp and alert to the wiles of the devil, even as I trust that You will have the ultimate victory in this spiritual battle.

January 30

My friend, what will you do when life is difficult to understand? when doubt pounds on the door of your mind? when believing God seems insane?

Will you follow the logical reasonings of man, or will you seek God in prayer, waiting to see what He will say? And when His answer comes, will you cling to His Word in faith?

When things become difficult, even unbearable, will you change your mood with the tide of circumstances, or will you rejoice in the God of your salvation? In the trial of your faith, will you turn to the arm of flesh, or will you allow God to be your strength, helping you walk above the difficulties of life?

Consider Jeremiah 17:7–8:

> **Blessed is the man who trusts in the LORD**
> **And whose trust is the LORD.**
> For he will be like a tree planted by the water,
> That extends its roots by a stream
> And will not fear when the heat comes;
> But its leaves will be green,
> And it will not be anxious in a year of drought
> Nor cease to yield fruit.

Every difficulty is a test—a test to see whether we will believe God, a trial to drive us into His arms and His promises, where we'll find Him all-sufficient. We need only to lay down our pride…and choose to cling to Him in faith.

Lord God, You are my salvation. I will trust in You and not be afraid. You are my strength and my song (Isaiah 12:2). You are my God, and I will cling to You and praise You—no matter what comes (Jeremiah 13:11).

January 31

Does it sometimes seem as if God is deaf to your cries? Are you frustrated by His delayed response and tempted to take things into your own hands, to strive for control of your circumstances or future, whatever it takes?

When we are discouraged or desperate, Hebrews 11:3 reminds us of a vital truth: "**By faith we understand that the worlds were prepared by the word of God, so that what is seen was not made out of things which are visible.**"

God is the One who is in control, the One whose Word is so powerful that it brought a universe into existence. If God can create the universe with a word, can't He also subdue all things by the Word of His power when He is ready to do so? Of course!

Would it do us any good to fight against God? to raise our puny fists in the face of Omnipotence and say, "What are You doing?" Would He need to answer us? Does He need to consult with us? Does God exist for us…or do we exist for Him? Can we lengthen our days? Can we keep ourselves alive if Elohim decides to take away our breath? Can we determine our destiny?

Let us remember that "all things have been created through Him and for Him" (Colossians 1:16). Because of this truth, my friend, we are called to submission. No matter what happens, we need to say, "From Him and through Him and to Him are all things. To Him be the glory forever" (Romans 11:36).

~

Father, I exist because of You and for You. Therefore, not my will but Yours be done. To You and You alone belong all glory and honor and power.

February 1

We can study for a lifetime and never mine all the precious gems of truth hidden in God's Word. Yet so few of us could honestly declare with the psalmist, "**I rejoice at Your word, as one who finds great treasure**" (Psalm 119:162, NKJV).

You can tell what is foremost in your life by what you give yourself to. How important is God's Word? How devoted are you to really learning it so that you can live by every word that proceeds out of the mouth of the Lord (Deuteronomy 8:3)? Are you spoon-fed, or are you learning to feed yourself? Do you flirt with Christianity, or do you love God with all your heart, all your mind, all your strength?

Oh, my beloved friend, how I pray that you will discover the riches, the strength, the peace, the power that are yours for the claiming if only you will search them out in God's Word. Why waste your time pursuing earthly treasures that will all too soon pass away and neglect the very words by which you are to live (Matthew 4:4)?

~

Take a few minutes to think over what you've just read. What does your daily schedule reveal about how much value you place on the Word of God? Talk to the Father about any ways in which you are failing to give Him and His Word priority in your life.

February 2

Idolatry does not necessarily mean worshiping something with six heads and twenty-four arms! Idols can be much more subtle and sophisticated than some crude stone statue with a ruby in its navel. Idols can also be television sets, houses, golf clubs, or careers. Idolatry can come in the form of a man, a woman, a child, a hope, a dream, or an ambition.

An idol is anything that stands between you and God and keeps you from following Him fully. It is anything that usurps the rightful place of God so that He no longer has preeminence in your life.

Note what Ezekiel 14:3 says: "Son of man, these men have set up their idols in their hearts and have put right before their faces the stumbling block of their iniquity." When you love and serve something or someone more than you love and serve God, it's an idol. There is One and only One who is to govern our passions, our desires, and our energy, and that is our Lord and King.

"Therefore if you have been raised up with Christ, keep seeking the things above, where Christ is, seated at the right hand of God. Set your mind on the things above, not on the things that are on earth" (Colossians 3:1–2).

Are there any idols in your heart that are keeping you from hungering and thirsting after righteousness? If so, in prayer, smash them at the feet of God. "**Therefore, my beloved, flee from idolatry**" (1 Corinthians 10:14).

Lord, reveal to me anything or anyone that has become a stumbling block in my pursuit of righteousness. Help me to lay aside every encumbrance and sin that entangles me and to worship You alone.

February 3

How often do you come to the end of your day and think, *How could I have possibly made such foolish mistakes?* Oh, friend, like you, I know the sadness of realizing that my words or actions were not guided by God's unfailing wisdom. Such times remind me of the truth that "**all of us like sheep have gone astray**" (Isaiah 53:6).

Over and over again God refers to us as sheep. Sheep are the dumbest of all animals. Helpless, timid, and feeble, they require constant attention and meticulous care. In my devotional book *Beloved: From God's Heart to Yours,* I wrote:

> The welfare of sheep depends solely upon the care they get from their shepherd. Therefore, the better the shepherd, the healthier the sheep. When you see weak, sickly, or pest-infested sheep, you can be sure that their shepherd really does not care for them.
>
> What is our Great Shepherd like? Learn that, and you will understand why you can confidently say, "The Lord is my shepherd; I shall not want." Believe it, and you will know a life of perfect rest.[1]

Even though we do dumb things, even though we are not perfect, even though we all stumble in many ways (James 3:2), we can succeed because the Lord is our Shepherd. In Him, we find all that we need. Thus, we can say with total confidence and conviction, "The LORD is my shepherd, I shall not want" (Psalm 23:1).

~

O blessed Shepherd, thank You for caring for me with tenderness even when I am foolish and stubborn. Lead me in the paths of righteousness, for Your name's sake.

February 4

Where do you turn first in the time of hurt, of need, of doubt?

So often we have a tendency to trust in mankind and make flesh our strength (Jeremiah 17:5) instead of turning to our God. We can be quick to run to counselors, psychologists, psychiatrists, or to the reasoning of man—and in the process we can miss what God has for us.

Where would God have you run in the time of need?

If you answered, "To Him," let me ask, what do you do when you turn to Him? Do you wait to see what He will lay on your heart? Do you seek Him through the counsel of His Word?

As you read God's Word daily, you'll find Him speaking to you in incredible ways, miraculously supplying just what you need for that specific time—or bringing to your remembrance what you have already read.

If you've spent time letting the psalms soak into your heart and mind, you can remain at peace even when trouble comes, knowing that God's help is only a prayer away: **"O Lord my God, I cried to You for help, and You healed me"** (Psalm 30:2).

If, however, you turn to alcohol, to pills, to drugs, to promiscuity, let me say that these will not help you. They will simply escort you into oblivion as they lead you into sin's bondage...into slavery and destruction.

Beloved, run to your Lord, who heals.

Thank You, Lord, that You offer healing for my wounds and relief from my pain. Help me stand strong when I am tempted to turn elsewhere for comfort.

February 5

I longed to be held in the arms of a man. I wanted security, and I thought it was to be found in a man who would become my protector, my sustainer for life. It was all I wanted. I went from one man to another. In the process, I became something I never dreamed I would be. I became an adulteress. Yet all I wanted was security.

When I was twenty-nine, my search ended on my knees beside my bed. There I met my El Shaddai. And I learned to say with David, "**How precious is Your lovingkindness, O God! And the children of men take refuge in the shadow of Your wings**" (Psalm 36:7).

Time and time again I have found Him to be my all-sufficient God, my protector, the unconditional lover of my soul. He held me through the suicide of my first husband. He held me as a single parent when, at times, I was overcome by loneliness and responsibility. He has held me through times of great financial need, both personally and in our ministry. He has held me when the pains of leadership have seemed almost overwhelming. He has held me when I've failed. He has held me when I've cried for my children and poured out my doubts about being a good mother. He has held me when I've run out of strength and wondered how I'd ever make it. He has held me when I've felt defeated by all that I had to do.

When I have run to my El Shaddai, I have never come away wanting. He is my all-sufficient One. Oh, beloved, have you experienced Him as your El Shaddai? If not, He is waiting—arms open wide—for you.

~

O El Shaddai, my all-sufficient God, I will trust You to meet my every need and to be the answer to my deepest longings.

February 6

After I came to know Jesus Christ, God sent a godly man named Dave to tutor me in the faith. One night as we sat studying in my living room, he took off his signet ring and put it in his hand, clenching his fingers around it until his knuckles were white. Then he said, "Kay, now that you belong to Jesus Christ, you are just like this ring, and my hand is just like the hand of God. God has you in His hand. No one can touch you, look at you, or speak to you without God's permission."

I didn't recognize it then, but Dave was teaching me about the sovereignty of God. Later as I came to understand that God is sovereign—in control of all so that nothing can happen without His knowledge or permission—I understood more fully what Dave had been saying.

I also came to understand that the God who held me in His sovereign hand is a God of love. I reveled in the wonderful truth of 1 John 4:16: **"We have come to know and have believed the love which God has for us. God is love, and the one who abides in love abides in God, and God abides in him."**

God is in control. He rules over all. He loves me. He desires my highest good.

Oh, dear child of God, do you see that no matter what happens in your life, in your family, or in your nation, you can rejoice in the God of your salvation? Everything that comes into your life is filtered through His fingers of love.

Loving heavenly Father, I thank You and praise You that everything that touches my life has been filtered through Your fingers of love. Help me to remember this and to rest in Your sovereignty today.

February 7

Does the enemy sometimes whisper in your ear, attempting to convince you that you don't really belong to God, that you're not worthy of His blessing—and never will be—because of your past?

Beloved, let me assure you that when you take God at His word and accept Jesus' sacrifice for your sins and, in faith, confess with your mouth Jesus as Lord and believe in your heart that God raised Him from the dead, *you are saved.* Jesus' death takes away Satan's power of death over you because you have received forgiveness of sins and, thus, eternal life. At that moment you pass from death to life. "But now having been freed from sin and enslaved to God, you derive your benefit, resulting in sanctification, and the outcome, eternal life. For the wages of sin is death, but the free gift of God is eternal life in Christ Jesus our Lord" (Romans 6:22–23).

Colossians 2:13–14 says, "When you were dead in your transgressions and the uncircumcision of your flesh, **He made you alive together with Him, having forgiven us all our transgressions, having canceled out the certificate of debt consisting of decrees against us, which was hostile to us; and He has taken it out of the way, having nailed it to the cross.**"

And what does this mean to you? Your sin was paid for in full at Calvary. Satan's power over you has been destroyed. What joy such assurance brings!

Lord, I cherish that "old rugged cross," where Jesus gladly bore my shame to cancel my debt of sin. Thank You for Your gift of forgiveness now and the promise of eternal life to come.

February 8

When we are saved, each of us becomes a member of Christ's body, forged with resurrection power and seated with Him in heavenly places above all rule, power, and authority. Nothing can alter our position. It is set forever in heaven. But position is one thing; living accordingly is another.

Although we're seated in the heavenlies, we still live on earth in bodies of flesh—bodies with very real appetites that we're not to succumb to. We are to walk in a manner worthy of God's calling upon our lives, as the apostle Paul admonished:

> Therefore I, the prisoner of the Lord, implore you to **walk in a manner worthy of the calling with which you have been called,** with all humility and gentleness, with patience, showing tolerance for one another in love, being diligent to preserve the unity of the Spirit in the bond of peace. (Ephesians 4:1–3)

We must remember we've put off the old self. We are not to participate in its unfruitful deeds of darkness. The days are evil—and short. We must be careful how we walk. As husbands, wives, children, parents, employers, and/or employees who belong to the Lord Jesus Christ, we should be filled with the Spirit and treat one another properly.

Although we are seated above the enemy, we're in an ever-present war. Thus, we need to stand firm in the Lord and put on the whole armor of God so that we can resist the devil.

~

Heavenly Father, I thank You that nothing can change my position as Your child. I pray that You will continually fill me with the Spirit so I may walk in a manner worthy of that calling.

February 9

Proverbs 4:23 counsels, "**Watch over your heart [mind] with all diligence, for from it flow the springs of life.**" The battleground in spiritual warfare is the mind. This is where the enemy sends his flaming missiles, because the mind is the epicenter of the body. So what is our strategy?

First, you must know truth so you can examine everything in its light. Remember Satan's kingdom is one of darkness. Lies bring bondage. Truth liberates: "You will know the truth, and the truth will make you free" (John 8:32).

Second, you must resolve to take "every thought captive to the obedience of Christ" (2 Corinthians 10:5). If what you think, hear, believe, or feel doesn't line up with the knowledge of God, then it has to go. If it isn't truth, you will not receive it or let it influence who you are and what you do.

Third, once your obedience is complete—once you do what God tells you to do, what truth commands—there's to be a punishment of "all disobedience, whenever your obedience is complete" (10:6). You are to confront the lie, exposing the underlying deception so that it will not destroy others.

Can you see how important it is that you guard your every thought, that you know the truth, and that you walk in it? The battle for your mind and emotions will continue to rage until you finally arrive in heaven. That's why you must saturate yourself in the Word of God.

Remember, truth takes down the devil's strongholds, brick by brick, until they're nothing but pieces of rubble.

~

Why don't you spend some time sitting quietly before God and asking Him to reveal to you any lies that you've embraced? Then ask Him to reveal the truth to you through His Word.

February 10

When the day's challenges seem overwhelming, when life doesn't go according to our plan, it brings such comfort to remember that the birthright of every child of God is grace—grace that saves and sustains, grace that will keep us and bring us to glory.

Yet with our birthright comes responsibility. We are responsible to have faith. We must believe that God means what He says and stands by His Word. The grace that has saved us to salvation is sufficient to take care of us. This is why Paul urges Timothy to **"be strong in the grace that is in Christ Jesus"** (2 Timothy 2:1).

When we fall back on the flesh during times of trouble or trials, we come short of the grace of God. And as Hebrews says, a "root of bitterness" can spring up in us and defile others. Or we can become immoral or godless like Esau, who sold his birthright for a single meal (Hebrews 12:15–16).

If we accept God's grace, but then, when the going gets rough, we cast it away in unbelief and return to life apart from it, we despise our birthright. Apart from grace there is no hope.

Beware of despising the birthright that belongs to every child of God. Remember, suffering is part of God's fatherly discipline. He disciplines us for our good. His goal is that we become holy or, as He puts it in Hebrews, that we might share in His holiness (12:10).

Loving Father, when temporal, fleshly needs or worries threaten to distract me from faith in You, keep my eyes focused on the birthright of grace that I can claim as Your child.

February 11

Do you look forward to spending time alone in prayer with God? Or do you tend to pray in the company of others rather than in private? Could it be that you don't fully comprehend the purpose and power of private prayer?

Jesus' instruction is clear: **"When you pray, you are not to be like the hypocrites; for they love to stand and pray in the synagogues and on the street corners so that they may be seen by men. Truly I say to you, they have their reward in full"** (Matthew 6:5).

Does that mean, then, that we are not to pray in public nor participate in public prayer meetings? I don't think so, for the Word of God has many other references to public praying. I don't believe Jesus' purpose was to condemn public prayer but to show us that true prayer is for communication between God and the individual—not for impressing others with our piety.

Dwight Pentecost in his book *The Sermon on the Mount* puts it so well: "Prayer is private communication."[2] Does this mean we can never carry on this communication publicly with God? Oh no. Public prayer can be private communication if our hearts are united, if we are aware that we have come into the presence of God and are actually praying and worshiping Him as a body. Yet we must always remember to Whom we are speaking!

Genuine prayer is for God, not other people. What place does such prayer have in your life?

~

I long for true communion with You, dear Lord. When I pray, help me to remember that I am in the presence of a holy and jealous God and that You deserve my full attention.

In the Korean War the majority of our men who were taken captive never tried to escape. They resigned themselves to prison because they saw no future. They had lost their vision. Their hope was gone.

Most Christians live this way. They have lost sight of the blessed hope, the glory of being absent from the body and at home with the Lord. They do not look to the time when they will reign with Jesus on earth (Revelation 5:9–10). They have lost their will to fight because they have forgotten that their "citizenship is in heaven" (Philippians 3:20).

They have sat down at the world's banquet table and glutted themselves with the things of this life, the things they can see and touch and taste and experience "now." They have little interest in the glories of heaven. Such Christians are no threat to the world that holds them captive.

How can Christians keep from being imprisoned by the world? How can we keep our vision and not lose hope? By obedience to God's Word, by clinging to it in faith. **"Therefore if you have been raised up with Christ, keep seeking the things above, where Christ is, seated at the right hand of God. Set your mind on the things above, not on the things that are on earth"** (Colossians 3:1–2).

Wherever you are, my friend, Jehovah is there, waiting, longing to be your future and your hope. Do not be absorbed by your captivity. Rather, be absorbed with your God!

~

I thank You, Lord, that my citizenship is in heaven. Help me to live with this in mind, conducting myself in a manner worthy of the gospel and remaining unsoiled by the things of this world.

February 13

Remember when Jesus told Peter that he would deny Him? Jesus said, "Simon, Simon, behold, Satan has demanded permission to sift you like wheat; but I have prayed for you, that your faith may not fail" (Luke 22:31–32). Satan had to get God's permission to sift Peter! Can you see the implication of that truth in your own life? Satan can never do anything to you without God's permission.

Therefore, according to 1 Corinthians 10:13, whatever temptation comes into your life will never be more than you can bear! You can overwhelmingly conquer through Jesus Christ in every circumstance of life (Romans 8:35–39)!

What blessed assurance it brings to remember that even when people intend to do evil against you, your sovereign God will work it out for your good. He's the Redeemer of your difficulties, trials, and tragedies. The comforting truth of God's sovereignty is what enabled the prophet Habakkuk to declare his faith in the midst of discouraging circumstances:

> **Though the fig tree should not blossom**
> **And there be no fruit on the vines,**
> **Though the yield of the olive should fail**
> **And the fields produce no food,**
> **Though the flock should be cut off from the fold**
> **And there be no cattle in the stalls,**
> **Yet I will exult in the LORD.** (Habakkuk 3:17–18)

No matter what happens, because God is sovereign, you can live above it all—if you are His child.

~

O Father, no matter what challenges today may bring, I will exult in You as my Redeemer and Savior.

February 14

Some of the sweetest words in any language are "I forgive you." It's really another way of saying "I love you with the love of the Lord." Remember the characteristics of a true follower of Christ:

> So, as those who have been chosen of God, holy and beloved, **put on a heart of compassion, kindness, humility, gentleness and patience; bearing with one another, and forgiving each other, whoever has a complaint against anyone; just as the Lord forgave you, so also should you.** (Colossians 3:12–13)

When we refuse to forgive, we become open targets for Satan's schemes. His devices are to divide: to cut us off from one another that he might devour us in sorrow or bitterness and to cut us off from the blessing of God that comes when we forgive as He commands.

When we don't forgive, beloved, rest assured Satan will take advantage of our disobedience and move in like a roaring lion. Not only that, but when we refuse to forgive—as God not only commands us to do but also modeled for us in our redemption—then God will not forgive us.

I know that sounds tough and maybe not like God, but those are the words of His Son Jesus Christ in Matthew 6:14–15: "For if you forgive others for their transgressions, your heavenly Father will also forgive you. But if you do not forgive others, then your Father will not forgive your transgressions."

Heavenly Father, I will not sin against You. Please give me the grace to obey, and I will forgive.

February 15

Beloved, do you understand why it's so crucial that you and I yield every day, every moment to God's will and ways? The enemy knows that when we walk in complete surrender to God, temptation cannot gain a foothold in our lives.

Just as Satan tried to get Adam and Eve to act independently of God, so he tried the same thing with the Son of Man: **"And the tempter came and said to Him, 'If You are the Son of God, command that these stones become bread' "** (Matthew 4:3). The devil was suggesting that as the Son of God, Jesus did not need to be dependent upon the Father. Satan was tempting Him to satisfy His own hunger, by His own power.

Jesus could have done it. He was God. He had the power. But Jesus knew He could not act independently of the Father. He was always and only to do those things that pleased the Father. He was to live by every word that came from the mouth of God. He was to walk by the Spirit, even as man is to walk by the Spirit. The flesh with its desires was never to control Him.

Sin has its roots in independent action. When we choose to walk independently of God and His Word, we fall into sin. And when we fall into sin, we are headed for the snare of the devil (2 Timothy 2:26) unless we repent and confess. If only we understood that unforsaken sin in the life of the believer gives Satan a "hold"! If we could truly comprehend the truth of that reality, we would quickly flee our youthful lusts!

~

Lord, help me to do and say only those things that are pleasing to You. When I'm tempted to act on my own initiative, let Your Spirit prompt me instead to seek Your will.

February 16

One of the most vital aspects of true surrender to God's ways involves yielding our minds, our thought lives.

Satan wants to focus our thoughts on things contrary to the truth about us as children of God, things contrary to the Word of God. Knowing that evil proceeds from the mind, he wants to bring lies or half truths into our thoughts so that we might dwell on them. He's crafty. He's subtle. He never announces who he is unless you desire to talk to him. He can disguise himself as an angel of light or as one of your thoughts. He'll drop suggestions in your mind that can throw you for a loop if you don't know where they come from.

Every thought and feeling that you and I have must be brought captive to the obedience of Jesus Christ. Our thoughts must submit to the truths of the Word of God or be refused.

We need to walk in obedience to Philippians 4:8: "**Whatever is true, whatever is honorable, whatever is right, whatever is pure, whatever is lovely, whatever is of good repute, if there is any excellence and if anything worthy of praise, dwell on these things.**"

When a thought comes knocking at the door of your mind, examine it to see if it meets the conditions of Philippians 4:8. If not, toss it out!

O God, help me to fix my mind and heart on the things above so I will recognize the lies of the enemy. When doubts and fears come, fill me with the knowledge of Your presence and protection.

What does God see when He looks into your heart? Does your innermost being shine with the joy of true surrender?

"For the eyes of the LORD move to and fro throughout the earth that He may strongly support those whose heart is completely His" (2 Chronicles 16:9).

God is looking for hearts that are fully His, totally dependent on Him, relying on nothing but His power. Hearts that are humbled by thorns and made strong in His grace.

And how do we keep our hearts like this? We guard our time of quiet, of being alone in His presence, reading and meditating on His Word and then talking with Him about all the issues of life. I cannot stress this enough. When we get in a hurry, when we're so pressured, so stressed out, so preoccupied by the affairs of daily living that we cannot have leisure in His presence and in His Word, then we're in grave danger of succumbing to temptation and pride.

The Lord's eyes are running to and fro across the earth. When He sees you meditating on His Word, taking time to commune with Him in prayer—He stops. He has found what He's looking for: a heart that's fully His.

Oh, precious one, do His eyes rest on you?

Lord, I long to have a heart that is wholly devoted to You. I surrender every corner of my life, every moment of my day to Your service. I choose to live in dependence on You and Your Word.

February 18

Did you awaken this morning with a heavy heart, wondering how you're going to accomplish the tasks ahead, how you can make it through this day and bring honor to your God?

The apostle Paul reminds us that "**we are a fragrance of Christ to God among those who are being saved and among those who are perishing; to the one an aroma from death to death, to the other an aroma from life to life. And who is adequate for these things?**" (2 Corinthians 2:15–16).

Who is adequate for victory, for triumph—to be the fragrance of Christ to God? to have Him see and sense again the pleasure that His Son brought Him? Paul was adequate, and he wants us to see that we are too: "God has chosen the foolish things of the world to shame the wise, and God has chosen the weak things of the world to shame the things which are strong…so that no man may boast before God" (1 Corinthians 1:27, 29).

Oh, my dear friend, do you see it? Our feelings of inadequacy are always true if we're trusting in ourselves or in any other human means to any extent. Our adequacy comes from God alone. "By His doing you are in Christ Jesus, who became to us wisdom from God, and righteousness and sanctification, and redemption" (1 Corinthians 1:30).

When we remember this truth, we'll recognize God as our source, our sufficiency, and our adequacy for any and every situation.

~

Thank You, dear Lord, for Your glorious gifts of wisdom and righteousness, sanctification and redemption. Please let me bring the fragrance of Christ into every life I touch today.

February 19

Have you despaired of being "perfect, as your heavenly Father is perfect" (Matthew 5:48)?

Have you cried out with Paul, "Who is adequate for these things?" (2 Corinthians 2:16)?

Have you looked into your own heart and sighed, "O God, when will I ever learn?"

Have you groaned, longing to be clothed with your new body from heaven, finally free of the flesh that keeps causing you to stumble?

Have you ever feared that someday you might stumble and never get up?

I understand, my friend, because I, too, live in a body of flesh. I know that although my spirit may be willing, my flesh is weak. Jesus told us this (Matthew 26:41).

Even more important, Jesus understands! He understands because He, too, lived in a body of flesh: **"We do not have a high priest who cannot sympathize with our weaknesses, but One who has been tempted in all things as we are, yet without sin"** (Hebrews 4:15).

As a man, He experienced the reality that the spirit is willing but the flesh is weak. He walked where you walk. He sat where you sit. And "since He Himself was tempted in that which He has suffered, He is able to come to the aid of those who are tempted" (Hebrews 2:18).

Jesus understands—and He stands ready to help you.

~

Some days I feel so inadequate, Lord, too weak to move forward. Thank You for reminding me that Jesus understands exactly how I feel and that He offers the mercy and grace I so desperately need.

February 20

Precious child of God, have you taken time recently to think on the life-changing gifts that are yours in Christ?

From death to life. From wrath to mercy. From earth to heaven. From futility to purposefulness. From enmity to peace. From isolation to family. And all because "**God, being rich in mercy, because of His great love with which He loved us, even when we were dead in our transgressions, made us alive together with Christ**" (Ephesians 2:4–5).

Read it again, beloved, and let yourself drink in the awesome reality of God's "great love with which He loved us."

And when did He love us? When we got our act together and cleaned up? No, He loved us when we were still sons of disobedience, children of wrath, dead in our transgressions. Read Romans 5, and remember you are saved through faith—and even faith to believe is a gift of grace. Dr. Charles Erdman says it well: "Faith is the instrument by which the gift is received. It is not the source of the gift."[3] How we need to remember that about faith.

Because Satan is the accuser and he loves to remind us of our sin, it's crucial that we understand God saved us when we were still sons and daughters of disobedience. Satan will do everything he can to keep us blind to the grace of God, trying to convince us that God won't or can't use us, bless us, or help us because of our sin.

Remember, God saved you when you were in sin. Nothing can take that away.

~

O Father, thank You that I am alive in every way because of Your great love. Help me to live in the knowledge that You have chosen me and You want to use me for Your divine purposes.

February 21

Will you be satisfied at the close of this day if you've lived up to *your* established standards of goodness? Will you weigh your words and actions against *your* set of dos and don'ts, *your* own little code of righteousness, to see how close you've come to the mark?

In the New Testament we read how the scribes and Pharisees had established a certain code of righteousness to which they insisted the people must adhere. In the Sermon on the Mount, Jesus pulled the rug out from under those false standards: "**For I say to you that unless your righteousness surpasses that of the scribes and Pharisees, you will not enter the kingdom of heaven**" (Matthew 5:20).

The righteousness of the scribes and Pharisees was a self-righteousness. Like so many of us, they had created their own list of requirements, based on external measures of righteousness rather than internal. That's why Jesus said, "Woe to you, scribes and Pharisees, hypocrites! For you tithe mint and dill and cummin, and have neglected the weightier provisions of the law: justice and mercy and faithfulness; but these are the things you should have done without neglecting the others" (Matthew 23:23). They were only keeping God's Law to the limit of their own desires. They were depending on their own righteousness.

What about you? What measure of righteousness will guide your life today? Your own…or God's?

Make clear to me, O God, the way of true righteousness, which can be found only in You. Let me not be led astray by my own interpretations or the false advice of others.

One of the enemy's tactics is to isolate people, to cut them off from fellowship with one another, to convince them that they are alone and that no one really cares about them. I believe that's one reason families are under such attack today.

Belonging is a basic need. We each need to be part of something beyond ourselves. Ephesians chapter 2 tells us that once we've been saved by grace we are in Christ Jesus. "**So then you are no longer strangers and aliens, but you are fellow citizens with the saints, and are of God's household**" (verse 19). You belong!

My beloved friend, Jesus has broken down all the barriers, all the walls between you and God. You have been brought near to God through the blood of Jesus Christ.

God is not some distant, supreme sovereign you can never communicate with. Jesus has brought you into peace with the Father, and now through the gift of the indwelling Holy Spirit, you have access to Him. Read Ephesians 2 and 3.

You are no longer an alien or a stranger. You are part of God's forever family. You've come home. You are in Christ, and He's in you. You're His dwelling place.

You'll never, ever be alone again. You are bone of His bone—an indispensable member of His body.

How comforting it is to know that because Your Son faced rejection on my behalf, I am accepted, welcomed without reservation into relationship with You. When I feel alone, help me to remember that I am forever part of Your family.

February 23

Jesus has called each of us to a righteousness that is impossible apart from Him. Who can reach this high level of righteousness? Who can walk where Jesus has walked? Only the poor in spirit, those who have acknowledged their utter spiritual poverty. Only those who have attained the kingdom of heaven and have been filled by God's own Spirit have a righteousness that exceeds that of the scribes and Pharisees.

Jesus revealed the secret for living in such righteousness: **"Ask, and it will be given to you; seek, and you will find; knock, and it will be opened to you. For everyone who asks receives, and he who seeks finds, and to him who knocks it will be opened"** (Matthew 7:7–8).

Here we see the keys in our relationship with God in the three words *asking, seeking,* and *knocking.* Each of these words is in the present tense in Greek, indicating a continuous or habitual action.

The Christian life is to be lived in continuous, total dependence upon God. The greater the dependence, the greater the righteousness. Let me repeat that for emphasis: the greater the dependence, the greater the righteousness.

Keep on asking, Jesus tells us. Keep on seeking. Keep on knocking. This is a life of persistent dependence. This is the only way to live in righteousness.

In my own strength, Lord, I continually fall short. But I ask today for Your Holy Spirit to demonstrate Your righteousness through me, and I have confidence that when I ask according to Your will, You hear me (1 John 5:14).

February 24

Do you realize God has gifted you in a unique way so that you might serve Him? The grace of God provides you with spiritual gifts by which you are to serve the body of Jesus Christ. As a steward of these gifts, you will be held accountable for using them: **"As each one has received a special gift, employ it in serving one another as good stewards of the manifold grace of God"** (1 Peter 4:10).

Every believer has been given one or more spiritual gifts. These gifts are not given according to merit or desire. Rather, "God has placed the members, each one of them, in the body, just as He desired" (1 Corinthians 12:18).

Every time God deals with the subject of spiritual gifts, He uses the analogy of the body. Why? Because the body is one entity. Yet its members are diverse and function in unique ways for the proper working of the whole. Its various members illustrate what the church of Jesus Christ is all about: unity in the midst of diversity, all under the headship of Jesus Christ.

As 1 Corinthians 12:4–7 shows, the gifts, the ministries, and even the effects are all from the Godhead. God supplies everything we need in order to do what He has called us to do. This, my friend, is grace. Our gifts "differ according to the grace given to us" (Romans 12:6). And we are given grace "according to the measure of Christ's gift" (Ephesians 4:7).

Remember, God not only calls you to serve Him, but He gifts you so that you can.

~

Show me how I can best serve You today, Lord, through the gifts and ministries You have given me. Let me find purpose and fulfillment in doing that which You have called me to do.

February 25

When people have been deeply wounded, they often feel as if they have no worth, no value as human beings. Feelings or thoughts like this do not come from God. They have their origin in Satan—the father of lies, the accuser, the destroyer.

Satan's primary target is the mind. It is for this reason that Ephesians 6 tells us the Christian's armor includes the helmet of salvation. When we understand our salvation, we see our purpose as human beings. We were created in God's image, marred though we may be. Through salvation, the work of the Holy Spirit, and the transforming power of the Word of God, a gradual transformation will take place, conforming us to the image of His Son.

Forget how you feel, what you think about yourself, and what anyone else has said about you. Here's what Jesus says about you: **"You did not choose Me but I chose you, and appointed you that you would go and bear fruit, and that your fruit would remain, so that whatever you ask of the Father in My name He may give to you"** (John 15:16).

According to this verse, your life as a child of God has worth and purpose. He has chosen and appointed you to bear fruit for His kingdom.

Will you walk in that joyous truth today?

Write out a prayer to God, affirming your commitment to live in accordance with the truth you have just seen in His Word. Remember, those who hear God's Word and don't live accordingly delude themselves and miss God's blessing.

February 26

Salvation is by pure grace—unearned, unmerited favor—given to us because of what Jesus Christ accomplished at Calvary. But that's just the beginning.

So often we quote Romans 8:28—"And we know that God causes all things to work together for good to those who love God, to those who are called according to His purpose"—then we stop. But our question should be, what is the good that God promises to bring about in our lives?

The answer: Christlikeness.

The very next verse declares, "**For those whom He foreknew, He also predestined to become conformed to the image of His Son, so that He would be the firstborn among many brethren**" (Romans 8:29). God predestined, or marked out before, that you and I should be conformed to the image of His Son. God not only saves us; He also begins to transform us into the image He intended for man when He created Adam and Eve. An image unmarred by sin.

How is that image restored in you and me? It begins at salvation with the indwelling of the Holy Spirit, and it continues to be achieved through three things: our proper relationship to God, our response to the Word of God, and the suffering that attends the life of every child of God.

Are your eyes open to how God is working today to conform your life to His Son's image?

~

I believe that You are actively working in my life, God, to conform me to the image of Your precious Son. Help me to remember that I have been called according to Your purpose and that You are transforming me day by day through Your presence, Your Word, and the circumstances of my life.

February 27

When we are walking in the light, our lives will reflect God's goodness and righteousness and truth. If they don't, something is clearly wrong. Ephesians 5:8–10 says, "For you were formerly darkness, but now you are Light in the Lord; **walk as children of Light (for the fruit of the Light consists in all goodness and righteousness and truth), trying to learn what is pleasing to the Lord.**"

First John 1 tells us that we cannot walk in darkness and continue to claim a share in the Great Light, the Lord Jesus Christ. Fellowship is sharing something in common. If we say we have fellowship with Jesus and yet we're walking in darkness—living in sin—we're obviously lying, because in Jesus there is no darkness. Light dispels darkness. The two are totally incompatible.

In addition to being marked by goodness, righteousness, and truth, our lives will be characterized by love if we are truly children of light: "The one who says he is in the Light and yet hates his brother is in the darkness until now. The one who loves his brother abides in the Light and there is no cause for stumbling in him" (1 John 2:9–10).

Those who have the life of God within them, who truly walk in the light, cannot walk in hatred. Why? Because God is not only light but also love (1 John 4:8).

~

Go to the Lord in prayer and ask Him if you are truly walking in the light. Ask Him to teach you to live in ways that are pleasing to Him, ways that clearly demonstrate His goodness, righteousness, truth, and love.

February 28

Do God's standards seem unreasonably high, perhaps even impossible for us to achieve? I agree. It's impossible for you and me to walk through this day with pure hearts, minds, and lives—unless the Holy Spirit lives within us.

In Romans 8:8–9, the apostle Paul contrasts two things: those who are in the flesh—who do not have the Spirit of God dwelling in them—and those who are in the Spirit: **"Those who are in the flesh cannot please God. However, you are not in the flesh but in the Spirit, if indeed the Spirit of God dwells in you. But if anyone does not have the Spirit of Christ, he does not belong to Him."**

He is saying that if the Holy Spirit is not in you, then you do not belong to God. You are not a Christian. But if you are now in Christ, you are no longer a slave. When the Holy Spirit, the Spirit of life in Christ Jesus, came to live inside of you, He set you free from slavery to sin. Romans 8:3 tells us God broke the power of sin by "sending His own Son in the likeness of sinful flesh and as an offering for sin."

God, through Jesus, condemned sin in the flesh. That means He took away the power sin needed to reign in your mortal body.

Man cannot straighten out man. Only God can do that! And that's just what He does by giving us the gift of His Holy Spirit when we enter into the New Covenant of grace.

~

Thank You for the gift of the Holy Spirit, who has freed me from sin to walk in righteousness. Help me to walk today not according to the flesh but by the strength and leading of the Spirit.

February 29

Are you ready to be used by God today to bring the good news to someone else?

God has given every child of God the ministry of reconciliation. He has committed to us the word of reconciliation, the gospel of Jesus Christ. Isaiah 52:7 says, "**How lovely on the mountains are the feet of him who brings good news, who announces peace and brings good news of happiness, who announces salvation, and says to Zion, 'Your God reigns!'** " The good news is the gospel of Jesus Christ, which brings forgiveness of sins.

Look at your feet. Are they lovely in the eyes of God? Jesus' feet were nailed to a cross so that your feet might someday walk streets of gold. Are you going to walk them alone? Or will others walk beside you—others with whom you have shared the good news so that they, too, might know how to have peace with God?

"But it's hard," you may protest. "I don't know what to say! I get so embarrassed!"

I know that it's hard and that it's difficult to know what to say. But those are not adequate excuses. Jesus said, "Go… and lo, I am with you always" (Matthew 28:19–20). Give Him your mouth, and He will give you His words! Be willing to be made a fool for Christ's sake, and He will make you an ambassador for the world's sake.

Put Your love in my heart and Your words on my lips that I may proclaim the good news of Your grace to everyone I meet. Give me a passion for bringing souls to You. Fill me with Your strength and wisdom so I may be effective in the ministry of reconciling others to You.

March 1

Are you saddened by how sin mars our world and destroys so many lives? Does your heart ache for individuals—perhaps your own children or grandchildren—who are stumbling in the darkness? How does God call you to live in the midst of a sin-sickened world?

The gospel of John tells us that Jesus came as the Source of light to lift humanity out of darkness (John 12:46). **"In Him was life, and the life was the Light of men"** (John 1:4).

Jesus, the Light of the world, has returned to the Father. Yet He has not left the world in darkness because we, His people, remain here as witnesses of the Light.

Matthew 5 says you and I are the light of the world. But did He leave us on earth to hide our lights under a basket? Of course not! The purpose of light is to be seen. "A city set on a hill cannot be hidden" (verse 14).

If you are a child of God, you are a part of that Holy City, the New Jerusalem, which will someday come down out of heaven from God. That city will have no need of the sun or moon to shine upon it, for the glory of God will illumine it. Its lamp will be the Lamb, and the nations will walk by His light (Revelation 21:2, 23–24). Until that glorious day, you and I, who are citizens of heaven, are to be like a city set on a hill that cannot be hidden. We are to let those who grope and stumble in the darkness know where the true Light can be found.

Lord, in a world full of darkness, embolden me through the Holy Spirit so I will not quietly hide away but instead will shine forth with Your truth.

March 2

My friend, are you suffering today? If not, then hold the following truths in your heart for another time, because the Bible tells us that suffering is a certainty for every believer.

The apostle Paul tells us that the gift of faith in Christ Jesus and the gift of suffering come together. And how are we to live in light of this truth?

> **Conduct yourselves in a manner worthy of the gospel of Christ…in no way alarmed by your opponents—which is a sign of destruction for them, but of salvation for you, and that too, from God. For to you it has been granted for Christ's sake, not only to believe in Him, but also to suffer for His sake.** (Philippians 1:27–29)

When you stand before your opponents firm and unshaken, it "is a sign of destruction for them." Why? Because they know that if they were in your shoes, they'd melt with panic! Your confidence alarms your opponents.

And for you, such confidence testifies to the reality of your faith: "Indeed, all who desire to live godly in Christ Jesus will be persecuted" (2 Timothy 3:12).

Suffering is a mark of our family relationship with God the Father and the Lord Jesus Christ (Romans 8:16–17), and suffering prepares us for glory. What a difference it makes when you and I grasp these truths and live by them!

~

Gracious Father, help me to embrace suffering and persecution as a gift as I conduct myself in a manner worthy of the gospel of Christ.

March 3

Are you distressed today over the choices a loved one has made? Or are you the one who is stumbling down the path of life?

How do we manage to so quickly mess up our lives? I believe it's because we have not esteemed God's Word as more precious than our necessary food. We have not known His Word so that it has become a light to our feet and a lamp to our paths. Therefore, we have stumbled in darkness.

I have been amazed, appalled, and grieved at the number of people who come to me after I have spoken and say, "But, Kay, I didn't know that's what God's Word said. I didn't realize I was going against the will of God!"

So many have conformed to the world instead of being transformed by the renewing of their minds. That's why lives, homes, and relationships are in such tragic disarray.

God's servant Job understood that the only way to walk safely through the trials, tragedies, and testings of this life is to set our feet firmly in the way of truth:

> **My foot has held fast to His path;**
> **I have kept His way and not turned aside.**
> **I have not departed from the command of His lips;**
> **I have treasured the words of His mouth more than**
> **my necessary food.** (Job 23:11–12)

Devoted time in God's Word is vital if you're going to have a pure heart.

~

Teach me to hold fast to the Word of life, dear Father. Give me a hunger for Scripture and fill me with discernment and understanding so that Your truths will shine light into my daily walk.

March 4

Do you ever hesitate to open the newspaper or turn on the television, dreading to learn of yet another tragedy or demonstration of humanity's capacity for cruelty and sin? Oh, my friend, I understand. At times it seems the world is spinning out of control—and yet we know that's not true: "**I am God, and there is no other; I am God, and there is no one like Me, declaring the end from the beginning, and from ancient times things which have not been done, saying, 'My purpose will be established, and I will accomplish all My good pleasure'**" (Isaiah 46:9–10).

El Elyon is the name that designates God as the sovereign ruler of all the universe. It was El Elyon, "God Most High, who…delivered" Abraham's enemies into his hand (Genesis 14:20). It was the Most High God who was and is the Redeemer of Israel (Psalm 78:35). And it is the Most High God who rules today over the affairs of men. "For His dominion is an everlasting dominion, and His kingdom endures from generation to generation.… He does according to His will in the host of heaven and among the inhabitants of earth; and no one can ward off His hand or say to Him, 'What have You done?'" (Daniel 4:34–35).

What difference does it make in your life to realize that God is sovereign and that ultimately nothing can happen without His sanction or permission? Will you let these truths guide your response to whatever happens today?

How comforting to know that "Yours, O LORD, is the greatness and the power and the glory and the victory and the majesty, indeed everything that is in the heavens and the earth" (1 Chronicles 29:11).

March 5

Did you awaken this morning with a thankful heart, beloved? If not, may I ask why?

As we saw yesterday, our God is the sovereign ruler over all the universe. He not only knows about every circumstance that touches your life, but He also ultimately uses it for His good purposes. When the reality of this truth takes hold of your heart, you'll find it easier to obey those New Testament commands to rejoice in all circumstances of life. God tells us that we are to "**be filled with the Spirit,...always giving thanks for all things in the name of our Lord Jesus Christ to God, even the Father**" (Ephesians 5:18, 20).

Isn't it easier to give thanks when you realize that your Father, El Elyon, God Most High, is in control and that nothing can happen in His universe without His permission? Even when we are wronged by others, we can still give thanks. Although we have been given a free will, still God so rules and overrules that no person, angel, demon, or devil, nor any circumstance of life can thwart His plan.

El Elyon rules supremely over all. And because He does, you can trust that all things "work together for good to those who love God, to those who are called according to His purpose" (Romans 8:28). In everything you can "give thanks; for this is God's will for you in Christ Jesus" (1 Thessalonians 5:18).

Thank You, sovereign God, for the assurance that You are in control and nothing can touch me without Your knowledge and permission. I thank You for working out Your purposes even in the difficult circumstances of my life.

March 6

Are you hurting or discouraged today? Are you worried about what the hours ahead may hold? May I ask, beloved, if you truly believe that God is in control of your every circumstance? And are you willing to trust Him to take care of you?

If God is not in charge—totally and completely—then whose hands are we in? If He were unaware of what was going to happen to us, then how could He work all things together for our good and our Christlikeness? Surely if man, Satan, accidents, or "fate" can do things to us without God's permission or knowledge, then we are in grave trouble, because it would mean that God is not in charge.

However, God *is* sovereign. And because of this truth, you need to know what this God who rules over all is like. One of His primary attributes is love. God loves you, my friend, no matter what you are like, no matter what you do. God is love, and it is His love that draws you to Him. He initiates love (1 John 4:10). God even says to disobedient Israel, **"I have loved you with an everlasting love; therefore I have drawn you with lovingkindness"** (Jeremiah 31:3).

Love desires your highest good and is willing to pay the ultimate sacrifice to attain it. That sacrifice was His Son.

Won't you accept God's love, His character, His sovereignty—and trust Him to work all things for His good purpose?

I believe in Your everlasting love, dear Father, and I accept it. I trust in Your sovereign control over the circumstances of my life, and I will rest in the knowledge that Your character is trustworthy and unchanging.

March 7

Have you ever been unjustly attacked? Did you react in anger or slip into depression? If so, that's a sure sign that you did not respond in meekness! Meekness doesn't get angry at what is done to it but at those things that offend God.

Yet meekness is not weakness. It is power under control. Moses, whom God chose to lead His people out of Egypt, demonstrated this truth: **"Now the man Moses was very meek, above all the men which were upon the face of the earth"** (Numbers 12:3, KJV).

When the sons of Korah challenged Moses' leadership, he fell on his face before the Lord (Numbers 16:1–4, 28–35). As God's representative, Moses could not yield his God-given leadership and allow rebellion against God. Therefore, in meekness Moses called down the judgment of God, and the earth opened and consumed the 250 men who were resisting the authority of God.

Never forget it: meekness is not weakness! Meekness holds its ground when God's honor and glory are at stake. Meekness does not become a doormat for sin. Never self-serving, meekness seeks only to bring glory to God.

As you walk through this day, no doubt you'll encounter many people—from rude drivers and difficult co-workers to a thoughtless spouse, an uncooperative child, or cranky neighbors—whose actions could provoke anger or outrage. Will you choose instead to surrender to the Lord in meekness, concerning yourself only with bringing glory to Him?

Almighty God, help me to respond with godly boldness and genuine meekness in even the most challenging circumstances rather than to live at the mercy of my emotions.

March 8

Many read Jesus' admonition in Matthew 7:1—"Do not judge"—as forbidding them to point out sin in another's life. So what do we do with other verses that encourage us to talk directly with those who sin and to urge them to repent? James 5:20, for example, says, **"He who turns a sinner from the error of his way will save his soul from death and will cover a multitude of sins."**

So are we to judge or not?

The answer lies with you, the one who is judging. What is your walk with Jesus like? Are you practicing the same sin that you condemn in others? Are you like those in Matthew 7 who went after little bits of dust in their brothers' eyes while they were afflicted with two-by-fours in their own? Have you met the qualifications of Galatians 6:1? "Brethren, even if anyone is caught in any trespass, you who are spiritual, restore such a one in a spirit of gentleness; each one looking to yourself, so that you too will not be tempted."

I do not believe God is forbidding the discernment and removal of specks and motes—the confronting of sin. Specks can and should be removed from others' eyes as long as the surgery is done in a spirit of gentleness by one who is spiritual—one who is not there to condemn but to restore.

There's a big difference!

~

Give me discernment, Father, that I may be used by You to bring hope and healing into the lives of others. Protect me from hypocrisy and instill in me a spirit of gentleness and love.

March 9

Does guilt or regret over your past actions cloud your perspective or diminish your joy?

One of Satan's most effective strategies is to remind us of sins we've already confessed or to tell us that, because of them, God can't use us. Sometimes he tries to convince us that our sins are so terrible God will never forgive us. At such times, we must cling to the truth: **"But you were washed, but you were sanctified, but you were justified in the name of the Lord Jesus Christ and in the Spirit of our God"** (1 Corinthians 6:11).

When you were a sinner—helpless, ungodly, and without hope—God justified you. When you repented and believed that Jesus Christ is God and that He died for your sin, God immediately transferred you from Satan's domain of darkness into His glorious kingdom. Instantly you were pardoned and declared righteous in the eyes of God. All your sins—past, present, and future—were forgiven.

Remember that "there is now no condemnation" because God's righteousness has been put to your account (Romans 8:1). So when condemnation comes, you must recognize who instigated those accusations. God does not condemn. God does not accuse. God convicts of sin and seeks to lead us to repentance. Satan is the one who accuses you night and day before the throne of God (Revelation 12:10). But do not fear, because Jesus sits at the right hand of the throne of God, where He lives to make intercession for you (Hebrews 12:2; 7:25).

Thank You, God, that my sins are absolutely forgiven, to be remembered no more. Help me to cling to that truth when the enemy tries to discourage and defeat me.

March 10

If you understand grace, you'll never turn away from the blessing of God because you feel you don't deserve it. If you understand grace, you'll never feel that you can't ask God for forgiveness or help because you've failed Him over and over and don't deserve to be forgiven or helped again. If you understand grace, you know that grace covers all your inadequacies, all your failures, all your human frailties...and all your sins.

Those who understand grace know we can never come to God on the basis of what we deserve. Nor do we come on the basis of what we have earned. Those who understand the grace of God are ready to appropriate His grace on the basis of faith and faith alone—faith in the God of grace!

> **But God, being rich in mercy,...made us alive together with Christ (by grace you have been saved), and raised us up with Him, and seated us with Him in the heavenly places in Christ Jesus, so that in the ages to come He might show the surpassing riches of His grace in kindness toward us in Christ Jesus.** (Ephesians 2:4–7)

Grace brings life, but it is also the means by which we are to live and to please our Father God. Grace is key to our relationship with God.

The believer never comes to God on any basis other than grace. I cannot emphasize this truth enough! What peace, what power, what confidence would be ours if we understood this truth and lived accordingly!

~

Help me, God, to comprehend and lay hold of the surpassing riches of Your grace, letting it work in and through my life daily.

March 11

When temptation confronts you today—and it will!—remember that you have a Savior who understands exactly what you're facing: **"Then Jesus was led up by the Spirit into the wilderness to be tempted by the devil"** (Matthew 4:1). You'll find great insight for defending your mind against the enemy's arrows by looking at Matthew 4:1–11 to see how Jesus dealt with Satan when He was tempted.

Our Savior's response shows that we must resist the enemy over and over again, rejecting thought after thought that is not pleasing to God or that is not in accord with His Word. We are not to allow the enemy to twist and pervert Scripture. Like Jesus, we are to resist the devil. We have that authority because of who is in us: "Greater is He who is in you than he who is in the world" (1 John 4:4).

When I deal with recurring thoughts that are contrary to Philippians 4:8, I often will say something like this: "Satan, those thoughts are not from God. You have no place in me. Therefore, in the name of Jesus Christ and by His blood, I command you to leave me alone." Why address Satan? Jesus did. He rebuked him and told him to leave.

If you're harassed by persistent evil or demoralizing thoughts, then verbally address Satan in this way. Claim the blood of Jesus Christ, which defeated Satan.

The devil may come back with a second round of fire—and maybe more. But when you continue to hold your ground in faithful obedience, you'll know the joy of victory.

Thank You that I can overcome the enemy's attacks through the power of the blood of Jesus. Help me to keep my shield of faith always at the ready and to be prepared with the truth of Your Word.

As we pursue a life of true surrender, it is absolutely vital that we keep our eyes on God. Only by looking continually to Him can we direct our focus away from our problems, away from our achievements or goals, away from our own strength or perceived wisdom. We need to remind ourselves frequently that "**God is opposed to the proud, but gives grace to the humble**" (1 Peter 5:5).

As the Holy Spirit renews our minds, we begin to think the way God thinks rather than according to man's reasoning. We see our need for total dependence. We recognize that the source of our problems is not a poor self-image or lack of self-esteem. Rather, when we see ourselves as we are—totally impotent and worthless apart from God—we realize the need to continually cast ourselves on the grace of God. As we see our poverty of spirit, we're released from thinking that our works could ever merit favor with God. We finally realize that all we receive from God is given—freely given—without any cause within ourselves.

It will help you tremendously, my friend, if you remember these things when you think of God's grace:

- God's grace is freely given without any cause within ourselves.
- Grace is always given because that is the heart of God.
- Grace is always given—never owed, never earned, never deserved.
- Grace is a benefit bestowed, released by faith alone.

~

Thank God for His grace, and ask Him to bring these truths to your mind continually, especially when you start to think or act in a way contrary to them.

March 13

Are you distressed at the seeming victories of the evil one and all his satanic host? Do you ever wonder why, if God is all-powerful and sovereign, He doesn't put a stop to all the rebellion, crime, and bloodshed? Do you wonder why He doesn't call a halt to drugs, alcohol, and all sorts of immorality and perversion? Do you have a hard time understanding why He allows evil men to rule and ungodly nations to persecute His people?

Do you weep over history? Do you fear what is yet to come and wonder where it all will end?

Weep not, beloved! The Lion from the tribe of Judah has overcome! The Lion is the Lamb, bearing in His body the marks of Calvary—marks that give eternal testimony that He has crushed the head of the serpent. The deceiver who usurped man's dominion is about to be evicted from the earth with all his demonic host because the Lamb is approaching the throne to take the title deed of the earth and break the seals.

> And they sang a new song, saying, "**Worthy are You to take the book and to break its seals; for You were slain, and purchased for God with Your blood men from every tribe and tongue and people and nation. You have made them to be a kingdom and priests to our God; and they will reign upon the earth.**" (Revelation 5:9–10)

Do not despair, my friend. Worthy is the Lamb—and He will have the victory!

This world is in such a dreadful state, Lord. It's so easy to become disheartened. Thank You for giving us a preview of the end of the story, for the assurance that Your power will overcome all evil.

March 14

Do you ever wonder where God is when bad things happen to you or someone you love?

Rest assured that God is not divorced from your pain. He's not a distant Creator who brought you into being and then abandoned you. "**The Lord is the one who goes ahead of you; He will be with you. He will not fail you or forsake you. Do not fear or be dismayed**" (Deuteronomy 31:8).

God doesn't stand on the sidelines and refuse to get involved because it's none of His business. Everything that concerns you is His business! He's not only your Creator; He's also your Sustainer.

Nor does He beat up on His kids. He disciplines them, but it is always for their good.

So when you wonder where God is when bad things happen, remember that God is in control. There is purpose in what He's doing, whether we see it or not. You have God's promise on that. What happens may not be good, but because He is God, He'll cause it to work together for your good (Romans 8:28).

Although you cannot understand why God did not intervene on your behalf in the midst of your trauma, you must believe God had a purpose. And if evil was done to you, it will be judged. "For the Lord is a God of recompense, He will fully repay" (Jeremiah 51:56). God is immutable; He never changes. He is consistent not only in blessing the righteous but also in judging sinners.

What a wonderful promise, dear God! To know that You will never forsake me, that You can never fail me. Thank You for being my Sustainer, my Shelter, my Strength.

March 15

Oh, beloved, what motivates you? What are your ambitions? Do you have a "need" to be in control? Are you constantly pushing yourself for recognition and achievement?

Have you seen self as the root of sin? Or have you been caught up in a doctrine that twists truth, urging you to practice positive thinking and to tap into "the potential" that lies within?

Is your vocabulary loaded with "I wills"? Or are you quick to say, "If the Lord wills"? Listen to James 4:13–16:

> Come now, you who say, "Today or tomorrow we will go to such and such a city, and spend a year there and engage in business and make a profit." Yet you do not know what your life will be like tomorrow.... **Instead, you ought to say, "If the Lord wills, we will live and also do this or that." But as it is, you boast in your arrogance; all such boasting is evil.**

If you are running your life rather than letting God run it, you are trying to be like the Most High. It is God's prerogative, and God's alone, to run our lives. We are the clay; He is the Potter. We are the created; He is the Creator. We are the servants; He is the Master. We are human; He is God.

Are you, in any way, trying to usurp His position?

~

Quicken my heart, Lord, to recognize any way in which I am striving for control, attempting to play a role that should be reserved only for You. Help me to break free of the desire to run my own life.

March 16

In the hours ahead, it's almost inevitable that some person or situation will provide ample opportunity for frustration and anger. Yet James 1:19 says, "**Everyone must be quick to hear, slow to speak and slow to anger.**" So how are we to respond in such circumstances?

1. Don't let your anger control you. "A fool always loses his temper, but a wise man holds it back" (Proverbs 29:11).

2. Be willing to overlook others' transgressions against you. This is meekness, not weakness. "A man's discretion makes him slow to anger, and it is his glory to overlook a transgression" (Proverbs 19:11).

3. Choose your words carefully. "A gentle answer turns away wrath, but a harsh word stirs up anger" (Proverbs 15:1).

4. Deal with your feelings. "Meditate in your heart upon your bed, and be still.… Offer the sacrifices of righteousness, and trust in the LORD" (Psalm 4:4–5). In other words, determine that you are going to sacrifice those emotions and desires for the sake of righteousness.

5. Trust in the Lord. Remember Joseph's words to the brothers who sold him into slavery: "As for you, you meant evil against me, but God meant it for good in order to bring about this present result, to preserve many people alive" (Genesis 50:20).

6. "Never take your own revenge, beloved, but leave room for the wrath of God" (Romans 12:19).

~

Take the next few minutes and pray these verses back to the Lord. Confess your anger and agree with Him that it is sin. Then forsake that anger, casting all your anxiety, bitterness, and hurt on Him who loves you so.

March 17

Have you ever been convicted of sin and felt like an absolute dog? I have. I know so much of the Word, yet I don't always live in the light of everything I know. At times, when something goes wrong, instead of bowing my knees in submission and getting up to move on in God's grace, I moan and grown over my ineptitude or wrong decision.

If I fail to put on the attire of the new person I am in Christ Jesus and I fail to walk in the Spirit, it is wrong. However, to compound it with another sin—ignoring the grace of God—is worse. I hate it when I sin, and that is the way it should be. But many times, because my flesh wants to "be perfect," I tend to stew over my lack of perfection and "what could have been if only" I had obeyed God in the first place. That should not be.

The proper response when we recognize sin in our lives is demonstrated by the psalmist who said, **"I acknowledged my sin to You, and my iniquity I did not hide; I said, 'I will confess my transgressions to the LORD'; and You forgave the guilt of my sin"** (Psalm 32:5).

When we confess our sin, we then need to go forward, believing that God is faithful and just to forgive our sins and to cleanse us from all unrighteousness (1 John 1:9).

Lord, You have promised to remove my transgressions "as far as the east is from the west" (Psalm 103:12). I choose to take You at Your word and receive Your grace, ignoring any false sense of guilt and living instead in the joy of Your presence.

March 18

If you expect to live a righteous life free of pain and disappointment, I'm afraid you're in for a rude awakening, dear one. Because of what Jesus was, they persecuted Him. Because of what Jesus makes you, they will persecute you also.

> **Remember the word that I said to you, "A slave is not greater than his master." If they persecuted Me, they will also persecute you; if they kept My word, they will keep yours also.** But all these things they will do to you for My name's sake, because they do not know the One who sent Me. (John 15:20–21)

The righteous lifestyle of those who belong to the kingdom of heaven will inevitably bring persecution, because it makes us radically different from the rest of this world, those who walk the broad path that leads to destruction (Matthew 7:13).

I believe that Christians in the United States of America will face an intense period of persecution in the not-too-distant future. My heart's burden and question for you is this: are you prepared to handle it? How I pray that you will dig deeper into God's Word on this subject. God's Word can prepare you to be adequate and equipped for whatever missiles Satan may throw at you in the coming days (2 Timothy 3:16–17).

~

Let me never be ashamed of the gospel, Lord. I believe it offers Your power of salvation to everyone who believes (Romans 1:16). Help me to stand strong in my faith, no matter what, remembering that You have not given me a spirit of timidity but of power and love and discipline (2 Timothy 1:7).

March 19

When things don't go our way, when God isn't giving us what we want, when we don't think our needs are being met, there is a great temptation to take the easy way out, to yield to our flesh, or to give up in discouragement.

These are the feelings the recipients of the letter to the Hebrews were experiencing. They didn't understand that their trials were part of God's discipline. So the author of Hebrews reminded them that the drama of redemption has not yet come to an end. If they wanted God's approval, they needed to continue in faith. Then he reminded them of the faithful saints who had come before, concluding:

> Therefore, since we have so great a cloud of witnesses surrounding us, **let us also lay aside every encumbrance and the sin which so easily entangles us, and let us run with endurance the race that is set before us, fixing our eyes on Jesus, the author and perfecter of faith,** who for the joy set before Him endured the cross, despising the shame, and has sat down at the right hand of the throne of God. (Hebrews 12:1–2)

Like these early believers, we need to remember that trials are part of God's discipline to refine us further, to free us from encumbrances and sins that are keeping us from His likeness. Grace does not exempt us from suffering and trials; it sees us through them. Our responsibility is to avail ourselves of the grace that flows from His throne.

~

Help me resist the temptation to look for an easy way out of my trials. Instead, open my eyes to what You want to accomplish in me and through me in the midst of difficult circumstances.

March 20

Oh, beloved, when you're overcome with regrets about the past, allow this truth to wash over your heart: **"He chose us in Him before the foundation of the world, that we would be holy and blameless before Him"** (Ephesians 1:4).

God knows all about you. Before the foundation of the world, He chose you. You may say, "But surely God would not have chosen me because ____________________."

Because of what you've done? Because of what was done to you? Were you going to say that if God had known what you would become—either by virtue of your own sin or by virtue of the sins others have committed against you—then He would not have chosen you?

You're wrong. God knows everything. He was there when you did what you did. He was there when others did what they shouldn't have done. God is your Creator and the Sustainer of your life. And He is the Righteous Judge, who gave His Son as the sacrifice for the sins of all mankind.

Because of grace, it doesn't matter what you were; it only matters where you are now...and that you are "in Him" and that "He is in you."

God, in His omniscience and sovereignty, allowed you to experience what you experienced. His intent was not to destroy you, because His thoughts toward you are precious. Rather, His purpose was to use it to make you into His child. A child upon whom He would delight to pour out His love. A child who would serve Him in the fullness of His grace.

Thank You, my God and my Father, that my past, present, and future are all within reach of Your sovereign grace. And thank You for choosing me and drawing me to Yourself.

What concerns are weighing on your heart and mind today, beloved? I think many of our problems overwhelm us simply because we do not set aside the time to be alone with God. I don't see how any Christian can survive, let alone live life as more than a conqueror, apart from quiet times alone with God.

Have you noticed how many voices clamor for our attention throughout the day? You and I are bombarded on every side by advertising, music, talk radio, news programs. We feel compelled to stay in touch with the world by reading the best-selling books and top magazines. If we're not careful, we can find ourselves spending hours in front of the television or computer, riveted to the images and messages on the screen.

If we do not turn them off and get alone with God, how can we hear His still small voice (1 Kings 19:12, KJV)?

The psalmist wrote, "**My soul, wait in silence for God only, for my hope is from Him**" (Psalm 62:5).

How important it is that we regularly seek refuge from the noise of life, my friend, and listen for the one Voice that truly matters. If you will learn to wait upon God, to get alone with Him and remain silent so you can hear His voice when He is ready to speak to you, what a difference it will make in your life!

~

Precious Lord, I come to You now and wait in silence for Your voice. Please speak to me and give me guidance for the day ahead.

March 22

Oh, beloved one, how many times we forget the cost our Lord paid to buy our redemption!

We forget that the beatings at the house of Caiaphas and the scourging of Roman soldiers marred His form more than any man, leaving Him unrecognizable as a human being (Isaiah 52:14).

We forget that flesh and bone hung by nails on a felled tree. We forget that the One who breathed life into man could breathe only as He pushed against the spike piercing His feet.

We forget the incomprehensible horror of bearing the sins of all mankind—past, present, and future. We forget that it must have been hell to have His Father turn His back on Him as He cried, "My God, my God, why hast thou forsaken me?" (Matthew 27:46, KJV).

We forget that our Kinsman endured all this and more. Isaiah 53:11 explains why He chose such agony: **"As a result of the anguish of His soul, He will see it and be satisfied; by His knowledge the Righteous One, My Servant, will justify the many, as He will bear their iniquities."**

Who would be willing to pay such a price to redeem people who were otherwise without hope—helpless, sinners, ungodly, and, on top of all that, enemies?

Only Jesus, who, "taking the form of a bond-servant, and being made in the likeness of men…humbled Himself by becoming obedient to the point of death, even death on a cross" (Philippians 2:7–8).

~

Spend some time alone with God. Read Psalm 22 and meditate on Christ's sacrifice on your behalf.

March 23

Have you ever meditated on the wonder of God's grace at work in your life? Consider Romans 8:32: **"He who did not spare His own Son, but delivered Him over for us all, how will He not also with Him freely give us all things?"**

God freely gives us all things—everything that pertains to life and godliness—through His abundant grace. Grace is unearned or unmerited favor. Some have defined it this way:

G—God's

R—riches

A—at

C—Christ's

E—expense

Grace is everything Jesus Christ is and has made available to us simply as an act of God's love. Everything we have in Christ is a gift of grace.

Because grace exists, I'm not afraid to tell you my shortcomings and my struggles. It's nice to know that struggling doesn't make us less spiritual, isn't it? Our spirituality shows in how we handle our circumstances.

Because of grace, I can share the lessons of my past. Grace covers every sin, every failure, every need. If I didn't know this truth, I don't think I could handle my past. I'd have so much guilt I couldn't move ahead.

But grace covers. God provides it—and it doesn't cost us a thing, because it cost God everything.

~

Out of the fullness of Christ, You have blessed me with grace upon grace. I thank You that today I can draw upon Your abundant provision for my every sin, every failure, every need.

March 24

If Christ's death on the cross has purchased forgiveness of our sins, then aren't we free to live this day however we choose? Can't we do or say whatever we want and simply ask forgiveness afterward? A thousand times no!

A biblical understanding of grace will cause us to live in such a way that we don't cheapen God's grace by seeking to turn it into a free pass for licentious living.

Grace doesn't permit a person to live an immoral lifestyle. Remember that the covenant of grace gives the believer the indwelling Holy Spirit. In Ezekiel 36:27, we read: "I will put My Spirit within you and cause you to walk in My statutes, and you will be careful to observe My ordinances."

If you think you can continue to live in sin because you are under grace, you insult the Spirit of grace (Hebrews 10:29). The apostle Paul cautions, "Do not grieve the Holy Spirit of God, by whom you were sealed for the day of redemption" (Ephesians 4:30).

Life lived according to the grace of God is not lawless! Rather, life under God's grace is evidenced by ever-increasing holiness: "**Sending His own Son in the likeness of sinful flesh and as an offering for sin, He condemned sin in the flesh, so that the requirement of the Law might be fulfilled in us, who do not walk according to the flesh but according to the Spirit**" (Romans 8:3–4).

Remember: grace is not license to sin; rather, it is power to overcome the flesh.

~

Guard my steps, that I may not grieve Your Spirit by walking in the flesh. Let me never take Your grace for granted but remember that it came at a high price—the blood of Your precious Son.

March 25

My friend, have you failed in your role as a parent, spouse, friend, brother, or sister? Are you weighed down with a burden of guilt and regret?

No matter what you've done, God has assured you of complete and absolute forgiveness. Through the blood of Jesus Christ, all your sins were paid for—once for all: **"By [God's] will we have been sanctified through the offering of the body of Jesus Christ once for all"** (Hebrews 10:10).

A guilty conscience can wreak havoc and destruction in our relationships with others, in our emotions, and even in our bodies. The cure for a guilty conscience comes in understanding and accepting the grace of God, which freely pardons all our sins through faith in the Lord Jesus Christ. A guilty conscience is shed like filthy rags at the foot of the throne of God. This is why the author of Hebrews wrote:

> Therefore, brethren, since we have confidence to enter the holy place by the blood of Jesus, by a new and living way which He inaugurated for us through the veil, that is, His flesh, and since we have a great priest over the house of God, let us draw near with a sincere heart in full assurance of faith, having our hearts sprinkled clean from an evil conscience and our bodies washed with pure water. (10:19–22)

There is no guilt that cannot be cared for at the mercy seat of God. Our part is to draw near.

~

What a wonderful gift, to know that You have completely forgiven my every sin, my every failure. Thank You, blessed Redeemer, that I walk not in guilt but in grace!

March 26

Have you endured times when it seems the Lord has forgotten you as His child—times when the pain, the hurt, and the rejection are so bad you can hardly stand it?

Oh, beloved, how I urge you to recognize and trust in the character of your loving Father, who says, "**Can a woman forget her nursing child and have no compassion on the son of her womb? Even these may forget, but I will not forget you. Behold, I have inscribed you on the palms of My hands**" (Isaiah 49:15–16).

Behold your Savior. Put your finger in the nail prints. Remember that God has loved you with an everlasting love. You are accepted in the Beloved (Ephesians 1:6, KJV). He'll never, never leave you nor forsake you. God will not—cannot—reject His own. Won't you run to the shelter of His Word?

"Who will separate us from the love of Christ? Will tribulation, or distress, or persecution, or famine, or nakedness, or peril, or sword?" (Romans 8:35).

Did you think these things were signs that God does not love you, that He has forsaken you?

"But in all these things we overwhelmingly conquer through Him who loved us. For I am convinced that neither death, nor life, nor angels, nor principalities, nor things present, nor things to come, nor powers, nor height, nor depth, nor any other created thing, will be able to separate us from the love of God, which is in Christ Jesus our Lord" (Romans 8:37–39).

Cling to God's promises, my friend.

~

Thank You, Father, for Your everlasting, unshakable love. No matter what comes, I believe You'll never leave me nor forsake me.

March 27

What's on your mind today, beloved? Is your thought life dominated by images you've seen on the Internet, songs you've heard on the radio, or items that caught your eye in a catalog? How much of your thought life centers on God and His Word?

Remember the admonition of Romans 12:2: "**And do not be conformed to this world, but be transformed by the renewing of your mind, so that you may prove what the will of God is, that which is good and acceptable and perfect.**"

When you dwell on things that are not of God or that are against God, you are giving the enemy ground on which he can erect a stronghold or a fortress. This is why the apostle Paul says, "We are destroying speculations [or imaginations] and every lofty thing raised up against the knowledge of God" (2 Corinthians 10:5). If Paul had not destroyed the thoughts that were contrary to the Word of God, they could have become the means of destroying him.

Paul goes on to say, "We are taking every thought captive to the obedience of Christ." In other words, whenever a thought came to Paul's mind, he evaluated it to see if it was pleasing to Christ and in accord with the Word of God.

Will you allow the enemy to set up camp in your mind by dwelling on unwholesome or defeating thoughts? Or will you follow the example of Paul and take every thought captive to the obedience of Christ?

~

Give me discernment, Lord, so I may be able to resist the wiles of the devil. Help me keep my mind and heart free of destructive or distracting thoughts.

March 28

What does it mean to live by faith, and how can we do so with confidence?

Faith is a firm persuasion, a conviction based on hearing. Therefore, according to Romans 10:17, faith comes from hearing God's Word: **"So faith comes from hearing, and hearing by the word of Christ."**

The Bible is God's word to man. It is God-breathed and God-preserved from the time that Moses, under the moving of God's Spirit, began to write the Pentateuch to the time the apostle John completed the Scriptures by writing in the book of Revelation the things which were, which are, and which are yet to come (Revelation 1:19).

When Jesus came to earth as the Son of Man, He never contradicted the Scriptures, nor did He ever imply they were inaccurate in any detail. What modern scholars have deemed mere stories recorded by man in order to illustrate a point, Jesus treated as actual, historical events.

Oh, my friend, never let anyone tell you that God's Word contains errors. Won't you believe the sovereign, omnipotent, omniscient God? Won't you believe His Son, who is one with the Father and called "the Truth"? Or will you believe men tutored by men more than the testimony of the One who, as the Son of God, has been forever with the Father—One who is called the very Word of God?

Only when you fully believe in God's Word can you live with bold, confident faith in its Author.

~

Thank You for Your Word, for the power of the truths it reveals. Thank You that I can feast on every word that proceeds from Your mouth and be strengthened for Your work.

March 29

Oh, beloved, have you ever been afraid that you might walk away from God? that at some dark point in your life you might turn away from Him? I understand. I used to be bothered by those fears too. But then I read Jeremiah 32:40, and my eyes were opened to God's wonderful keeping power: **"I will make an everlasting covenant with them that I will not turn away from them, to do them good; and I will put the fear of Me in their hearts so that they will not turn away from Me."**

In the New Covenant, God promises us that He will put the fear of Him in our hearts so that we will not turn away! Praise the Lord!

This reminds me of what Paul wrote in 2 Timothy 1:12: "I know whom I have believed and I am convinced that He is able to guard what I have entrusted to Him until that day."

God writes His laws on your very heart. Isn't that wonderful? As a result, you have a deep, inner knowledge and awareness of what pleases God and what displeases Him.

If you truly long to honor God with your life this day, He will honor that desire and equip you to walk in faithfulness.

Almighty, gracious God, I thank You that I am not under bondage to sin. Thank You that Your divine power has granted me everything I need pertaining to life and godliness (2 Peter 1:3). Help me stand firm in that knowledge today.

March 30

Weakness is often a source of shame and embarrassment. We tend to look at our inadequacies, our weaknesses, and say, "I can't." "Not me; it will never happen." "There's no way!" When we do that, do you think we may be limiting God?

The apostle Paul wrote, "If I have to boast, I will boast of what pertains to my weakness" (2 Corinthians 11:30).

When we think about boasting, we usually focus on our strengths and analyze how they can best be used in our quest for whatever. To look at our weaknesses seems ludicrous, defeating! Certainly contrary to what the world would tell us to do. And yet Paul had learned to boast in the insults, distresses, persecutions, and difficulties he experienced, because his weakness threw him to his knees—and there he came to know the incredible power of God.

First Corinthians reminds us that God revels in using unlikely people for His glorious purposes: "**God has chosen the foolish things of the world to shame the wise, and God has chosen the weak things of the world to shame the things which are strong...so that, just as it is written, 'Let him who boasts, boast in the LORD'**" (1:27, 31).

As we, like Paul, turn to God in our weakness, our inadequacy, we become aware of the difference between the wisdom of the world and the wisdom of God. And we learn that He has all the strength we need.

Loving God, thank You for choosing me just as I am to serve You. Lead me to draw upon Your strength to complete the work You give me so that You and only You will receive the glory.

March 31

Is God using you in the lives of those around you? Are you willing to be open and vulnerable so that others will find you approachable? Romans 12:15 urges us to **"rejoice with those who rejoice, and weep with those who weep."** By entering into the joy and pain of others, we serve as vessels of God's love and comfort.

Remember, you cannot continue in sin and be used. However, once you have allowed God to heal you through His Word, you are ready to be used by God in the healing of others. You don't have to be a professional counselor to help; you have the Word of God. In Psalm 119:24, we read, "Your testimonies also are my delight; they are my counselors" or, to put it literally, "the men of my counsel."

You also have the Holy Spirit. His ministry is to guide you into all truth, to bring to your remembrance the truths you've learned. God's truth sanctifies and sets people free. So, when you minister, ask the Holy Spirit to show you what truths the person needs.

Being used by God to minister to others is one of the greatest privileges of a believer. And He's equipped you with all you need. You only have to be willing and sensitive to His leading.

~

Take a few minutes to talk to your Father. Make yourself available to Him to be used to minister to others—even if it's just being available to listen, to pray, or to encourage, reprove, or exhort from God's Word. Then watch what God does!

April 1

As you anticipate the day ahead, have you considered how you'll respond to any disappointments that come your way? Amid stress, suffering, or rejection, what's the most important thing anyone could ever see in you? It is Jesus. His life in you. When that happens, He alone gets the glory.

Consider the words of the apostle Paul:

> **We are afflicted in every way, but not crushed; perplexed, but not despairing; persecuted, but not forsaken; struck down, but not destroyed; always carrying about in the body the dying of Jesus, so that the life of Jesus also may be manifested in our body.** (2 Corinthians 4:8–10)

When difficulties come, we can be assured of several things:

- You and I can be pressured by our circumstances—but we cannot be crushed. Why? Because there's a stronger power within us than without.
- Though we may be perplexed, we need not despair or give up. We have within us the God of all hope.
- We may be struck down and brought low, but we'll never be destroyed. Even physical death cannot destroy the child of God, for death merely places us immediately in the presence of Christ.

These are our assurances, recorded forever in the Word of God. This is our legacy in the difficulties of life. Will you live today so that Christ's life might be dramatically seen in you?

Thank You, faithful Lord, that I can never be destroyed by the circumstances of my life. Use me to demonstrate Your resurrection power to those who need a reason to hope.

April 2

Precious child of God, may I ask you to consider what underlying thoughts and beliefs direct your decisions and lifestyle?

Living in daily surrender and being transformed into the image of Christ involves a continual renewing of our minds, allowing God to free us from any worries, worldly concerns, or mistaken philosophies that have enslaved our thinking. **"So also we, while we were children, were held in bondage under the elemental things of the world"** (Galatians 4:3).

People can be held in bondage by wrong thoughts, worldly philosophies, worldly wisdom, wrong doctrine, and all sorts of lies from the father of lies. These are fortresses of wrong thinking, which need to be torn down, destroyed. Any thinking that is contrary to God, to His Word, and to our position in Christ and what God says about us is to be destroyed. We are not to allow these thoughts to continue. If we do, Satan will be the victor. Any thought that would lead us to disobedience or unbelief is not from God, and it, too, must be dealt with. We have the weapons to bring down these strongholds.

The key is found in Paul's example: "We are taking every thought captive to the obedience of Christ" (2 Corinthians 10:5). This, then, is what we must do with every thought: take it captive and subjugate it to Christ! And we must do it continually.

God of all truth, free my mind from wrong thinking, from anything that is contrary to Your will, Your character, Your Word. Let Your truths be my meditation all the day long so that I will not fall victim to the lies of Satan.

April 3

Beloved, can you declare with certainty that you possess a righteousness born of faith in Jesus Christ? And how is this reflected in your daily living? Remember, **"No one, after putting his hand to the plow and looking back, is fit for the kingdom of God"** (Luke 9:62).

When I share the gospel, I hear all sorts of reasons why people who live in sin still think they are going to heaven. I also hear people say they aren't really interested in the rewards of godly living. They simply want to "make it into heaven" when life is over.

These people bring to mind the story of the rich young ruler in Mark 10:17–27. The young man wanted eternal life—but on his own terms. He loved his riches more than he loved God!

"Jesus felt a love for him," but He could not let him enter His kingdom. The way is narrow, the gate small, and those who enter His kingdom are few.

It's so important, my friend, to examine your beliefs and lifestyle in the pure light of God's holy Word. So please consider seriously a few questions:

- What is your relationship with Jesus Christ?
- Do you want the kingdom of heaven—now? On whose terms?
- Who must be your Master?
- Is anything keeping you from forsaking all to follow Him? If so, is it worth missing the kingdom?

I urge you, my friend, to give these things serious thought.

~

Take these questions to God in prayer, and ask Him to open your eyes to the truth.

April 4

Are you concerned today about a friend or loved one who has not yet claimed Jesus as Savior? Are you entrusting that person to God's holy but loving care, or have you been pushing for a decision? Remember, Jesus has promised, "**My sheep hear My voice, and I know them, and they follow Me; and I give eternal life to them, and they will never perish; and no one will snatch them out of My hand**" (John 10:27–28).

Sometimes we're so quick to try to get people into heaven that I think we go after a profession of faith rather than allow the Holy Spirit to bring conviction. We fail to let others grapple with their total inability to save themselves through their good deeds, religious sacraments, and impotent wrestling with fleshly desires. We present the blessings of belonging but fail to point out the consequences of rejecting Christ.

We're in such a hurry to "get them saved" (as if we ourselves could save them) that we don't wait for God to shine His light into the darkness of their souls.

The Good Shepherd is not going to lose one single lamb that belongs in His fold. He promises that they shall never perish. No one can snatch them out of Jesus' hand.

Will you rest in this hope and surrender your loved one into God's hands?

~

Lord, You have promised that not one of Your sheep will be lost. Shine Your light into the souls of my unsaved loved ones and convict them of their desperate need for You. And please help me not to get in the way of what You're doing!

April 5

Are you facing a difficult time in your marriage or perhaps in one of your friendships, beloved? How can you respond with righteousness and grace in this situation?

When relationships get rough—when we become disillusioned, disappointed, or hurt—the first thing we tend to do is quit communicating. The second thing is to withhold affection. It's the way we punish, making sure the person knows he or she has failed us.

This is what the Corinthians did to Paul. But Paul would not react in kind. Instead he said, "**Our mouth has spoken freely to you, O Corinthians, our heart is opened wide. You are not restrained by us, but you are restrained in your own affections**" (2 Corinthians 6:11–12). When he wrote that his mouth was "open to them," which is the literal translation, he meant that he was still writing, still communicating. And his heart was open as well. Their wrong behavior couldn't quell his love, because it was God's love flowing through Paul—unconditional, never-ceasing love.

How critical this is, for so often people wrongly attempt to control others by their communication or lack of it. Or by withholding their affection every time someone displeases them. As servants of God we cannot control our loved ones this way. We each are to be controlled only by God.

As you seek to honor God in your daily interactions, remember that healthy relationships are not manipulated. They're based on honesty and integrity.

~

Lord, give me grace to be kind and loving in my most difficult relationships. Help me to have a tender heart, to forgive freely rather than take offense.

April 6

When we, or those we love, have suffered unjustly at the hands of another, it's hard to forgive, especially if the perpetrator won't admit or apologize for the offense. And yet that's exactly what God requires of us: "**Be kind to one another, tender-hearted, forgiving each other, just as God in Christ also has forgiven you**" (Ephesians 4:32).

So what do we do when we feel that we can't forgive—or don't have the desire to?

First, we must realize that forgiveness is a matter of the will, not the emotions. God has commanded us to forgive, so refusing to do so is disobedience. Commands are not options or suggestions that we can pick or choose from on the basis of our emotions or desires. Rather, our Lord's commands are to be obeyed, regardless of what we feel or think.

Second, we need to realize that our forgiveness of others doesn't exempt them from the just judgment of God. It doesn't mean they won't be held accountable.

If you're still having a hard time, if you're wrestling with forgiving another, you need to take a good, hard, objective look at the Lord's forgiveness of you. Remember that when you forgive someone, it's one sinner forgiving another. Neither you nor the other person is or has been what you ought to be. By contrast, when Jesus Christ forgives us, He is forgiving people who have sinned against His perfect holiness! Calling to mind that truth should help you gain a fresh perspective on forgiveness.

Precious Lord, give me a spirit of gentleness and humility and compassion so that I may live—and forgive—out of the abundance of grace You have shown toward me.

April 7

If you and I are seeking peace in our daily lives, we must choose to respond in meekness to whatever frustrations, challenges, or disappointments come our way: "**But the meek shall inherit the earth; and shall delight themselves in the abundance of peace**" (Psalm 37:11, KJV).

What does it mean to be meek? How does meekness fit with the sovereignty and character of God?

Meekness speaks of a submissive and trusting attitude toward God. It is an attitude that accepts all of God's ways as good. It does not murmur or dispute. It neither rebels nor retaliates. It realizes that what comes to us from the hand of man has been permitted by God's sovereignty, has been filtered by His fingers of love, and will be used by God for His glory and our ultimate good.

Meekness looks beyond circumstances—no matter how upsetting and hurtful—and bows the knee to the sovereign God. And in doing so, meekness taps into the peace that passes all understanding.

I am convinced that if we are to walk in meekness, we must know our God. We must accept His sovereign rule. We must grapple with the character of this One who rules over the affairs of men and the hosts of heaven. Of all the truths I've ever learned, none has brought me more assurance, boldness, calmness, devotion, gratitude, and humility than the sovereignty of God. I pray it will do the same for you.

Lord God, I choose to trust You with the circumstances of this day. Fill my heart and mind with the peace that comes from walking in meekness down whatever path You lead me on.

April 8

Have you been cheated, treated unfairly, ignored, or harmed in some other way? No matter the cruelty or pain, beloved, as a child of God your pathway is clear: you must forgive.

To the very depths of your heart, you must fully forgive whoever has wounded you, deceived you, or transgressed against you.

"But I can't!" you say. No, my friend, it's not that you can't but that you won't. There's a big difference. Know this: if you do not forgive others, God cannot forgive you. Remember Jesus' words in Matthew 6:15: "**But if you do not forgive others, then your Father will not forgive your transgressions.**" So you can forgive, and you must forgive. The question is, will you?

Or if your complaint is against God, if you are bitter toward Him, then you need to ask Him to forgive you for your lack of meekness.

Meekness is the sure cure for bitterness—bitterness toward God or bitterness toward man. Meekness is strong medicine indeed. And though it may be hard to swallow in some cases, once you have ingested it, you will taste the sweet, healing flavor of life itself.

~

Ask God to show you any root of bitterness in your heart. Tell Him you want it gone. Give Him permission to remove it—even if the roots are deep! Then wait on Him in prayer, and do everything He puts in your heart to do.

April 9

What role, if any, should anger have in your life and mine? Is it possible to be angry without dishonoring God?

The answer is yes, but we need to understand the crucial difference between a righteous anger and an unrighteous anger. We see righteous anger demonstrated in the life of Jesus Christ when He overturned the tables of the moneychangers in the temple. We see righteous anger in God when King Solomon disobeyed and allowed his heart to be turned toward other gods.

Obviously, when Paul wrote, "**Be angry, and yet do not sin; do not let the sun go down on your anger**" (Ephesians 4:26), he was referring to righteous anger. By contrast, when Jesus said that "everyone who is angry with his brother shall be guilty before the court" (Matthew 5:22), He was speaking about a wrong and sinful kind of anger.

What's the difference? What makes anger wrong? In the context of Scripture, we see that it is wrong because it is directed toward the sinner rather than the sin. It is an anger that, if unchecked, could lead to murder. Therefore, if you are going to be righteous before God, you cannot permit this kind of anger in your heart.

~

Give me the wisdom to distinguish between righteous anger and unrighteous anger. Let my emotions be guided by Your Holy Spirit so that I am angered by what offends You rather than by what offends me.

April 10

When you come up against disappointment, temptation, difficulties, or defeat, will you trust in your loving God—or will you take matters into your own hands?

The apostle Paul reminds us that such challenges cannot be conquered through human wisdom or methods: "**For though we walk in the flesh, we do not war according to the flesh, for the weapons of our warfare are not of the flesh, but divinely powerful for the destruction of fortresses**" (2 Corinthians 10:3–4).

Although Paul walked in a fleshly body—as we all do—he did not walk "according to the flesh," that is, under the dominion of the flesh. Nor did he war "according to the flesh," because he knew it was a spiritual battle: "Our struggle is not against flesh and blood, but against...the world forces of this darkness, against the spiritual forces of wickedness in the heavenly places. Therefore, take up the full armor of God, so that you will be able to resist in the evil day, and having done everything, to stand firm" (Ephesians 6:12–13).

The armor of God is truth, righteousness, peace with God, faith, salvation—and the sword of the Spirit, which is the Word of God. Equipped with all this, we then "pray at all times in the Spirit...on the alert with all perseverance and petition for all the saints" (Ephesians 6:18).

These are the divinely powerful weapons that destroy the fortresses, the strongholds of the enemy.

~

As I encounter frustrations and temptations today, help me to remember who the enemy is and to be mindful of his tactics. Remind me that my struggle is against things unseen and that I can experience victory only by taking up my spiritual armor.

April 11

Is prayerful petition a vital part of your daily life? Do you deliberately lay your needs before your heavenly Father each morning, not in a rote prayer but sincerely seeking His divine care and sustenance?

Not only has Jehovah foreseen your need for salvation and made provision through the death and resurrection of His Son, but He also sees your day-by-day needs. Thus, Jesus left these instructions: "And when you are praying, do not use meaningless repetition as the Gentiles do, for they suppose that they will be heard for their many words. So do not be like them; **for your Father knows what you need before you ask Him**" (Matthew 6:7–8).

Yes, our Father, Jehovah-jireh, both sees and knows our needs. Yet He instructs us to pray, "Give us this day our daily bread" (Matthew 6:11).

Do you feel silly asking God for bread when you can get it yourself? Do you feel that it is unnecessary to come to the sovereign ruler of the universe with your seemingly trivial needs? Do you wonder why God would even bother with you?

Oh, beloved, Jehovah-jireh bids us to come. We are coming to the One who is for us! "He who did not spare His own Son, but delivered Him over for us all, how will He not also with Him freely give us all things?" (Romans 8:32).

He is a God who is for you, not against you. In any test you can worship Jehovah-jireh in obedience and know that whatever you need, the Lord will provide it.

Jehovah God, You are my provider, sufficient for my every need. Please give me today just what You know I need.

April 12

In my walk with God, I long to develop a spiritual disposition that causes me to seek Him immediately in every situation. I want to come to a place where I always think of how my God would have me respond because of who He is and because of what He has said. But often I simply react to a situation. Do you, too, find yourself reacting over and over again to the circumstances of life rather than responding to the knowledge of God?

Yet, if we are new creations in Christ Jesus, we can't do whatever we want. Instead, as Galatians 5:25 directs, **"If we live by the Spirit, let us also walk by the Spirit."** If we walk by the Spirit, we will come under His control even in our emotional responses. According to Galatians 5:22–23, if I am filled with the Spirit, the fruit of love, joy, peace, patience, kindness, goodness, faithfulness, gentleness, and self-control will be seen in my walk. Not one of these characteristics will be missing!

How I pray we will each learn to turn to Him immediately. I pray that we will not react to the natural but that we will respond to the spiritual.

O loving Father, how easy it is to react in the flesh when I am disappointed or frustrated. Please fill me with Your Holy Spirit and let me walk by His power so that my words, attitudes, and actions today will reflect Your grace and truth.

April 13

Are you serious about guarding your heart, beloved? If so, you must remain alert against temptation, which so often worms its way into our lives through subtle means.

Adultery is awakened by what the eye sees or what the hand touches. For this reason, Jesus said, "If your right eye makes you stumble, tear it out and throw it from you.... If your right hand makes you stumble, cut it off and throw it from you; for it is better for you to lose one of the parts of your body, than for your whole body to go into hell" (Matthew 5:29–30).

Is Jesus telling you to literally pull out your eye? to literally cut off your hand? I don't believe so. I think He's using hyperbole to make His point that adultery is a sin that can take you to hell. Consider the warning in Galatians 5:19, 21: "Now the deeds of the flesh are evident, which are: immorality, impurity, sensuality,...and things like these, of which I forewarn you...that **those who practice such things will not inherit the kingdom of God.**"

God isn't saying that a single act of adultery condemns a person to an eternity in hell. He's saying that if adultery is the practice of your life, you won't enter the kingdom of heaven.

Therefore, get rid of anything that would cause you to commit adultery. Do not put yourself in a position of vulnerability. The spirit is willing, but the flesh is weak. Whatever you have to do, bring it under control. If you don't, sin will destroy you!

~

Before You, dear Lord, I make a covenant with my eyes, just as Job did (Job 31:1, 9–12). I refuse to let my gaze linger on anything that could entice me to sin. Let my eyes look only on that which is pure.

April 14

Will your words and actions today reveal you to others as a man or woman of integrity and honesty? Is your Christian walk honest before God? Can others trust you…or do you cheat?

Cheating can take all sorts of forms. It doesn't necessarily have to be in school when you take an exam. You can cheat the government. You can cheat on contracts. You can fail to tell the whole truth. You can pad the statistics for emphasis. You can advertise and exaggerate. You can tell "little white lies."

You can do all these things, but then where is your integrity?

Isn't that the issue in our world today—integrity?

Job determined not to lower his standards or to buy into the justification that "it's just how things are done these days." He declared, **"Till I die I will not put away my integrity from me"** (Job 27:5).

Can you say the same? What's your contribution to the moral fiber of our nation? Can you say what Paul said in the midst of a corrupt Roman Empire? "Be imitators of me, just as I also am of Christ." "Join in following my example, and observe those who walk according to the pattern you have in us" (1 Corinthians 11:1; Philippians 3:17).

Holy Lord, I choose not to set my mind on earthly things but to pursue Your standards of righteousness. With the psalmist I pray, "Let integrity and uprightness preserve me" (Psalm 25:21).

Do you worry about your financial future? Are you preoccupied with saving money for the days ahead? Tell me, beloved, just what kind of Father do you have? Is He faithless or faithful? Can He lie?

Of course He cannot lie. And, yes, He is always faithful. As Paul wrote to Timothy, "If we are faithless, He remains faithful, for He cannot deny Himself" (2 Timothy 2:13). You can trust Him, so quit being anxious! It's so unnecessary. It's also a sin. It's an accusation against the very faithfulness of God.

Remember the reassuring words of Jesus: **"Look at the birds of the air, that they do not sow, nor reap nor gather into barns, and yet your heavenly Father feeds them. Are you not worth much more than they?"** (Matthew 6:26).

What then is the bottom line when it comes to our needs, the basics of life? Jesus made it clear: "Do not worry about tomorrow" (Matthew 6:34).

We are to live one day at a time. That's why Jesus taught us to pray, "Give us each day our daily bread" (Luke 11:3). If He took care of you today, will He not take care of you tomorrow?

~

Loving Father, I thank You for the assurance that my loved ones and I are Your precious children, for whom You will be faithful to provide. Convict me when I sin by giving way to anxious thoughts and worries rather than trusting You with my tomorrows.

April 16

In our commitment to continually surrender our moments and days to God, fasting can be a powerful tool for focusing ourselves more fully on Him. But this spiritual discipline requires us to first examine our hearts.

Consider Jesus' words on this subject: **"When you fast, anoint your head and wash your face so that your fasting will not be noticed by men, but by your Father who is in secret; and your Father who sees what is done in secret will reward you"** (Matthew 6:17–18).

It seems to be a given with Jesus that God's children will fast. And as with other spiritual disciplines, we see that this action is directed toward our Father and has nothing to do with putting on a show for others. When we fast, we must not do anything to draw attention to our hunger or our dedication. Fasting is between each of us and our God.

Fasting implies abstinence. It usually refers to doing without food for a limited period of time. As you move through the Bible and examine each reference to fasting, you will see that people fasted for various reasons and in different ways. Sometimes individuals fasted; at other times people were gathered together for the sole purpose of fasting and seeking God.

Fasting can be sincere and done for proper reasons. It can also be done for selfish purposes. "Are you seeking Me?" God asks. "Or are you trying to manipulate Me?" It's a good question to ask ourselves when we fast.

~

Ask God to reveal any hidden motives in your fasting. If fasting is not a regular habit for you, ask God how He would have you incorporate this discipline in your life.

April 17

Fasting is usually born out of a need. Jesus brings this out in His answer to the disciples of John, who asked why Jesus' followers didn't make a practice of fasting: "The attendants of the bridegroom cannot mourn as long as the bridegroom is with them, can they? **But the days will come when the bridegroom is taken away from them, and then they will fast**" (Matthew 9:15).

In essence, Jesus said, "I'm here, supplying their needs. Therefore, they don't need to fast. But when I'm gone, they will." When people fast, it is generally because they feel moved by a need!

Fasting calls us to break from our normal preoccupations with the body. It summons us into such serious communion with our Lord that we voluntarily abstain from our normal absorption with such needs as food and drink. Could this be why more of us don't fast? Could it be that we're too busy? too self-sufficient? too self-absorbed?

Instead of seeking the Lord in time of need, we first try fixing it ourselves. Before we know it, we're over our heads in planning, scheming, and manipulating to bring about what we need and desire. If we're that busy, who has time for fasting? Fasting is for those who will put aside all else, including food, to seek God on some particular issue or need.

When was the last time you deemed something so important, so critical, that you sought God in prayer and fasting?

~

Speak to my heart, Lord, and show me where I've grown complacent. Reveal my deep need for You, and equip me for the discipline of fasting so that I may seek You with single-minded focus.

April 18

As we consider the pain in this world, the suffering endured by those around us, and even the heartbreak we face ourselves, we may wonder if some wounds are so great that they can never be healed. Is healing possible...no matter how bad the hurt? no matter if it was self-inflicted, the consequence of sin?

It is. Whether you believe it or not, you are beloved of God. He desires your wholeness, your healing.

About twenty-five hundred years ago, God had the prophet Jeremiah record His burden for His people who were hurting. Listen to the anguish of Jeremiah's heart: **"For the brokenness of the daughter of my people I am broken; I mourn, dismay has taken hold of me"** (Jeremiah 8:21).

Why the anguish? Was it because of the greatness of their wound? No, beloved, it was because there was a cure for their hurts, and they were unaware of it. Or perhaps it was because they knew where to turn but refused for some reason.

Consider Jeremiah's cry of dismay: "Is there no balm in Gilead? Is there no physician there? Why then has not the health of the daughter of my people been restored?" (Jeremiah 8:22).

Can you relate to the anguish of Jeremiah's heart? Do you long for healing and restoration? Have you been hurt so badly that you wonder if the pain will ever go away?

There is balm in Gilead, my friend. The Great Physician awaits with healing for every wound of your soul!

Thank You that You care, God, that You know every detail of my pain, my suffering. And thank You for Your healing power at work in my life.

April 19

My prayer is that God will show you today how precious you are in His sight, not because of who or what you are, but simply because of who He is and because of the unmerited favor He has chosen to bestow upon you as a vessel of His mercy.

And yet I must give you the other side of the coin. There are those who cling to their impurities of bitterness, hate, and anger, even in the fire of increased suffering. The result is that they become what God calls rejected or reprobate silver. This is what happened in Jeremiah's day when the people refused God's healing:

> All of them are stubbornly rebellious.... They, all of them, are corrupt. The bellows blow fiercely, the lead is consumed by the fire; in vain the refining goes on, but the wicked are not separated. **They call them rejected silver, because the LORD has rejected them.** (Jeremiah 6:28–30)

If you and I do not allow the truths of God's Word to transform us into His image, then God can do nothing more with us. Don't let this happen to you. If you do, you'll never know His healing.

You can come through any difficulty or trial and be conformed to the image of Jesus Christ. Remember, He lives to intercede for you, and He understands you.

Thank You for the example of Your Son, who learned obedience from the things He suffered (Hebrews 5:8–9). Help me to follow His pattern of trusting submission so that I will emerge from the fire of my trials, purified and holy.

April 20

Have you ever felt that you couldn't be good even if you wanted to? Have you hated the things you were doing, but you couldn't stop yourself? That's exactly the way it was for me before I was saved.

When I finally faced my immorality for what it was, I simply knew that a holy God could not accept me into heaven. So I determined to change my lifestyle. And I did try. But it didn't work. I would say, "I'm not going to do that anymore." But I would! I'd go out and be immoral again. Little did I realize how well my frustration would one day help me relate to Paul's cry, **"Wretched man that I am! Who will set me free from the body of this death?"** (Romans 7:24).

I was a slave to sin. I made resolution after resolution, but resolutions couldn't unlock my chains. Finally one day I fell to my knees. "O God, I don't care what You do to me," I sobbed, "if You will only give me peace."

There on my knees, I received the Prince of Peace.

In the days that followed, I knew that I was clean and that Jesus was with me. I had been set free. My perspective on life was different. I was no longer a slave. I had the power to say no and to live according to God's commandments.

I'm not saying that I didn't sin. I did. But not like I used to. Sin was now a matter of free choice, and sin was not something I casually chose! I wanted to please my God. And I was able to do so because the Godhead had taken up residence within (John 14:23).

Thank You that through Your power I've been set free from the chains of sin. Help me to live according to this truth, choosing to obey and honor You.

April 21

When we start our days by giving each moment ahead into God's keeping, we acknowledge our utter dependence on His amazing grace—and our utter inability to be righteous in our own strength.

It is the presence of the indwelling Holy Spirit that enables us to keep God's statutes and ordinances. Thus, Paul could write, "**Walk by the Spirit, and you will not carry out the desire of the flesh**" (Galatians 5:16). And it is the Spirit within that causes us to fear God, to have a reverential respect for Him. It is the Spirit who keeps us from turning away from God.

It is grace, grace, grace. God does it all. Ours is only to believe. Even the faith to believe is of grace. It is all of grace.

It is by grace that we are saved.

It is by grace that we know Him intimately.

It is by grace that we live day by day.

By grace we deal with the traumas of life.

By grace we serve God.

By grace we please God. By grace we deal with our sins when we do not walk by the Spirit but yield to the flesh.

By grace, and grace alone, we approach God and receive the things we need—whether spiritual, emotional, or physical.

Through faith, we lay hold of the grace of God, believing and walking in obedience to Him, no matter what.

Lord, it is truly humbling to realize that I cannot live a life of faith on my own. And yet how freeing to know that, through Your grace, You offer everything I need!

April 22

Oh, dear friend, have you grasped the immensity of the gift we've been given? God so loved us that He sent His only begotten Son from heaven to become flesh and blood and to be sacrificed for our sins!

Blood had to be shed, for without the shedding of blood there can be no remission of our sins. (See Leviticus 17:11; Hebrews 9:22.) God could not redeem us with corruptible things like silver and gold. Redemption could come only one way: with the precious blood of a Lamb unblemished and spotless, the blood of Christ (1 Peter 1:18–19).

So after He was tried, tested, and in all ways tempted such as you and I are, yet without sin, Jesus continued in obedience, yielding Himself into the hands of His Father. And God took His Son, nailed Him to a cross, and there made Him who had never sinned to be sin for us.

"He Himself bore our sins in His body on the cross, so that we might die to sin and live to righteousness; for by His wounds you were healed" (1 Peter 2:24).

God laid on Jesus Christ the iniquity of all mankind—every human being from the time of Adam and Eve through the millennium yet to come. He was forsaken so that you might never be forsaken. He was made sin so that you, in exchange, might have His righteousness.

God in Christ did this for you, not by counting your sins, your trespasses, against you but against His innocent Son. How will you respond today to His gift of mercy and grace?

~

What an awesome, unspeakable gift. Thank You, blessed Redeemer, for the sacrifice of Your Son on my behalf. Let me live every day in gratitude for Your incomprehensible love and grace.

April 23

As you prepare spiritually for a new day, remember the counsel of Paul: **"And take the helmet of salvation, and the sword of the Spirit, which is the word of God"** (Ephesians 6:17).

When you put on your helmet of salvation, you acknowledge that the enemy cannot do anything to you without your heavenly Father's permission. If the enemy seems to gain the upper hand, remember that Jesus Christ will ultimately lead you in triumph.

The helmet of salvation covers the three tenses of salvation: I have been saved, I am being saved, and I shall be saved.

The first is justification—you have been saved from sin's penalty. That's the past tense. It has already happened, and because of this, you'll never be condemned.

The second is sanctification—the present tense of salvation. You are being saved from sin's power moment by moment as you live under His control and allow the indwelling Holy Spirit to lead you into all righteousness.

The third is glorification, and it is future. You will be saved from sin's presence and given a new body. Someday you'll die and be at home with your heavenly Father and the family of God.

No matter the battle, stand with your helmet on, confident because of your identity with Christ. The devil's blows will bounce off your head. You're on the winning side!

I praise You and thank You, dear Lord, that not only have You saved me from my past sin, but You also are saving me from sin's power today, and one day You will save me from death so that I can live for all eternity with You.

When life seems unjust, when you come smack up against disappointment, when you want to cry out, "It's not fair," go back to the character of God as described in His Word: **"The Rock! His work is perfect, for all His ways are just; a God of faithfulness and without injustice, righteous and upright is He"** (Deuteronomy 32:4).

God's actions are always consistent with His character, including His love, righteousness, holiness, and justice. He cannot lay aside any one of His attributes and act independently of it. It is part of His being to be just. In all His actions, God acts with fairness. If He did less, He would no longer be God!

Please don't think I'm saying that God decrees or orders men to do evil. This would be contrary to His nature. Remember the warning of James? "Let no one say when he is tempted, 'I am being tempted by God'; for God cannot be tempted by evil, and He Himself does not tempt anyone" (James 1:13).

Those who want everything set down in some logical, five-step presentation (complete with graphs and pie charts) will always struggle with these divine mysteries. This is where meekness and faith come in!

Meekness realizes that holy God, perfect and pure in every aspect, also is merciful and long-suffering. The longing for the highest good for His creatures restrains His holy justice. "The Lord is...patient toward you, not wishing for any to perish but for all to come to repentance" (2 Peter 3:9). And so meekness whispers through its tears, "God, I trust You."

~

God, I know You are sovereign, loving, and just. I may never understand in this life, but I will not accuse You, slander You, nor alter a single one of Your words to fit my poor, limited perspective.

April 25

In our dealings with those ensnared by sin, we must always realize that we could have fallen too! The flesh is the flesh, and any Christian who does not walk in the Spirit will fulfill the lust of the flesh (Galatians 5:16).

It is essential, therefore, that whenever we seek to restore a fellow believer, we do so without a holier-than-thou attitude. As Paul reminds us, we all are judged by God: "**But you, why do you judge your brother? Or you again, why do you regard your brother with contempt? For we will all stand before the judgment seat of God**" (Romans 14:10).

Many times I have sat with dear brothers and sisters who have given in to the lust of their flesh. My heart was grieved over their sin. I winced to think of the blasphemy it would bring to the name of God. They were wrong. They knew it. And yet I wept for them and with them and expressed my understanding. After all, I live in a body of flesh too!

As I write this, I cannot help but think of our great High Priest, tempted in all points as we are, yet without sin, the One who did not come to judge but to save (Hebrews 4:15; John 3:17).

The next time we see a speck in our brother's eye, let's remember to examine our own hearts first. Is our judgment for the purpose of condemnation or restoration? As we seek to restore, will we go in meekness, gentleness?

~

Pride is such a sneaky and dangerous thing, Lord. Guard my heart and mind against believing that I am safe from certain temptations. Let my conversations with others be free of self-righteous judgment, filled instead with Your message of grace and redemption.

April 26

Years ago, in the early days of our ministry, I delivered a very strong message to more than 250 young people, calling them to holiness of life. That night as my husband, Jack, and I crawled into bed, he said to me, "Kay, I didn't hear any love in your voice tonight."

"But those teens know I love them!" I retorted.

"I know," he persisted, "but I still didn't hear any love in your voice."

I didn't say another word. I simply turned to my side of the bed. But Jack's words rang over and over in my mind: *I didn't hear any love in your voice tonight.*

Finally despairing of sleep, I got up, pulled out my concordance, and looked up every reference to *gentle.* I'll never forget the verse I discovered that night: "Your gentleness makes me great" (Psalm 18:35). How I wept before God, pleading for His forgiveness. The next week I stood before those same young people and asked their forgiveness as well.

Oh, beloved, no matter how grievous the sin, we are not to correct anyone except in meekness. Otherwise, instead of our erring brother or sister seeing the character of God and being drawn to Him, they will be repulsed by our behavior and excuse their own sin! Instead, let's follow the direction of the apostle Paul: **"If anyone is caught in any trespass, you who are spiritual, restore such a one in a spirit of gentleness; each one looking to yourself, so that you too will not be tempted"** (Galatians 6:1).

~

O long-suffering One, let my words and actions reflect a gentleness that can come only from You. Let me be always meek, never arrogant or cruel, when I point others toward Your truth.

Beloved, when the enemy brings to mind sins of the past, remember, "**Although you were formerly alienated and hostile in mind, engaged in evil deeds, yet He has now reconciled you in His fleshly body through death, in order to present you before Him holy and blameless and beyond reproach**" (Colossians 1:21–22).

I have a note written to me on lined paper, hastily torn from a three-ring notebook on January 17, 1986.

> Before I was saved, I was an adulteress, stole the man who lived next door to my parents from his wife and children, had his child out of wedlock, and finally succeeded in getting him to marry me when our child was two years old. When I came to the Lord, I was devastated to realize what pain my sin had caused so many, but especially how I had grieved my Lord. God has redeemed much of the hurt to so many and in His miraculous ways has brought us to a place of loving one another, but I still have felt that He let me slip in the back door and that never could I be truly special to Him.
>
> But, oh, Kay, I know that He chose me with full knowledge of how wretched I would be and that I am now called holy and blameless by the blood of my precious Jesus.

Here is the testimony of a woman who has been set free of the past. Free because she believed God!

O gracious and merciful Lord, how wonderful to know that You see me as beyond reproach! Please help me resist the lies of the enemy that would hold me prisoner to the past.

April 28

Have you ever felt like quitting because the hassle of Christianity was too much?

Do you ever doubt the truth of God's Word or the reality of Christianity? Have you ever been tormented by blasphemous thoughts against God?

Have you ever felt captivatingly drawn to the things of the world?

Are you bombarded with doubts about God's goodness—His love toward you? Have you been plagued by feelings of worthlessness or inadequacy?

Even though you've confessed past sins, do you live under a cloud of condemnation?

Are you filled with anger, bitterness, or unforgiveness? Even though you realize you are wrong to harbor these feelings, do you feel powerless to deal with them?

Are you physically sick, yet the doctor cannot find the cause?

Have you ever been joyfully serving the Lord and suddenly been attacked unjustly?

Have you remembered that the Christian life is warfare?

Resist and remember, although our adversary, the devil, "prowls around like a roaring lion, seeking someone to devour" (1 Peter 5:8), you've nothing to fear if you are standing firm in the faith. Don't be afraid of the lion's roar. The Lord is on your side! Instead, **"be on the alert, stand firm in the faith, act like men, be strong"** (1 Corinthians 16:13).

I will not fear what man—or Satan—can do to me, because I am sheltered in Your mighty arms. Help me to stand firm in the faith even when life seems overwhelming.

April 29

If you're ever tempted to despair over the future, take a moment to consider the past.

All the pain and suffering we now see started with a single act: sin and death began through one man, a man named Adam, who disobeyed God after his wife was deceived by Satan in the form of a serpent. Romans 5:12 says, "**Therefore, just as through one man sin entered into the world, and death through sin, and so death spread to all men, because all sinned.**"

From that point on, the whole world lay in the power of the evil one (1 John 5:19). Because we were all born in sin, Satan had the power of death over every human being, for the wages of sin is death (Hebrews 2:14; Romans 6:23).

It looked as if the serpent had won. And he had won a battle, but the war had just begun. God had a plan—a Lamb in the wings, behind the curtains of time, slain before the foundation of the world. In the fullness of time God would come, clothed in humanity, bearing the title "the last Adam." And as the nails pierced and bruised the heels of Jesus' feet, Satan's head was bruised with the same act and his power over us broken. The ruler of this world was cast out (John 12:31)!

Remember, dear one, the God who has already conquered sin and death holds all your tomorrows in His sovereign plan.

I praise You, O gracious Father, that You have conquered the ruler of this world. I thank You that death and sin no longer have a hold on me because of the sacrifice of the Lamb of God.

April 30

Do you give simply out of your surplus, my friend? Maybe you tithe and call it done? You've done what God requires, and you're finished?

That's not the way it should be.

Remember what Jesus said of the widow who dropped just two small coins into the temple treasury while those around her gave large sums of money? "**Truly I say to you, this poor widow put in more than all the contributors to the treasury; for they all put in out of their surplus, but she, out of her poverty, put in all she owned, all she had to live on**" (Mark 12:43–44).

Do you realize that nowhere in the New Testament does God tell the church to tithe? Tithing was the law—the way God supplied the Levites and the temple. We're in a new era, where giving is a ministry of grace.

We're to give according to what God has given us. He doesn't expect us to bring ease to others while bringing greater pressure on ourselves so that we have a difficult time making it. Paul makes that clear to the Corinthians when he reassures them that "this is not for the ease of others and for your affliction, but by way of equality" (2 Corinthians 8:13).

Our giving should help bring about equality within the body of Christ so that no brother or sister ever has a genuine need that goes unmet while others have an abundance.

Beloved, what does your giving reveal about your relationship with God?

~

Search my heart, O God, and reveal any hidden corners of selfishness, any reluctance to give generously. Let Your Holy Spirit guide and direct my giving.

May 1

You're probably familiar with God's commandment **"You shall have no other gods before Me"** (Exodus 20:3). But have you taken time recently to examine your daily schedule for evidence that other gods might have taken His rightful place in your life?

"For I, the LORD your God, am a jealous God, visiting the iniquity of the fathers on the children, on the third and the fourth generations of those who hate Me, but showing lovingkindness to thousands, to those who love Me and keep My commandments" (Exodus 20:5–6).

To fail to love God above all else is to play the harlot with other lovers. When we love something or someone else more than we love God—whether a husband, wife, child, friend, profession, pleasure, or intellectual pursuit—God calls it harlotry. And yet rather than abandoning us, our gracious Lord calls us to return: " 'Only acknowledge your iniquity, that you have transgressed against the LORD your God…and you have not obeyed My voice… Return, O faithless sons,' declares the LORD…'and I will bring you to Zion' " (Jeremiah 3:13–14).

Have you played the harlot with God, beloved? Won't you return to Him today with all your heart, soul, mind, body, and strength?

Merciful Lord, I acknowledge my sin, my failure to put You first in my life at all times. Forgive me, I pray, and through Your Holy Spirit heal my faithlessness and strengthen me to obey Your voice.

May 2

So many of us spend our days chasing after those things that seem to promise "the good life." But if our definition of "good" doesn't match up with God's, we'll never find lasting satisfaction.

If you and I want what is "good," where will it be found? James 1:17 gives the answer: **"Every good thing given and every perfect gift is from above, coming down from the Father of lights, with whom there is no variation or shifting shadow."**

God is the only One who is good. Because He is our Father and because He is good, He wants us to have what is good.

When Jesus tells us to continue asking, seeking, and knocking, He reassures us that our persistence will pay off because of the character of the One to whom we are coming (Luke 11:9–10). God is the Father of fathers—the very epitome of fatherhood—and, as Jesus explains, He delights to give what is good to those who ask Him: "If you then, being evil, know how to give good gifts to your children, how much more will your heavenly Father give the Holy Spirit to those who ask Him?" (Luke 11:13).

Earthly fathers, for the most part, seek to give their children good things. How much more will our heavenly Father give us what is good—truly good and able to satisfy our soul's deepest longings?

Father, thank You for the joy of knowing I can come to You with every request. I will trust Your answer, whatever it may be, because I know that You delight to give me what is good.

May 3

Have you developed such a heart for God that you seek Him immediately in every circumstance of life? Have you learned to trust Him in all things, knowing that "**[He] is able to do far more abundantly beyond all that we ask or think**" (Ephesians 3:20)?

How quickly we sometimes forget God's promise to care for us. Instead of surrendering ourselves into His hands, we react out of fear or frustration, much like the children of Israel. They had seen God's works with their own eyes. He had brought them "out from under the burdens of the Egyptians" (Exodus 6:6). He'd drowned their enemies in the Red Sea. He'd rained down manna from heaven and provided quail for meat. After witnessing all this evidence of God's protection and provision, how could they murmur and complain? Why didn't they rest in all that they knew about God?

And what about you and me, beloved? Oh, we haven't seen what the Israelites saw, but they never read all that we've read in the Bible. They saw His Shekinah glory in the cloud and knew He was with them. But we have His Spirit dwelling in us. Also, we have the promise "for He Himself has said, 'I will never desert you, nor will I ever forsake you,' so that we confidently say, 'The LORD is my helper, I will not be afraid. What will man do to me?'" (Hebrews 13:5–6).

It's one thing to know about God and another to live in the light of that knowledge.

~

Gracious heavenly Father, help me to remember that, no matter what comes, I have sufficiency in everything, an abundance for every good deed to which You call me (2 Corinthians 9:8).

Have you ever despaired of pleasing God? Do you often come to the end of a day feeling defeated, knowing that you haven't lived up to God's standards for living?

Oh, beloved, you're absolutely right in thinking you can never hope to attain God's holy standards—at least not in your own strength.

"Why the Law then?" you may ask. And Paul has the answer: **"It was added because of transgressions.... The Law has become our tutor to lead us to Christ, so that we may be justified by faith"** (Galatians 3:19, 24).

The Law was given for two reasons, according to Galatians 3. First, it defined our transgressions. It revealed our total inadequacy to be righteous on our own. Second, it acted as a tutor to bring us to Christ, who would give us the gift of His indwelling Spirit. The Spirit within would provide all that we needed to overcome our flesh. He would make us complete in Christ, adequate for every good work.

God sent His Son to earth to take away the sins of the world! Through Him we are made adequate. And so we stand with unveiled faces beholding in a mirror the glory of the Lord, and in the process—the wonderful, awesome process of sanctification—we're being transformed into the same image.

You are complete in Him, beloved. Your adequacy is of God. Doesn't that make you want to get on your knees and praise Him?

~

Glorious Lord, I thank You for the witness of the Spirit in my life and for His power to transform me into the likeness of Christ. I praise You for freeing me from the Law and the snare of sin.

May 5

As you enter into this day, will you once again surrender your life into God's hands and walk each step in faith?

Faith is simply taking God at His word. It's believing all that He says whether you understand it or not, whether you can explain it or not.

Faith is believing God, no matter how you feel, no matter how you read the circumstances, no matter what anyone else tells you.

God cannot lie. All that He says is truth. For that reason the very plumb line of our faith is the Bible. Anything or anyone that contradicts the unadulterated Word of God is wrong.

When the Bible talks about faith, it means more than intellectual assent. As you study God's Word, you see three elements involved in true faith or belief. They are (1) a firm conviction that fully acknowledges what God has revealed, (2) a surrender to what God has revealed, and (3) conduct that results from a personal surrender to what God has revealed.

To live by faith means to believe what God says, surrender to it, and live accordingly. **"Without faith it is impossible to please Him, for he who comes to God must believe that He is and that He is a rewarder of those who seek Him"** (Hebrews 11:6).

Do you believe that the Bible is the inerrant, verbally inspired Word of God? If so, then how are you going to live?

~

I believe that You are Almighty God and that You are a rewarder of those who seek You. I surrender this day to You in faith, choosing to believe Your Word no matter what my feelings or circumstances are.

May 6

How will you respond when life doesn't go according to plan?

When my father entered the hospital for surgery on an aortic aneurysm, I asked God for a scripture concerning him. I felt God gave me Psalm 20 and, with it, the assurance that my sixty-eight-year-old father would not die. But almost a month later, Daddy died.

Had my faith failed? Had God failed? No, I had simply misunderstood God's plans.

If we're going to trust in the Lord without wavering, we must remember that His ways are often beyond our understanding: **"Can you discover the depths of God? Can you discover the limits of the Almighty?"** (Job 11:7).

Has something happened that you think God shouldn't have allowed? Rather than descending into despair, listen to God's words in Isaiah 40:28–29:

> Do you not know? Have you not heard?
> The Everlasting God, the LORD, the Creator of the
> ends of the earth
> Does not become weary or tired.
> His understanding is inscrutable.
> He gives strength to the weary,
> And to him who lacks might He increases power.

When God doesn't deliver you out of a trial, He promises it will never be more than you can bear. He'll help you to live as more than a conqueror, for your good and His glory.

Father, please give me unshakable, immovable, abundant faith in Your love and Your promises.

May 7

Do you ever wonder about your purpose, about how someone like you can play a role in God's kingdom?

Oh, beloved, it's so important to remember that every child of God receives a spiritual gift from God, many times more than one. These gifts given by the Spirit are what make us adequate for the work He has for us. Paul taught this very clearly in 1 Corinthians 12–14 when he explained that there are varieties of gifts but the same Spirit, varieties of ministries but the same Lord, and varieties of results but the same God, who works all things in all persons. What we are given we are given not for ourselves, **"but to each one is given the manifestation of the Spirit for the common good"** (1 Corinthians 12:7).

What does this mean practically? It means that we aren't to compare ourselves with each other. We aren't in competition with one another. We belong to one body. "If the foot says, 'Because I am not a hand, I am not a part of the body,' it is not for this reason any the less a part of the body.... God has placed the members, each one of them, in the body, just as He desired" (1 Corinthians 12:15, 18).

If we remember this and that God is sovereign, then we'll stop feeling inadequate. We'll stop seeking our own promotion and leave that to God.

All God would have us seek is His heart, His will. When we do this, we'll know contentment and fulfillment—a peace that passes all understanding.

Thank You for the gifts You have given me. Lead me in using them for Your glory and for the good of Your people. Speak to my heart, I pray, and show me how You want to use me today.

May 8

It's one thing to serve God in the work of ministry when glory comes your way, when everyone says what a fine job you did, when you're well known, hailed, honored, respected. But it's another to continue doing what God has called you to do while people dishonor you, bring evil reports about you, and call you a deceiver when that is anything but true—and when nobody knows or cares who you are. To continue when you, like Jesus, are despised and rejected.

When you persevere during times like these and when you can handle the plaudits, admiration, and honors of men—when it goes either way and you stand firm commending yourself as a servant of God—then the ministry will not be discredited. God rewards His faithful, and in time He will certainly vindicate them in the eyes of their enemies. Ours is to stand firm in His all-sufficient grace, "**in everything commending ourselves as servants of God**...by glory and dishonor, by evil report and good report; regarded as deceivers and yet true; as unknown yet well-known, as dying yet behold, we live; as punished yet not put to death" (2 Corinthians 6:4, 8–9).

These can become deathlike situations—death to self, crucified with Christ. Nevertheless you live, yet not you but Christ in you (Galatians 2:20). And in His living, while death works in you, you show yourself to be a servant of your Lord. For no servant is greater than his Lord; it is simply enough to be like Him (John 13:16; Matthew 10:24–25).

Lord God, help me to stand firm even when others condemn me or misunderstand. Equip and strengthen me to serve You without pride and without shame.

May 9

As we go about our day with the eyes of our heart open, searching out opportunities to serve, we must continually be mindful of our dependency on the Father. As the apostle Paul explained to Timothy:

> **[God] has saved us and called us with a holy calling, not according to our works, but according to His own purpose and grace....** For this reason I also suffer these things, but I am not ashamed; for I know whom I have believed and I am convinced that He is able to guard what I have entrusted to Him until that day. (2 Timothy 1:9, 12)

God has called us not according to our degree of adequacy but according to His purpose and grace. This is what makes us adequate, able to do the work of ministry. Paul knew what God had appointed for him, just as you and I are to discover what God has appointed for us.

So where do we begin? First, we must resolve not to "lose heart" or give up. The Christian life is not for the fainthearted but for those who are strong and courageous with a strength and courage that come from knowing the truth.

Second, we're to renounce the things hidden because of shame. Our lives are to be lived openly. The past is forgiven; we are declared righteous because of the power of the Spirit bestowed on us through the New Covenant in His blood. We are adequate, and there's nothing to cover up or compensate for. We only have to be what God would have us to be.

~

Hallelujah! Thank You, Lord! Help me to remember that You are the only One I must answer to.

May 10

Why is it that in times of trouble we so often seek the counsel of others rather than run to the arms of our all-sufficient God? I think it's because most of us don't really know our God. Why do many collapse in the day of trouble and testing? Why are they immobilized? Why don't they take an aggressive stand in the face of fear? Because Christians, for the most part, can't boast in the name of their God. And yet we are called to say with David, "**Some boast in chariots and some in horses, but we will boast in the name of the LORD, our God**" (Psalm 20:7).

In Old Testament days, chariots and horses were means of protection and escape during times of war. Today our "chariots and horses"—our visible means of help, escape, or protection—come with different labels, shapes, and forms. Yet are they really a source of safety? No. "The horse is prepared against the day of battle: but safety is of the LORD" (Proverbs 21:31, KJV).

So what does it mean to boast in the name of our God? In the Hebrew language the phrase *to boast in* means "to have confidence in, to trust in." Therefore, to boast in God's name means to have confidence in His name. God's name represents His character, His attributes, His nature. To know His name is to know Him. To boast in His name is to have confidence in who He is!

In the day of trouble or need, let us run to our God, beloved, and put our trust in Him.

~

Lord, thank You for Your invitation to call upon You in the day of trouble (Psalm 50:15). Thank You for Your promise to deliver and protect me. I place my confidence and trust solely in You.

May 11

Every day the words we speak reveal something about the condition of our hearts and the level of our commitment to pursuing righteousness.

The author of the book of James reminds us of the need for the integrity of our lips: "**But above all, my brethren, do not swear, either by heaven or by earth or with any other oath; but your yes is to be yes, and your no, no, so that you may not fall under judgment**" (5:12).

May I make a suggestion? Spend some time today in prayer. Ask your Father to show you if you are failing in any way to let your yes be yes or your no, no.

Do you keep your word to your children?

Do you keep your word to your mate?

Do you hedge?

Are you like me in that many times you promise things you have a desire to do and yet you are not absolutely sure you can fulfill them? Sometimes it seems that my heart's desires go far beyond my abilities and a twenty-four-hour day.

I'm going to search my heart. Why don't you search yours? I'm going to tell God to remind me, over and over, to watch the commitments I make with my mouth.

~

Holy and righteous God, with David I pray, "Set a guard, O LORD, over my mouth; keep watch over the door of my lips" (Psalm 141:3).

May 12

Confession is the acknowledgment of our debt to God. Somewhere, somehow, you and I have failed to walk in righteousness, and when we fail, when we transgress the word and will of God, this must be acknowledged and forsaken.

The Bible tells us, "**He who conceals his transgressions will not prosper, but he who confesses and forsakes them will find compassion**" (Proverbs 28:13).

It's a wonderful feeling to be right with God and right with man. It's freeing! There is nothing like a clear conscience. The load is gone. You can breathe deeper, walk with a lighter step, and smile from the inside out. Why? Because you know there is nothing between you and God. You have done what is right, what pleases Him, and in doing so you have rolled the whole situation over onto His shoulders.

Oh, dear friend, how I urge you that if anything stands between you and God, or you and your fellow man, settle it right away.

Keeping a clear conscience, a right relationship with God and others is to be a daily exercise. Just as we come before Him day by day, asking Him to supply our needs, we must also examine our hearts daily to see if we owe any debt of righteousness to God. If so, we need to confess it immediately.

Lord, You search all hearts and understand every intent of the thoughts (1 Chronicles 28:9). Please reveal to me any hidden sin so that I might be cleansed and have a pure conscience before You.

Precious one, do you realize that the very blessings of the Lord can seduce our affections away from the Giver to the gifts if we do not hold them in an open hand?

The Bible says, **"From everyone who has been given much, much will be required"** (Luke 12:48). As you travel abroad, you begin to realize just how much God has lavished on the United States of America in both material and spiritual blessings. We have more freedom than others, more access to the media, more Bibles in all varieties, more literature, more schools, more training, more churches, more missions, more professing believers, more...more...more.

And yet in our prosperity it seems we have turned from God. We have forgotten that Jesus said no one can serve two masters. Our affections cannot be divided.

Is this why so many Americans who profess to know Him simply give Him lip service? Might this be why so many reflect the lukewarm attitude of the church at Laodicea, which said, "I am rich, and have become wealthy, and have need of nothing"? Do we, like they, fail to realize that we are "wretched and miserable and poor and blind and naked" (Revelation 3:17)?

Have our hearts become captivated with the seductiveness of "things" rather than with a fervent, sacrificial love for our God and for the furtherance of His kingdom?

How I need You, Lord. You have blessed me in so many ways. Let me never lose sight of the Giver in my enjoyment of Your gifts. Show me how best to honor You with all my substance.

May 14

"I'm not interested in being rich; I just want to survive! Is anything wrong with that?"

If that's your question, my answer is this: it depends on how you intend to survive. If surviving means you don't have time to seek God's kingdom and righteousness, then you're not serving God but mammon. And God says that's wrong.

Have you forgotten that you have a heavenly Father and that it's His responsibility to take care of His children? How I love the fact that Jesus so often referred to God as our heavenly Father. It is not by accident but by design. Fathers are expected to give their children the basics of life, to provide them with food and clothing. Since you are a child of God, it's His responsibility as your Father to take care of the necessities of your life.

When the cares of life close in, it helps to focus on Jesus' words to the disciples: **"Do not be worried about your life, as to what you will eat or what you will drink; nor for your body, as to what you will put on. Is not life more than food, and the body more than clothing?"** (Matthew 6:25).

We need not be anxious about our lives or our bodies. Why? Because we are God's children, and He promises to supply all our needs "according to His riches in glory in Christ Jesus" (Philippians 4:19). Our responsibility is simply to seek first His kingdom and His righteousness and know that in doing so "all these things will be added" (Matthew 6:33).

Precious heavenly Father, I thank You that You have promised to supply all my needs. Thank You that I have no need to worry as long as I am trusting in and following You.

May 15

Describing our responsibilities and priorities in light of God's promise to supply all our needs, Jesus urged His disciples, "**But seek first His kingdom and His righteousness, and all these things will be added to you**" (Matthew 6:33).

Does this promise liberate us from all responsibility for earning a living? Does it mean that all I need to do is pray, study, and meditate—and expect God to feed and clothe me?

I think it's obvious from the text that Matthew 6:33 is not a license for an undisciplined life. Rather, Jesus is saying that we are to habitually seek first God's kingdom and His righteousness.

The word I really want you to notice is the word *first.* In all things God is to have the preeminence. The priority of our lives is to be His righteousness. God is not saying that you and I cannot do anything else. He knows that we have other responsibilities. For example, men are responsible to provide for their households. If they do not, Scripture says they're worse than infidels. A married woman is to be a keeper of her home, according to Scripture. If she fails in keeping a proper home, then she has failed in what God has ordained for her to do.

These things cannot be neglected—nor does God expect us to neglect them for His kingdom. He does, however, expect us to keep them in proper perspective. Our devotion to Him is to supersede all else. And when it does, we have the blessed promise: "All these things will be added to you."

Father God, please grant me the wisdom to organize my life carefully so I will neither neglect my responsibilities nor allow them to take precedence over You.

My beloved friend, do you know without a doubt that you truly belong to Jesus? Do your daily actions, words, and choices reflect a surrendered heart?

The issue is so critical that Jesus made His point unmistakably clear: "**Not everyone who says to Me, 'Lord, Lord,' will enter the kingdom of heaven, but he who does the will of My Father who is in heaven will enter**" (Matthew 7:21).

Calling Him "Lord" is not enough. Just because we say we are Christians does not mean that we are. Just because we have joined the church and sit in church every Sunday does not mean we possess the kingdom of heaven. As the old saying goes, sitting in a church does not make you a Christian any more than sitting in a garage makes you a car!

Yet isn't this what many believe? They believe that because they sit in church and go through the motions and the rituals, they are children of God. They believe that because they've been baptized or confirmed or because they take communion, they'll go to heaven when they die. They believe that because they "prayed the prayer," they possess eternal life, regardless of the way they live!

That is not what Jesus says. He tells us that it's not those who say "Lord, Lord" but those who habitually—not perfectly, but habitually, as a lifestyle—do the will of the Father who will enter His kingdom.

What about you, my friend? Are you practicing a life of obedience?

Father, I thank You for the marvelous gift of salvation, a gift that not only brings me the hope of heaven to come but the strength to do Your will here on earth.

Oh, beloved, I pray that you have discovered for yourself the power of God's Word to bring life and healing.

In Jeremiah's day the Word of God had become a reproach to His people. The nation, for the most part, was spiritually sick. There was no healing for them because "**from the prophet even to the priest everyone practices deceit. They heal the brokenness of the daughter of My people superficially, saying, 'Peace, peace' but there is no peace**" (Jeremiah 8:10–11).

The prophets prophesied falsely. The priests ruled on their own authority. And God's people loved it (Jeremiah 5:31).

To describe their almost hopeless condition, God metaphorically told His people that they had forsaken the healing, living water of the Word of God for the filthy waters of the Nile and the Euphrates (Jeremiah 2:14–19).

What they did in Jeremiah's day, we've done in ours. Many drink the waters of psychology, philosophy, and psychiatry instead of the Water of Life. We have run to men and women trained in the world's wisdom, but we have not run in prayer to the One whose name is "Wonderful Counselor, Mighty God, Eternal Father, Prince of Peace" (Isaiah 9:6).

This is not to say that we should never go to others for help. Rather, we should not fail to go to God. And when we turn to others, what real and lasting help can they give us if their counsel is contrary to God's Word?

~

Lord, You have promised to give wisdom to those who ask, generously and without reproach. I ask today for Your counsel and direction. Give me the discernment to find true healing.

May 18

So many best-selling books these days are committed to undermining the authority and reliability of Scripture. Popular novelists, academics, and even theologians promote theories suggesting that the Bible was created solely by men and driven by human agendas. Popular opinion has declared "ignorant" and "misguided" those who choose to believe the Bible's own declaration that **"no prophecy of Scripture is a matter of one's own interpretation, for no prophecy was ever made by an act of human will, but men moved by the Holy Spirit spoke from God"** (2 Peter 1:20–21).

Do you believe the Bible is what it claims to be: the very Word of God, without error, and the very bread by which the child of God is to live? Or do you believe it is filled with myths, exaggerated stories passed down from generation to generation? Do you believe that the Bible can be sorted through by theological scholars to determine which select words are truly God's?

Your view of God's Word directly affects how you choose to live. Many of us, although saved by faith, behave as if faith is not enough to sustain us day by day, as if we need something in addition to God's Word to live successfully.

But what a difference it makes when we believe that 2 Timothy 3:16–17 is true, when we trust that the Bible is sufficient so that the child of God might be perfect, thoroughly equipped for every good work.

Whose word are you going to accept regarding the Word of God—man's or God's?

Everlasting God, help me to live daily in the knowledge that only by following Your words will I lead a life of purpose and meaning.

May 19

Have you ever really understood that there's nothing you can do to merit or earn God's favor? Can you identify with the apostle Paul, who wrote, **"For I know that nothing good dwells in me, that is, in my flesh; for the willing is present in me, but the doing of the good is not"** (Romans 7:18)?

What are you trusting for your salvation? And if you are sure that your salvation is all of grace, how then do you relate to God on a daily basis—on the basis of grace or on the basis of the Law?

Grace is key to your relationship with God. The believer never comes to God on any basis other than grace. Therefore, if you are going to live by grace, you must understand—really understand—the grace of God that has appeared and, in its appearing, brought salvation to all men. Once you have a clear, biblical understanding of grace, you will have a solid foundation upon which to construct a life lived totally in the grace of God rather than one based on whether or not you deserve His blessing, His favor.

This is why it's such a powerful, life-changing practice to start each day by giving all that it holds over to God. As you deliberately surrender your moments and hours to Him, you'll experience for yourself the incredible grace that He offers.

O Father, open the eyes of my understanding. Remove the veil of the Old Covenant of the Law so I might see the glory of the New Covenant of grace. I ask this for Your glory and for my peace so that through understanding I might be released into greater service for You.

May 20

Why do so many Christians live in defeat? I believe they don't understand the grace of God, which not only brings us to salvation but which also enables us to live as more than conquerors! They don't know how to appropriate grace on a daily basis.

But you may say, "Kay, you don't know what I've done! You don't know how weak I am. You don't know how often I've failed. How can God forgive me, accept me, use me?"

It is grace, beloved! Not cheap grace, costly grace. Grace that cost the death of Jesus Christ, the innocent for the guilty. Grace that banishes condemnation and brings justification. Grace that covers the inadequacies and the sins of the justified for the remainder of their days. Grace that can do all that and whatever else you need, because of its great capacity!

Let us exult in such grace and claim its power to redeem our every weakness and failure, as did Paul, who wrote:

> I thank Christ Jesus our Lord, who has strengthened me, because He considered me faithful, putting me into service, even though I was formerly a blasphemer and a persecutor and a violent aggressor. **Yet I was shown mercy…and the grace of our Lord was more than abundant, with the faith and love which are found in Christ Jesus.** (1 Timothy 1:12–14)

Do you live in defeat? Are you spiritually impotent because you're ignorant of the abounding grace of God? Oh, my friend, please don't let His grace be poured out on you in vain.

~

Thank You, Lord, for Your abundant grace that frees me to walk in newness of life.

May 21

Jesus doesn't turn the clock back on your life when you're saved by grace through faith. He doesn't change what you've done. But He does take away the guilt! When your guilt's gone, you have peace.

If peace eludes you, one or both of two things may be hampering you—unbelief or the devil.

If it's unbelief, you'll remain miserable and probably ineffective until you determine to believe God's declaration in Isaiah 43:25: **"I, even I, am the one who wipes out your transgressions for My own sake, and I will not remember your sins."** What more can God say, what more can He do than what He's done to blot out your sins and convince you of His forgiveness? Until you decide in faith to believe God, you're in sin: "Whatever is not from faith is sin" (Romans 14:23).

The other possible explanation for your feelings of guilt is the enemy. If he can heap guilt on you, he'll flatten you with it. Remember that *Satan* means "adversary." He'll get you any way he can.

However, don't make him your focus. Don't live in fear of his attacks. Simply be aware of his devices, his schemes to get you. Remember that one of those schemes is unremitting guilt. If you'll learn to live in the light of God's truth, you can handle him attack by attack and have victory after victory, "strengthened with power through His Spirit in the inner man" (Ephesians 3:16).

Father, strengthen me through the Holy Spirit so I can resist the devil's deceptions and enjoy a guilt-free, peace-filled relationship with You.

Have you experienced times when fears assailed you? Have you doubted whether you've ever heard God? or even if you're saved?

Have you felt like a failure as a mate, a parent, a son or daughter, a lover, a child of God? Has someone you loved failed you or hurt you?

Are you tempted to throw up your hands and say, "What's the use?" Have you thought of finding solace or oblivion in what you know is wrong for a child of God?

Are all sorts of thoughts clamoring for attention? Does vengeance keep pushing its way through your thoughts, wanting to share its plan for getting even?

Have you thought of simply ending it all? Have you gone so far as thinking of a way to do it?

Listen! Can't you hear the trumpet? It's war! Those are the flaming missiles of the evil one. Heed the call of Ephesians 6:11: "**Put on the full armor of God, so that you will be able to stand firm against the schemes of the devil.**"

Get off your bed. Get dressed. Where's your belt, your breastplate? Pick up your shield. Put on your helmet. Don't forget your shoes! Call your Commanding Officer. Ask Him to bring to your remembrance His commandments and precepts. Cry out His promises. Take your thoughts captive. Do not run away. Do what you're supposed to do—stand firm.

~

I thank You, Almighty God, that You have not left me defenseless against the enemy but have equipped me with everything I need to stand firm in the midst of today's battle.

May 23

Beloved, do you know what Jesus is doing right now? According to Hebrews, His ministry on our behalf is simply to continually intercede for us! That is what He lives to do for us. "**Therefore He is able also to save forever those who draw near to God through Him, since He always lives to make intercession for them**" (7:25).

What a wonderful, awesome thought. As I teach the Bible, I can be assured, *Right now, Jesus is interceding for me.*

As I am witnessing and feel at a loss as to what to say next, I can know that Jesus is making intercession for me.

When I find myself in difficult situations, I can breathe a sigh of relief because I remember that Jesus is interceding—that's what He lives for now.

When I'm hurting, I know I can go on, because Jesus understands—and He's interceding.

And I know the Father hears and answers His prayers.

What a divine and incomprehensible mystery! What a marvelous reality to live, moment by moment! You and I are never alone in any situation—never left to our own wisdom, prowess, ability, or endurance. Jesus is interceding! Because of that, no situation lies outside His knowledge, control, or purpose.

~

O Father, teach me to continually draw near. Let me always remember that the One who loves me with an everlasting love is continually interceding on my behalf.

Beloved, have you discovered for yourself the deep joy of nurturing a healthy prayer life?

Prayer isn't meant to be a dry exercise or discipline. It's the joyful privilege of communicating with your Father about every matter of life, an ongoing conversation that brings confidence and quietness to your soul as you confront the complexities of daily living. Prayer serves as your compass, giving you direction for the course of your life. Prayer gives you the opportunity to be alone with God, where you can focus on Him alone.

Prayer can follow a certain pattern. At the same time, however, it is not to be the repetition of meaningless words. Jesus makes this clear in Matthew 6:7: "**And when you are praying, do not use meaningless repetition as the Gentiles do, for they suppose that they will be heard for their many words.**"

Prayer is to be honest, heartfelt communication between you and your heavenly Father. Genuine prayer isn't about saying a lot of words or jumping through the hoops of some set formula. When you pray, you are simply talking to your Father, who knows what you need before you ever ask!

Over the next few days, we'll look at how Jesus instructed His disciples to pray, but don't wait until then to talk to your Father. He's eager to hear from you!

~

Why don't you take a long walk or go wherever you can be alone, quiet, and undisturbed before God. Talk to Him, beginning with reflecting on who He is. From there, see where He leads the conversation. Why delay? Your Father is waiting.

Today and for the next several days, we're going to look together at what we often refer to as "the Lord's Prayer," learning from Jesus how we can draw closer to the Father through our time alone with Him.

The first sentence—"**Our Father who is in heaven, hallowed be Your name**" (Matthew 6:9)—calls us into the presence of the One who alone is worthy of our praise and adoration. It brings us before the Sovereign of the universe, who can meet our needs and satisfy the deepest longings of our hearts.

What is our relationship to this God whom we worship? It is nothing less than that of a child to his father. Can you imagine calling Jehovah, the self-existing, sovereign God, "Father"? To an Old Testament Jew, calling God "Father" would have been unthinkable!

So with the very first two words of this prayer, Jesus introduced a shocking new concept! "Our Father..." Those words opened up a whole new realm of intimacy. Together, we can cry out with John, "See how great a love the Father has bestowed on us, that we would be called children of God" (1 John 3:1). His Spirit living within us enables us to cry out to Him with all the trust of a little child, in devotion, love, admiration, confidence, and security.

Prayer is your privilege, your birthright as a child of God. Won't you talk to your Father today, beloved, and tell Him all that's on your heart?

Lord, I enter Your presence in awe that You are my loving Father. What a privilege it is to speak with You. I thank You and praise You for all that You are and all You have done.

May 26

Let's look today at the second sentence in the Lord's Prayer, which declares our allegiance to God and to His kingdom: "**Your kingdom come**" (Matthew 6:10). Had Jesus not continued with "Your will be done, on earth as it is in heaven," this phrase would cover the topic adequately. For after all, in giving God our allegiance, we're choosing to submit to His will.

After we have seen God and reverenced Him as the only One worthy of our praise, is it not logical that we would bow the knee and say, "Father, we want Your kingdom to come"?

Here is our opportunity to affirm daily our allegiance to His kingdom, acknowledging we have but one God, and He must rule today above all else.

Here also is our opportunity in prayer to expedite the coming of His literal kingdom to earth. The Good Shepherd cannot come until all His sheep are inside the fold. When we pray "Thy kingdom come," we are praying that Jesus' lost sheep would hear His voice, come to Him, and receive eternal life.

If you and I could catch a glimpse of how crucial our prayers are in preparing people's hearts to receive the seed of God's Word, I believe we would spend much more time on our knees! That's where effective evangelism begins.

Will you pray today for the coming of God's kingdom—and live in allegiance to His reign?

~

Majestic and sovereign God, I eagerly await Christ's return, when every tongue will confess You as Lord. In the meantime I pray that my loved ones will call upon Your name and receive eternal life.

Yesterday we saw that the Lord's Prayer leads us to affirm our allegiance to God by praying for His kingdom to come. So it's logical that we would next pray, "**Your will be done, on earth as it is in heaven**" (Matthew 6:10).

Consider what this means, beloved: before we bring any petition before God's throne, before our prayers can be effective, we must submit to God's will. John 9:31 tells us that God does not hear sinners, but if anyone fears God and does His will, then God hears him.

In the pattern of the Lord's Prayer, petition follows on the heels of submission. The order cannot be reversed! After all, how can we expect God to grant us our desires when we refuse to submit to His will?

Submission to the will of God is the key to the storehouse of answered prayer. "This is the confidence which we have before Him, that, if we ask anything according to His will, He hears us. And if we know that He hears us in whatever we ask, we know that we have the requests which we have asked from Him" (1 John 5:14–15).

If you would know the will of God, you must understand the Word of God! The two cannot be separated, for through His Word we are sure of His will. Jesus puts it very succinctly: "If you abide in Me, and My words abide in you, ask whatever you wish, and it will be done for you" (John 15:7).

Today will you surrender your mind and heart to God's Word—and your life to His will?

Father God, help me to follow Christ on the path of submission, doing nothing on my own initiative but always seeking Your will and accomplishing Your work.

Whatever needs or concerns are heavy on your heart today, beloved, your heavenly Father does not expect you to deal with them on your own.

As a child of God, you have the right to ask your Father to meet your needs. Yet notice the pattern Jesus revealed through the Lord's Prayer, which we've been reviewing these past few days: petition comes after we've worshiped our Father, given Him our allegiance, and submitted to His will. Only then are we spiritually ready to ask Him to supply our needs: **"Give us this day our daily bread"** (Matthew 6:11).

Our petitions must coincide with who He is and with who we are as His children. Understanding this will keep us from thoughtlessly claiming a verse like John 14:13: "Whatever you ask in My name, that will I do, so that the Father may be glorified in the Son." Whatever we ask must be in accordance with His character. Reverence for His name governs our petitions.

And what are these petitions for? It's interesting to me that the petition is "give us this day our daily bread." This isn't a request for next week's bread nor for the coming year. It's a petition for the daily needs of life. I believe Jesus uses the term *bread* because it was considered the staff of life. Bread symbolizes all our physical needs, the things necessary to sustain our lives.

God wants us to keep coming to Him day by day, doesn't He?

Heavenly Father, I trust You to supply everything I need for this day. Help me not to be distracted by unnecessary wants or desires but to rest in Your care.

May 29

God's forgiveness of us is linked to our forgiveness of others. Does that seem harsh to you, my friend? Is there someone you can't imagine forgiving? I understand that this can be a difficult truth to accept, but Jesus' words in the Lord's Prayer are very clear: "**Forgive us our debts, as we also have forgiven our debtors**" (Matthew 6:12).

To fail to forgive others is a sin, and if we are walking in sin, how can we expect God to hear our prayers? Failing to forgive others shows that we have no comprehension of the magnitude of our own debt to a holy God. So many people want to skirt the truth of these verses. They either ignore them completely or attempt to explain them away. Perhaps this is the reason for Jesus' words immediately following this model prayer: "For if you forgive others for their transgressions, your heavenly Father will also forgive you. But if you do not forgive others, then your Father will not forgive your transgressions" (Matthew 6:14–15).

Why do you think we tend to resist this truth?

Could it be that we want to come to God on our own terms? If so, we need to remember that we've already prayed, "Your will be done, on earth as it is in heaven." If we have prayed this, then we should be ready to forgive our debtors, even as God forgives our debts.

And if we're still unwilling to forgive, if we refuse to obey in this matter, how can we expect a holy God to answer our prayers?

~

Gracious and merciful God, thank You for Your clear word on forgiveness and for the gift of Your Holy Spirit, who gives me the power to obey. I choose Your forgiveness by forgiving.

May 30

What truth was Jesus exploring when He prayed, **"And do not lead us into temptation, but deliver us from evil"** (Matthew 6:13)? Is He indicating that God would ever lead us into temptation? Obviously not. So what are we to understand?

I refer to this portion of the Lord's Prayer as "preventative prayer" or "prayer for deliverance." I see it as the heart cry of a child of God who longs for righteousness and yet is all too aware of the weakness of his flesh.

Remember when Jesus warned His disciples about sleeping in the Garden of Gethsemane instead of keeping watch? Rather than catching up on their rest, they should have been praying, "Lord, my spirit is willing...but I know and understand the weakness of my flesh. And, Lord, I'm crying to You to keep me from temptation and to deliver me from evil."

In light of this, I personally believe this aspect of the Lord's Prayer is a means of watching and praying so that you might not enter into temptation.

In the Old Testament, in another "model prayer," a godly man named Jabez prayed, "Oh that thou wouldest bless me indeed...and that thou wouldest keep me from evil, that it may not grieve me!" Scripture goes on to record that "God granted him that which he requested" (1 Chronicles 4:10, KJV).

It delights the heart of our Father when we cling to Him for holiness.

Holy and righteous God, full of grace and truth, I pray that You will rescue me from every evil deed and bring me safely to Your heavenly kingdom (2 Timothy 4:18).

May 31

The closing sentence of the Lord's Prayer brings us full circle. We began with worship. We close with worship: **"For Yours is the kingdom and the power and the glory forever. Amen"** (Matthew 6:13).

To me, worship is the act of looking at God's Word in order to focus on who God is. The Word of God gives us the perfect revelation of who He is, making worship the basis of all true prayer. "He who comes to God must believe that He is and that He is a rewarder of those who seek Him" (Hebrews 11:6). All our prayers must have this belief at their center.

Notice also that this closing sentence of the Lord's Prayer begins with the word *for.* To me this suggests that all that has gone before is because of His kingdom, because of His power, because of His eternal glory. And we, His children, the sheep of His pasture, the people of His hand, shout, "Amen! So be it!"

As my beloved friend and ofttimes partner in ministry Alicia Williamson Garcia says, "Worship is a response to the truth." May we respond to the truth of who God is, remembering, "For from Him and through Him and to Him are all things. To Him be the glory forever. Amen" (Romans 11:36).

In every aspect of my day, may I bring glory to You and to Your Son, to whom belongs the glory and dominion forever and ever. Amen (1 Peter 4:11).

June 1

As you prepare for the opportunities and challenges of a new day, are you rejoicing that you need not face anything on your own? You have God's precious resources at your disposal!

You have God's promise to Israel but applicable to us: **"Moreover, I will give you a new heart and put a new spirit within you; and I will remove the heart of stone from your flesh and give you a heart of flesh. I will put My Spirit within you and cause you to walk in My statutes, and you will be careful to observe My ordinances"** (Ezekiel 36:26–27).

When you come to God in genuine repentance, He gives you the kingdom of heaven by giving you the Holy Spirit. The Spirit is not only your guarantee of redemption; He is the very means of living righteously so you can enter God's kingdom.

Listen again to Ezekiel 36:27: "I will put My Spirit within you and cause you to walk in My statutes, and you will be careful to observe My ordinances."

Here is the promise of God's indwelling Holy Spirit, the Enabler who gives us the power to keep God's laws and walk in obedience to His commandments. Here is the promise of the Spirit of life in Christ Jesus, the One who sets you free from the law of sin and death (Romans 8:2), the One who gives you a new heart!

Remember, beloved, you need not walk through this day alone but in the awesome presence and power of the Holy Spirit.

~

Precious Lord, I rejoice to know that Your Spirit lives within me, enabling me to live righteously and preparing me for Your kingdom.

Do you ever hesitate to enter God's presence? Do you feel unworthy to make your requests known to Him?

If your sins have been cleansed by the blood of Jesus, then you have no reason to fear, no reason to hesitate on the threshold of prayer. The author of Hebrews tells us that we can have confidence to enter into the presence of God and stand before the throne of mercy. Why? Because the blood of Jesus Christ has been put on that mercy seat, and He is our High Priest, preparing our way to the Father.

> **Therefore, brethren, since we have confidence to enter the holy place by the blood of Jesus, by a new and living way which He inaugurated for us through the veil, that is, His flesh, and since we have a great priest over the house of God, let us draw near with a sincere heart in full assurance of faith, having our hearts sprinkled clean from an evil conscience and our bodies washed with pure water.** (10:19–22)

You might say, "Oh no, Kay, I couldn't approach God. I'm too filthy. My presence would be repugnant to Him."

And I would reply, "Beloved, if you're a Christian, that's not true. According to Hebrews 10:22, your heart has been sprinkled clean from an evil conscience, and your body has been washed with pure water. You've been sanctified."

You have all that you need to draw near to God with confidence!

Holy God, thank You for the assurance that I am welcome in Your presence because of Jesus Christ, my High Priest and Mediator. What a privilege to be able to draw near to You, without shame or fear.

June 3

Have you learned for yourself that, though God's grace does not exempt us from trials, it is more than enough to take us through them? This confidence has enabled countless suffering Christians to live their faith boldly: **"We are not of those who shrink back to destruction, but of those who have faith to the preserving of the soul"** (Hebrews 10:39).

One saint who refused to shrink back but instead boldly pressed into the sufficiency of God's grace was Madame Jeanne Guyon. During the extravagant reign of Louis XIV, she became a thorn in the flesh of her king, who lived in debauchery. Though born into nobility, Madame Guyon's soul had been awakened to the things of God during her childhood years in a convent.

When she fell in love with the One who died for her, her pen became a sword, slashing through the sin of the times, revealing the heretical teachings of the church. Louis XIV winced, writhed, and then came to the end of his endurance.

Madame Guyon was imprisoned in a cell lit only by a candle. After ten years in her dungeon, she moved her quill across the paper to write a poem that testifies to the sufficiency of God's grace.[4] Here's a brief excerpt:

> A little bird I am, shut from the fields of air
> Yet in my cage I sit and sing to Him who placed me there;
> Well pleased a prisoner to be,
> Because, my God, it pleases Thee.[5]

~

Almighty God, help me to face every difficulty, secure in the knowledge that You will use it for Your divine purposes.

June 4

Oh, beloved, how I long for you to know without a doubt that nothing can separate us from the love of God—and to rest in that truth.

The tribulations, distresses, and persecutions that come into our lives are not meant to destroy us. They are designed to drive us into His everlasting arms of love.

God is love, and everything that comes into your life must be filtered through His fingers of love. No one can touch you, speak to you, look at you, or do anything to you without His permission. If adversity comes into your life, it comes with His permission (Isaiah 45:7). And if it comes, it will work together for your good. It will be used to conform you to His image (Romans 8:28–29). It will not keep you from the kingdom of heaven.

> But in all these things we overwhelmingly conquer through Him who loved us. For I am convinced that **neither death, nor life, nor angels, nor principalities, nor things present, nor things to come, nor powers, nor height, nor depth, nor any other created thing, will be able to separate us from the love of God,** which is in Christ Jesus our Lord. (Romans 8:37–39)

Whatever God allows to come into your life, you can know it is not designed to embitter, disfigure, or destroy you. It is permitted by a loving God for the purpose of conforming you to the image of His Son, Jesus Christ.

Help me to live today in the awareness that, through Your power and because of Your love for me, I can overwhelmingly conquer any trouble that comes my way.

June 5

Is your life a whirlwind of activity? Are you constantly on the go—yet never really getting anywhere? Are you continually searching for that elusive solution—the perfect diet, the right church, the fulfilling job, the ideal mate—that will pull your life together and give you lasting satisfaction?

Could it be that you're looking to the wrong things to quench your thirst? Jesus said, "**Whoever drinks of the water that I will give him shall never thirst; but the water that I will give him will become in him a well of water springing up to eternal life**" (John 4:14). To experience true fulfillment, we must keep coming to Him, the wellspring of life.

Consider the invitation of Isaiah 55:1–2: "Ho! Every one who thirsts, come to the waters.... Why do you spend money for what is not bread, and your wages for what does not satisfy? Listen carefully to Me, and eat what is good, and delight yourself in abundance."

Don't you love that line, "Why do you spend money for what is not bread, and your wages for what does not satisfy?" Doesn't that describe America? Have you ever stood in a mall and watched the people looking...desiring...whipping out that plastic and buying?

Oh, if only we would lay aside our iPods and turn off our televisions and computers. If we would leave the malls, head out of the fitness clubs, and go be alone and quiet before the Lord. If we would just come to Him, then we would find that satisfaction we so long for.

~

Lord, You satisfy the thirsty soul, and the hungry soul You fill with what is good (Psalm 107:9). Help me to remember that and to seek refreshment in You throughout my day.

June 6

Do you tend to fixate on your weaknesses, wondering how God could use someone like you? Do you realize that everything you need to live a life of faith—absolutely everything—is yours in Christ Jesus?

When you and I feel inadequate for any task God sends our way, we can bring to mind the words of Paul: **"I thank my God always concerning you for the grace of God which was given you in Christ Jesus, that in everything you were enriched in Him, in all speech and all knowledge, even as the testimony concerning Christ was confirmed in you, so that you are not lacking in any gift"** (1 Corinthians 1:4–7).

We have a tendency to associate grace only with salvation. Either we forget or don't realize that grace is the ever-present commodity of God's unmerited favor that we're to live in. Grace is everything Jesus Christ is and has, made available to us so we will not lack anything we need.

Grace can never be earned, bought, or won; it can only be appropriated by faith, believing God says what He means and means what He says. Romans 5 says we have "obtained our introduction by faith into this grace in which we stand" (verse 2). In other words, once we're God's children, we forever stand in His all-sufficient, lavish, extravagant grace, which more than satisfies our every need. Awesome, isn't it! Really incomprehensible, yet attainable just for the believing!

And it's our weaknesses that help us realize how attainable this grace is.

Thank You, God, for the grace You have freely given to me, grace that supplies everything I need to live this day without regret or fear.

June 7

Are you plagued by a problem that just won't go away—perhaps a health issue, a challenging relationship, or a stagnant career? Are you allowing this problem to draw your eyes away from the Lord—or is it leading you to rely even more fully on His grace?

In 2 Corinthians 12:1–10 Paul tells about a time when the Lord disciplined him after he was given a staggering vision of heaven. Paul had seen revelations so celestial and magnificent that God was concerned for His servant. He didn't want Paul to become puffed up with pride or self-importance.

As a result, God gave Paul "a thorn in the flesh," a messenger of Satan to torment him. Whatever that "thorn" was, it was painful and distressing. Paul went to the Lord three times, pleading with Him to take it away. What was God's answer? **"And He has said to me, 'My grace is sufficient for you, for power is perfected in weakness' "** (2 Corinthians 12:9).

Essentially God said, "Don't ask Me again to remove this thorn. This is My answer, and it stands. My grace is sufficient for you, Paul, for power is perfected in weakness."

Oh, beloved, do you see it? What God was saying to Paul, He is saying to you and me. When we come under the discipline of the Lord, when God takes us through the refining process to make us into the image of His Son, we can know that His grace is enough! It is completely adequate.

We can endure anything because His grace is sufficient!

~

All-sufficient Lord, help me to live this day in the power of Your strength rather than in the weakness of my flesh. Teach me to trust wholly in Your grace alone.

June 8

Have you ever looked at your mate and wondered if you married the wrong person? Be honest now! I think the majority of us would say yes. I would have to say yes—and I'm sure my husband would say the same!

Such thoughts can be troubling, can't they? Could you somehow have missed the will of God?

Or if you're a single person, have you found yourself running hither and yon, trying to be at the "right" place at the "right" time so you might cross paths with the mate of your dreams? Have you traveled from church to church, surveying the prospects, then absolutely panicked for fear you're somehow going to miss God's best?

Thoughts like these can unleash sheer mental torture, eventually spinning you into depression and despair. Yet what you may not realize is that this is a missile from the enemy's arsenal—a destructive tactic as old as the Garden of Eden.

He will try to make you question God's goodness. Question God's timing. Question God's care and concern for you. Question God's control of life's tiny yet momentous details. So what's the solution? You'll find it in Psalm 37:4–5: **"Delight yourself in the LORD; and He will give you the desires of your heart. Commit your way to the LORD, trust also in Him, and He will do it."**

Run to the sovereignty of God, beloved! Rest in His loving control of every particular of your life.

~

O Father, help me not to fret over the details—or the big things—of my life. Whenever worries enter my thoughts, remind me of Your sovereign care and Your unchanging goodness and love.

June 9

I enjoyed twenty-twenty vision right into my late forties. Yet gradually, as I grew older, I experienced more difficulty focusing on things up close. It became a bit of a struggle to read a magazine, follow a recipe, or thread a needle. How frustrated I used to get over my blurry vision! But contact lenses gave me an entirely new perspective.

In a similar way many of us are so focused on the future that we can't understand the things happening to us now. Our circumstances don't appear to be taking us in the direction we want to go. Our immediate relationships seem strangely out of focus. We strain to see our lives more clearly.

This is why some people have problems with the sovereignty of God. They look at the future, imagining they see it clearly. Because of their cherished goals and high expectations, they have difficulty accepting and handling hurts, setbacks, and adversities in daily life. How could these bumps and bruises possibly be coming from God?

One reason we have problems with God's sovereignty in the face of adversity, evil, or calamity is that our vision is temporal and limited. God, however, sees everything under the heavens, from eternity past to eternity future: **"For He looks to the ends of the earth and sees everything under the heavens"** (Job 28:24).

What we need are spiritual contact lenses. We need a proper perspective on the present in light of the eternal. Only faith will do.

~

Sovereign Lord, help me to live this day in light of Your eternal purposes, trusting You with the things beyond my vision as well as those things I think I see clearly.

June 10

In dark moments of disappointment, we may find it challenging to keep our eyes on God rather than on our circumstances—or those who may have created them. And yet only by focusing on our faithful Almighty God can we hope to see the purpose He's bringing out of our difficulties.

Do you remember how Joseph's brothers plotted his demise? Because of his brothers' jealousy, Joseph was sold to be a slave in Egypt. There, in the house of Potiphar, he was falsely accused and put in prison for two years. It was enough to make any normal man bitter at God. Joseph had been faithful to God and suffered because of it. He seemed to be the victim of the whims and plots of men. And yet, during all this time, Joseph did nothing to dishonor his God.

He knew the Most High stood in the shadows, ruling over all. Joseph knew that God had a purpose in everything he endured. How can I say that? Because of what Joseph said to his brothers when they found themselves standing before him as the appointed ruler over all Egypt:

> Now do not be grieved or angry with yourselves, because you sold me here, for God sent me before you to preserve life.... Now, therefore, it was not you who sent me here, but God.... As for you, **you meant evil against me, but God meant it for good in order to bring about this present result, to preserve many people alive.** (Genesis 45:5, 8; 50:20)

Quit striving, beloved, and simply rest. God has a purpose.

Almighty God, I praise You for Your power to redeem even the darkest moments and work Your purposes through them.

June 11

Are you troubled by the prevalence of evil in our culture? Have you trembled in fear that it will touch your home, your loved ones?

What encouragement we can find by considering how Jesus responded to evil during His time on earth! The Gospels present sixteen accounts of Jesus and His disciples encountering demons. However, we know that in His three and a half years of public ministry, there were other confrontations with the kingdom of darkness.

Confronting the enemy and setting captives free were integral parts of our Lord's mission. Remember what took place when Jesus visited the synagogue in Nazareth:

> And He opened the book and found the place where it was written, "**The Spirit of the Lord is upon Me, because He anointed Me to preach the gospel to the poor. He has sent Me to proclaim release to the captives, and recovery of sight to the blind, to set free those who are oppressed, to proclaim the favorable year of the Lord.**"... And He began to say to them, "**Today this Scripture has been fulfilled in your hearing.**" (Luke 4:17–19, 21)

The kingdom of God had come. With it came the authority of heaven—authority that had to be obeyed.

Satan is strong, but he is not strong enough to resist God! Don't tremble or be alarmed. God has seated you with Christ, above all Satan's dominions (Ephesians 1:20–21).

~

What a reason to rejoice! You have all authority under heaven and on earth, and You've made it available to me as Your child.

June 12

Did you know that anger in itself is not a sin? It can even be righteous. As a matter of fact, the majority of references to anger in the Bible refer to God's anger. God hates sin. His righteousness and holiness don't leave Him passive in respect to unbelief and disobedience. Nor should sin leave us passive. If God gets angry over sin, then so should we. I believe the more we become like Him, the more we will abhor sin.

Even so, we need to heed the Bible's warnings about anger, which can become a dangerous, habitual response if unchecked by the Holy Spirit: "**Do not be eager in your heart to be angry**" (Ecclesiastes 7:9).

Anger is an emotion. But when anger rules, we're in trouble! According to Galatians 5:19–20, outbursts of anger are works of the flesh, and when the flesh controls us rather than the Spirit, that's sin.

Harboring anger is also sin. Anger, justified or not, must be given to God. He can handle it righteously and justly; we cannot. If we harbor anger and don't deal with it biblically, then we're giving the devil an opportunity to attack. When we harbor sin, it wears away at our hearts and at our relationships, and it opens the door to the enemy.

~

Ask God to show you if there is any unresolved anger in your heart. If there is, write down whom you're angry with or what you're angry about. Then tell God how you feel about letting go of your anger. If you want to be at peace with God and with others, tell Him. If you don't, tell Him why. Be honest. Say it aloud. He'll listen. And He'll help, if you genuinely want His help.

June 13

When other people wound us, deliberately harm us, or leave us disappointed, it does no good to lash out in anger or respond in kind. Instead, our responses must be guided by the wisdom of Psalm 37:1, 3–4: "**Do not fret because of evildoers, be not envious toward wrongdoers....** Trust in the LORD and do good; dwell in the land and cultivate faithfulness. Delight yourself in the LORD; and He will give you the desires of your heart."

Fretting over the behavior of others leads to anger and to sin. Instead, rather than wallowing in frustration and anger over evildoers, you and I are to delight ourselves in our Lord.

When God tells us to delight ourselves in Him, He is turning our attention to our one and only source of satisfaction—Him. Our hurts have come or been compounded when we have placed our expectations of happiness and fulfillment in people or things rather than in God. He is the One who gives us the desires of our heart, not man.

Have you ever thought that maybe the reason you have been hurt so badly is because you sought from man what only God could give? Maybe that's why you're so angry at your loved one. Your delight has been in imperfect, fallible flesh rather than in the Lord Himself, who will never fail.

It is God who shapes your future, not man. Therefore, don't allow man to frustrate you or cause you to do evil. Trust in your God, the One who causes all things to work together for your good (Romans 8:28).

~

Lord, I choose this day to commit my way to You. When I'm disappointed by others, give me the strength to resist anger, choosing instead to trust in You and to continue to do good.

June 14

If you've been wounded through verbal, emotional, or physical abuse, you are in the midst of warfare. Your spiritual life is under siege.

Satan will fight long and hard to hold a soul in his dominion of darkness (Acts 26:18). However, when the Spirit begins the process of bringing God's lost sheep to salvation, Satan must let them go.

Satan's power over a soul is broken because sin has been completely paid for by the blood of Jesus Christ. However, salvation does not end a person's battle with the forces of the evil one. Satan desires to sift us as wheat, to make us weak and ineffectual servants in the kingdom of God. Having lost us to God, he knows that we are God's forever, yet the reality of that truth does not stop him from attacking us.

And where does the enemy attack first? If you answered, "In our minds or in our thoughts," you are so right! Satan wants to fill your mind with thinking that is contrary to God's Word. Evil comes from the mind, the heart: "**As [a man] thinks within himself, so he is**" (Proverbs 23:7).

Oh, beloved, this is why the Bible warns us, "Watch over your heart with all diligence, for from it flow the springs of life" (Proverbs 4:23).

Protect my heart and mind, dear Father. Help me fill them with Your truth, leaving not even a sliver of room for the enemy's lies to take hold.

June 15

Beloved, are you able to rejoice in the midst of trials? Have you discovered the gift that accompanies suffering?

> **In this you greatly rejoice, even though now for a little while, if necessary, you have been distressed by various trials, so that the proof of your faith, being more precious than gold which is perishable, even though tested by fire, may be found to result in praise and glory and honor at the revelation of Jesus Christ.** (1 Peter 1:6–7)

Suffering gets rid of the dross in our lives; it is God's crucible of purification, as symbolized by the ancient art of mining and purifying silver.

When first extracted from the earth, silver is tainted by various impurities. Purification occurs in a crucible over a hot flame where the metal is heated to a molten state, and the silversmith skims off the dross that floats to the top. Looking into the pool of molten metal, the craftsman searches for his own reflected image on the surface. At first the image is very dim, and he knows that impurities remain. So he builds the fire to an even greater intensity. He never leaves the crucible unattended but hovers beside it, watching closely. He repeats the process over and over—with each purifying fire more intense than the last—until, finally, he can see a clear and perfect image of himself. The silver is pure.

This is how suffering prepares us for glory. It is the fire God uses to consume the dross in our lives so that we finally reflect a clear and perfect image of Him.

Holy God, help me to see darkness and difficulty as Your purification process, for my good and Your glory.

June 16

Whether we're leaping on spiritual mountaintops or slogging through despair, drawing close to God in prayer serves to protect and strengthen our faith.

The psalms are an especially wonderful resource for guiding our prayer lives. Psalm 42, for example, leads us into an honest encounter with God, where we lay open the longings of our heart and entrust them to God's loving care. **"Why are you in despair, O my soul? And why have you become disturbed within me? Hope in God, for I shall again praise Him for the help of His presence"** (verse 5).

Throughout the psalms, the psalmist tells God exactly how he feels, but he does not stop there. Once he's laid his heart and needs before God along with his questions and doubts, he finds peace in the act of trusting God. The psalmist looks at his past relationship with God. He remembers and rehearses what God has done, who He is, and what He will do. He recognizes that this time of despair will pass and that he will again praise God. He recognizes that if help is going to come, it is going to come from God.

Whenever you're in despair, run to the psalms. Pray them back to God—aloud—until the sweet relief of faith comes. You'll find their truths taking root in your heart and bringing forth hope.

~

O Father, my heart pants for You as the deer pants for the water brooks. I pour out my heart, my soul to You. Help me in times of despair to stop and remember the joy that I have known with You in the past. O Lord, You are greater than all my failures, greater than all my fears. You can help me in every situation. I thank You and praise You for all You are and for all You do.

As we seek to live our days with purpose, to be effective in our work and relationships, we can certainly benefit from books, articles, and other resources that provide helpful advice. Yet always we must compare the words of the so-called experts to the truth of God's Word, our only infallible source of guidance.

John 6:63 records Jesus saying, **"It is the Spirit who gives life; the flesh profits nothing; the words that I have spoken to you are spirit and are life."** God's Word is life-giving because it is literally the Word of God. It didn't originate with man. "No prophecy of Scripture is a matter of one's own interpretation, for no prophecy was ever made by an act of human will" (2 Peter 1:20–21). When you read the Word of God, you're not looking at man's analysis. The Bible is God's book, given to us through men who as they were "moved by the Holy Spirit spoke from God" (2 Peter 1:21).

In 2 Timothy 3:16 we read, "All Scripture is inspired by God and profitable for teaching, for reproof, for correction, for training in righteousness." The Greek word for *inspired* is *theopneustos,* which means "God-breathed." Thus, the Word of God is unique. It is the only book that is supernatural, divine in its origin. That's why it is living—its words originated with God. Therefore, God's words are exactly what Jesus said they were—spirit and life.

So what better place than the Bible to find the wisdom you need for the day ahead?

Lord, may it be a priority in my life to meditate on Your Word, knowing that man does not live by bread alone but by every word that proceeds from Your mouth (Deuteronomy 8:3).

As we saw yesterday, **"All Scripture is inspired by God and profitable for teaching, for reproof, for correction, for training in righteousness"** (2 Timothy 3:16). The Greek word used here for *inspired* means "breathed." Since the Bible is God-breathed, it is profitable for teaching or, as the King James Version says, "for doctrine." Doctrine is what people believe, what they adhere to, the creed or truth by which they live.

Every day we're bombarded by information—through advertisements, news programs, music, Web sites, books, and other sources—that we filter, often unconsciously, through our personal doctrine and either discard as meaningless or accept as a truth upon which we will base future decisions.

If you and I want to know what's right and what's wrong, what's truth and what's a lie, then we need to know what the Word of God has to say about it, either in specific words or in principle or precept.

Jesus prayed to the Father, asking that God would sanctify us in truth, and then Jesus made this statement: "Your word is truth" (John 17:17). Anytime you come across something contrary or contradictory to the Word of God, you can know immediately that you do not have the truth. Whoever wrote it, said it, or taught it was wrong.

The Bible is the only book that, in its entirety, is composed of the very words of life, the very precepts of God. Oh, beloved, won't you let God's precious Word be your counselor, guide, and teacher for every situation?

Lord, move my heart to delight in Your Word. Give me a hunger for the Bible and the understanding to apply its truths to my life.

June 19

We've been looking at 2 Timothy 3:16, which tells us not only that God's Word is truth—the doctrine or teaching by which we are to live—but that it's also profitable for reproof. The Bible reproves us because it shows us where we are wrong, where we are off track. God's Word is our plumb line by which we are to measure everything we hear, everything we believe, everything by which we live.

If you're seeking advice from others or help in healing wounds of the past, but the counsel you're receiving doesn't agree with Scripture, either in specific teaching or in principle, then the counsel is not accurate. Your counselors may be lovely people. They may have impressive degrees and professional training. They may have helped others. But their counsel is not from God if it in any way is not in accord with God's Word.

Colossians 3:16 urges us, "**Let the word of Christ richly dwell within you.**" It is vital that we know God's Word and that we allow it to dwell in us richly. We need to know the Word of God so that we can identify counsel that would lead us into ungodly reasoning and unbiblical behavior.

Let me close today with two questions: What priority does the Bible have in your life? Have you given yourself to a diligent study of its precepts?

~

Lord God, the Author of all truth, thank You for the gift of Your Word and the counsel it offers. Help me to apply its precepts and to walk in Your wisdom today.

June 20

Let's continue today in our consideration of 2 Timothy 3:16. According to this verse, God's Word is not only profitable for doctrine and reproof but also for correction. Correction is knowing how to take what is wrong and make it right so that healing can begin.

So often when people are wounded by someone, they harbor hurt and bitterness, nursing those feelings rather than releasing them. They don't know that bitterness and unforgiveness will keep them from being healed. How often I've seen people in this situation! And, bless their hearts, they don't know how to let go of their bitterness. They wonder how they can ever forgive.

God's Word is so thorough that it not only gives us truth and shows us where we are wrong, it also shows us how to take what is wrong and make it right. **"For whom the LORD loves He reproves, even as a father corrects the son in whom he delights"** (Proverbs 3:12).

And do you know what? If you will do what God says, it will work. You can be healed. When I say healed, I don't mean you'll never experience pain again. Nor do I mean that the past will never again rear its ugly head. I mean you'll be able to deal with your hurt in such a way that you will "overwhelmingly conquer" in all things (Romans 8:37).

You have God as your Great Physician, and you have the Word of God, which corrects and heals. All you need is faith to obey.

~

God, I believe. Help my unbelief (Mark 9:24). Give me the strength to bear Your loving correction, knowing that it will draw me closer to You and to a life of wholeness.

June 21

Dear friend, through our discussion of 2 Timothy 3:16, are you beginning to see the rich resource we have in the Bible—if we will mine its treasures?

In addition to everything else we've seen, the Word of God is profitable for training in righteousness. To live righteously is simply to live according to God's Word. **"For whatever was written in earlier times was written for our instruction, so that through perseverance and the encouragement of the Scriptures we might have hope"** (Romans 15:4).

And this, once again, is where healing begins—in doing what God says to do, no matter how you feel, no matter what you think. This is faith, "and without faith it is impossible to please Him, for he who comes to God must believe that He is and that He is a rewarder of those who seek Him" (Hebrews 11:6).

You cannot outtrust God! His name is Jehovah-rapha, the God who heals. He is the Physician in Gilead, and you can cry, "Heal me, O LORD, and I will be healed; save me and I will be saved" (Jeremiah 17:14). He will heal; He will save. I know—I have seen it in my own life, and I have seen it again and again in the lives of others. His Word is true. His name is a strong tower; the righteous run into it and are safe (Proverbs 18:10).

As we spend time studying the Bible, letting its truths soak into our hearts, we'll gain all we need "to live sensibly, righteously and godly in the present age" (Titus 2:12).

I praise You, Lord, for offering in the pages of Your Word clear direction on how to lead a righteous life that brings honor to You and health to my spirit.

June 22

In the past several days we've seen in 2 Timothy 3:16 that the Word of God is profitable for doctrine, reproof, correction, and instruction in righteousness. And what is the purpose of all this? So that you and I "may be adequate, equipped for every good work" (verse 17).

The Greek word translated here as *adequate* is *artios,* which means "perfect or complete." And *equipped* is translated from *exartizō,* which means "to equip fully, to accomplish, to thoroughly furnish."

Do you see what God is saying? The Word of God has the practical answers for all of life's needs. It will thoroughly furnish us for every good work of life. The living and enduring Word of God is ultimately all you and I need in order to be what we need to be. **"You have been born again not of seed which is perishable but imperishable, that is, through the living and enduring word of God"** (1 Peter 1:23).

God's Word is truth. It is alive. It can heal if we will accept it in faith and walk accordingly.

If God is able to save man from himself and his sin, if God is able to save man from hell, and if God is able to make a person a new creature in Christ Jesus all through faith in His Word alone, then can't God enable us to live above our hurts as we take Him at His word?

~

Thank You, Lord, for sending Your Word to heal me and deliver me from those things that threaten to destroy me (Psalm 107:20). I praise You for the knowledge that I have been reborn through Your Spirit, made adequate and equipped for every good work.

June 23

Whatever your regrets, whatever past sins darken your memories or hold you ensnared in the present, you need to know this truth, beloved: forgiveness belongs to God and comes only from God. God is the One you sinned against, for all sin is ultimately against God. "**To the Lord our God belong compassion and forgiveness, for we have rebelled against Him**" (Daniel 9:9).

Remember when King David slept with Bathsheba, got her pregnant, and then strategically plotted her husband's death? David finally came face to face with his sin when he was confronted by Nathan the prophet.

Psalm 51 records his response for those who, like David, want to get rid of their guilt. As you read it, you'll see that David's confession wasn't motivated by the fact that he messed up his life and got caught. Rather, David confessed because he was grieved. He knew that "against You, You only, I have sinned and done what is evil in Your sight, so that You are justified when You speak and blameless when You judge" (verse 4).

If you see your sin as against God, if you have a godly sorrow that leads to repentance, and if you confess your sin to God, then He forgives. That's what God says, and God cannot lie. Whether it is guilt because of your days prior to believing on Jesus or because you've sinned as a Christian, only the blood of Jesus Christ takes care of your sins.

Help me to deal with my sense of guilt, Lord, to determine whether it is rooted in unconfessed sin or is simply a lie of the enemy to make me doubt Your promise of forgiveness. I know that with You lies the power of forgiveness, and I want to be blameless in Your sight.

Beloved friend, do you ever wonder if God has abandoned you?

How often people write to me in anguish, feeling that they have blasphemed the Holy Spirit and are cut off from God forever. They disregard Christ's promise that the one who comes to Him will never be cast away but will be raised up in that last day to live with Him forever: **"All that the Father gives Me will come to Me, and the one who comes to Me I will certainly not cast out"** (John 6:37). Instead, they buy a lie from the enemy. And Satan shrieks with delight. If the destroyer can persuade us that we are cut off from the Father, where is our hope, our power?

Satan also plants doubts about our salvation. I'm not saying you don't need to examine yourself for signs of genuine faith. I'm talking about people who have repented and believed in Jesus Christ and whose lives give evidence that they have become new creatures, yet they are plagued with doubts. They depend on their feelings—and they don't feel saved.

If you're being tormented in these areas, do what James 4:7–8 says: "Submit therefore to God. Resist the devil and he will flee from you. Draw near to God and He will draw near to you." Audibly agree with God regarding your sinfulness and inability to please Him. Thank Him for His mercy and grace. Tell Him that you live to do His will.

Then resist the devil. Command him aloud in the name and authority of Jesus Christ to be gone. "Resist the devil and he will flee from you."

Read Ephesians 1–3 aloud as a prayer to God, and thank Him in faith for these truths.

Friend, when was the last time you mourned—not because of what someone did to you or because of something that happened to you, but because what you did was wrong and it hurt God?

When did you last cry over the sins of others? When have you hurt because God hurt? Is it hard for you to imagine a God who truly hurts in the depths of His great heart? When did you last weep in your prayers for others, lamenting over the awful degradation of humanity? or grieve the persecution of our brothers and sisters in Christ? or mourn because God's holy name had been mocked and blasphemed?

Listen to God's words to King Josiah after he led his nation in a time of repentance:

> **"Because your heart was tender and you humbled yourself before God when you heard His words against this place and against its inhabitants, and because you humbled yourself before Me, tore your clothes and wept before Me, I truly have heard you," declares the LORD.** (2 Chronicles 34:27)

It's time for tears, beloved. It's time to cry. It's time to humble ourselves before God and weep in mourning for all the groanings of creation brought on by the sins of mankind. Only in repentance can we find salvation and peace.

O God, break my heart with the things that break Your heart. Open my eyes to the dreadful consequences of sin, and fill my heart with the sorrow that leads to true repentance.

Will you pause for a moment and think with me about the standards of our day? Who sets them? Who determines what is right? moral? correct? socially acceptable? just? fair? how we should dress, think, act, behave?

Let me challenge you to sit in front of your television for a couple of hours and listen with an analytical ear to what's being said. Jot down what you see and what you hear. And as you do, bring each thing up against the standard of God's Word. What are the differences, the discrepancies? Or are there any?

Then take a good look at yourself. Where do you want to be? What do you admire? What do you want to imitate? What is your dream? your desire? What gives you your sense of worth?

Where are you in this world? in the flow of our culture? Who sets the standard for you? Whose standard do you come closer to—God's or the culture's? How does that feel? Does it alarm you at all? Why?

Consider Paul's words to the Corinthians: **"I am afraid that, as the serpent deceived Eve by his craftiness, your minds will be led astray from the simplicity and purity of devotion to Christ"** (2 Corinthians 11:3).

Is there any danger, beloved, that possibly you've been "led astray from the simplicity and purity of devotion to Christ"? If so, what will you do about it?

Examine me, O holy and righteous Lord. Test my mind and heart and show me any way in which I have strayed from my devotion to You.

June 27

Are your relationships endangering your spiritual health? It's one thing to be in the world; it's another to be in it but not of it. Thus we're warned of the danger of yokes—believers and unbelievers harnessed together in partnership: **"Do not be bound together with unbelievers; for what partnership have righteousness and lawlessness, or what fellowship has light with darkness?"** (2 Corinthians 6:14).

To harness a believer with an unbeliever is dangerous, because you're trying to harness opposites, and it doesn't work. Righteousness and lawlessness have a totally different set of moral codes. Light and darkness cannot exist together—light is either present or it's not. Can there be harmony between the true God and an idol? What do believers have in common with unbelievers? One group believes that Jesus is the Christ; the other doesn't.

When you're bound together in a yoke with someone who doesn't hold your same values and beliefs, you're so locked into that relationship that you can no longer act independently. You're harnessed to another who will eventually want to go in a direction you can't follow and still honor God. What are you going to do then?

The believer is a brand-new creature in Christ Jesus. Consequently there must be a separation. This is what sanctification is all about, beloved. Because of who you are, because of Who is in you, there can be no compromise.

Protect my heart from dangerous relationships, dear God. Open my eyes to temptation, to the wiles of the enemy. Let Your light shine undimmed in my life that others may be drawn to You.

How can we hope to be salt and light to a hurting world if we don't interact with unbelievers and seek ways to touch them with God's truth and love?

Paul's instruction in 2 Corinthians 6:14 to avoid being bound with unbelievers is not an instruction to remove ourselves and shut out communication, dialogue, or even friendships with nonbelievers. God isn't telling us to run to our ecclesiastical sanctuaries and isolate ourselves from the world. Paul strives to clarify this in 1 Corinthians 5:9–10: "**I wrote you in my letter not to associate with immoral people; I did not at all mean with the immoral people of this world, or with the covetous and swindlers, or with idolaters, for then you would have to go out of the world.**"

Remember that Jesus sent His disciples into the world to make disciples of all nations (Matthew 28:19). You can't make disciples if you aren't going to be with people, befriend them, and share their grief and joy as well as the gospel. We have a ministry of reconciliation, and reconciliation reunites rather than separates.

We stand in the world in Christ's stead, urging people on His behalf to be reconciled to God (2 Corinthians 5:20).

If God is your Father, then invite the world to "visit" His home—to hang around you, for you are where He dwells, and you obey the rules of the house—so they can get to know the Father of the house. Who knows? They may want to move in permanently under His authority and love!

Give me wisdom, Lord, as I interact with unbelievers. Let my words reflect Your love and grace so that they will long to enter into relationship with You.

June 29

If you're a Christian who boldly lives in faith and seeks to draw others to Christ, how I rejoice in your passion, beloved. These days it seems few share Paul's sense of urgency in proclaiming the gospel: "**I did not shrink from declaring to you anything that was profitable,...solemnly testifying to both Jews and Greeks of repentance toward God and faith in our Lord Jesus Christ**" (Acts 20:20–21).

However, I urge you to be sure your efforts are rooted in the full truth of God's Word. Sharing the good news of Jesus Christ doesn't mean simply urging people to determine where they'll spend eternity. When we deliver the gospel, we need to proclaim the following:

First, out of bottomless love, *God took our sin and placed it upon Jesus.* Jesus literally became sin for us. Thus, we can receive His righteousness (2 Corinthians 5:21).

Second, *it is necessary to repent,* to have a change of mind evidenced by a change of direction. A person coming to salvation is no longer a law unto himself but is willing to submit to God and to God's holy commandments.

Third, people cannot make themselves righteous. *Only God can transform man,* and He does it by grace through faith (Ephesians 2:8). If a person will believe that the Lord Jesus Christ is who He says He is, God will do the rest.

~

Ask God to give you someone with whom you might share the gospel of grace this week. There is such joy in proclaiming God's gospel. Don't worry about leading the person to Him; that is God's job.

June 30

If we ever wonder if we have what it takes to live in victory, we have only to look at the life of our Savior. Jesus walked by the Spirit, the same Holy Spirit who lives in us! When we walk under His control, not quenching or grieving Him, we will do the works that Jesus did. Why? We have the same Spirit, the same authority, and the same power.

Our problem is that we don't know it, or we know it and don't appropriate it, or we don't believe it's for today. Our faith is small. It moves sandcastles, not mountains.

Read the book of Acts; there is your example. Some would say we can't live that way today, but I would have to ask when or where God tells us differently. Don't just live in the Epistles; consider the whole counsel of the Word. If the Old Testament was for our learning, what about the Gospels and Acts as well as the Epistles and Revelation?

Just before Jesus ascended, He said:

> **All authority has been given to Me in heaven and on earth. Go therefore and make disciples of all the nations, baptizing them in the name of the Father and the Son and the Holy Spirit, teaching them to observe all that I commanded you; and lo, I am with you always, even to the end of the age.** (Matthew 28:18–20)

The One who has all authority told you to go, and He promised to be with you always, "even to the end of the age." Take up your sword and go—the gates of hell will not overpower you.

~

Show me how to walk boldly and faithfully today in the power and authority of the Holy Spirit.

July 1

Have you ever stretched out flat on your back in the grass on a warm summer day and gazed at the heavens? Have you found yourself wondering what it's like beyond that deep blue dome of sky? Sometimes I've gazed into a clear night sky, dazzled by the brilliance of stars cast like diamonds on black velvet, thinking of the time when Jesus will come to take me home.

The apostle Paul longed for heaven. His heart's desire was "to depart and be with Christ" (Philippians 1:23). He groaned, longing "to be absent from the body and to be at home with the Lord" (2 Corinthians 5:8).

At home with the Lord!

Where is "at home with the Lord"? Paul says it's in the third heaven, Paradise (2 Corinthians 12:2–4). Is it through the empty space in the north of the heavens (Job 26:7)? It could be!

Wherever it is, I know home is where God is! Jesus promised, "In My Father's house are many dwelling places; if it were not so, I would have told you; for I go to prepare a place for you. **If I go and prepare a place for you, I will come again and receive you to Myself, that where I am, there you may be also**" (John 14:2–3).

What security this brings when things on this earth seem so temporal—and so shaky! God's children have a New Jerusalem awaiting them, a heavenly city where they will dwell forever in the very presence of God and His Son.

What a wonderful thought, that the Creator of heaven and earth waits to welcome me one day into His presence! Thank You for the marvelous promise that You are preparing a home for me in heaven.

Did you know that water, which is necessary for life, has always been symbolic of God?

For the Israelites, God was to be their wellspring, the One to whom they turned for all their needs.

> **O Lord, the hope of Israel,**
> **All who forsake You will be put to shame.**
> **Those who turn away on earth will be written down,**
> **Because they have forsaken the fountain of living water, even the Lord.** (Jeremiah 17:13)

God's people were to depend on Him as their source of life and satisfaction, their Fountain of Living Waters. Instead, in the days of Jeremiah, they turned to other sources.

That's an Old Testament parallel to you and me walking in the flesh instead of walking in the Spirit. God alone is to be our life, our source, our sufficiency. Jesus said, "If anyone is thirsty, let him come to Me and drink. He who believes in Me, as the Scripture said, 'From his innermost being will flow rivers of living water'" (John 7:37–38). "Come" and "drink" are in the present tense in the Greek, which implies continual or habitual action. You and I are to live in total, continuous dependence upon God.

Are you depending upon God, beloved? Or are you turning to a person, to a position, to material possessions—what you drive, what you wear, where you live—to give you a sense of worth, purpose, satisfaction? At what fountain are you drinking to quench your thirst? Has it really satisfied?

Lord, I thank You that You have promised to meet all my needs, to satisfy my longings. Forgive me for seeking fulfillment elsewhere.

July 3

Our society has lost its conscience. Have you ever wondered why? I believe it's because we as believers have lost our conscience and have discredited Christianity.

Where is that constraining, controlling love that reins in our emotions, passions, and ambitions, holding them tight in a determination that we will not—no matter what—discredit the ministry of reconciliation to which God has called us?

The world has covered itself with its cloak of sin and not even blushed, because we, by our willful, self-centered lifestyles, have discredited Christianity. And in doing so, we've put obstacles in the way of others.

And what will you do? What will I do? How will we live so we do not discredit the ministry?

Paul says that in every aspect of our lives, in every single thing we do, we're to give no cause for offense but are to commend ourselves as servants of God: "**We also urge you not to receive the grace of God in vain...giving no cause for offense in anything, so that the ministry will not be discredited, but in everything commending ourselves as servants of God**" (2 Corinthians 6:1, 3–4).

May we know the cry of a heart that says, "Search me, O God, and know my heart; try me and know my anxious thoughts; and see if there be any hurtful way in me" (Psalm 139:23–24).

O Father, shine Your light of holiness into my heart, revealing any way in which I am blemished, spotted by wrong thinking or wrong doctrine. Wash away any "hurtful way" with the water of Your Word.

July 4

As you look around our society today—even in our churches—it's clear that Satan has targeted the family unit for destruction. His success is phenomenal.

Why the family? Satan has targeted the family because the relationship between the husband and wife and between the parents and children are to be earthly examples of our heavenly Father and His family. "**But as the church is subject to Christ, so also the wives ought to be to their husbands in everything. Husbands, love your wives, just as Christ also loved the church and gave Himself up for her**" (Ephesians 5:24–25).

If people want to know what it's like to belong to God, they should be able to look at Christians' relationships and homes and get a taste of heaven.

One of the greatest threats to Satan's progress will be a committed Christian husband and wife who are determined to raise godly children for the furtherance of the kingdom of God. Families such as these will be on Satan's bombing run. The family is the backbone of any nation, because families produce the nation's leaders. The more committed Christian families there are in a nation, the greater will be their collective influence upon that nation.

How vital it is, then, that we pray regularly for God's protection and guidance for our families!

Protect and preserve my family, O Lord, and raise up strong families of faith, courage, and conviction throughout our nation. Let young men and women, parents and children stand up and call our country back to morality and virtue.

July 5

If we want to protect our families, we need to be alert to the dangers we face, to the tactics of the enemy.

What is the tempter's strategy for breaking up the family unit? He knows the weakness of our flesh. He's going to do everything he can to entice us to sin. One of his most wicked devices is pornography; it's destroying marital relationships because it leads to sexual perversion. This is why it's imperative first that we fulfill our sexual roles in marriage (1 Corinthians 7:3–5) and second that we remember that looking upon others to lust after them in our heart is adultery—and God judges adultery (Matthew 5:28). **"Marriage is to be held in honor among all, and the marriage bed is to be undefiled"** (Hebrews 13:4).

Satan will also do everything he can to prevent us from fulfilling our family responsibilities and to keep parents from loving and nurturing their children. His desire is to turn the hearts of the fathers from their children, and the children from their fathers. Alienation is his game. That's why Paul warns, "Fathers, do not provoke your children to anger, but bring them up in the discipline and instruction of the Lord" (Ephesians 6:4).

Oh, beloved, guard your family, guard your marriage. "Be careful how you walk, not as unwise men but as wise" (Ephesians 5:15).

Bind the hearts of my family together in love and unity and faith. Let the fruit of the Spirit—love, joy, peace, patience, kindness, goodness, faithfulness, gentleness, and self-control—reign in our relationships.

July 6

I wonder how many more we could see set free from sin, from the power of the enemy, if we understood the offensive dimension of prayer. The apostle Paul exhorted his readers:

> **With all prayer and petition pray at all times in the Spirit, and with this in view, be on the alert with all perseverance and petition for all the saints,** and pray on my behalf, that utterance may be given to me in the opening of my mouth, to make known with boldness the mystery of the gospel…that in proclaiming it I may speak boldly, as I ought to speak. (Ephesians 6:18–20)

I wonder how many more nations we could evangelize and disciple if our Wednesday night prayer meetings focused on global intercession rather than personal needs.

I wonder where our government officials and our nation would be morally if we had diligently obeyed our Lord's injunction to pray for kings and rulers and all in authority so that we might live peaceable and godly lives.

Yes, God is sovereign. But mystery of mysteries, prayer affects the work of God in the lives of men and nations. I don't understand—I don't have to. I am simply to obey.

As I write this, I confess that I have not prayed as I should have. I cling to Romans 8:28–30, but I know I need to be more diligent in prayer for family, friends, ministry, our government, our nation, our world. What about you?

~

I ask that You would move my heart, O God, and the hearts of many others to "devote ourselves to prayer and to the ministry of the word" (Acts 6:4) that we may see Your power at work.

July 7

So often I have groaned and wept over my own inadequacies, my own failures, my own stupidities, and I have thought, *If only I had...* or *If only I hadn't...*

Not all of my mail consists of love letters! Not everyone who talks to me is always pleased with me. Not every member of my family loves me or accepts me the way I am. And try as I may, I'm not all I should be. I have to deal with rejection, some of which comes because of my personality and inadequacies and some because of the gospel.

How do I handle it?

By accepting that "by the grace of God I am what I am" (1 Corinthians 15:10) and by believing that I am in the process of being conformed to His image. By trying to learn from my mistakes and seeking to turn from that which is not Christlike in character and behavior.

At all times, but especially when faced with criticism, I must remember that I am God's bond-servant—not man's—and He is the One to whom I am accountable: "For am I now seeking the favor of men, or of God? Or am I striving to please men? If I were still trying to please men, I would not be a bond-servant of Christ" (Galatians 1:10).

Beloved, you and I must remember to let this truth daily guide our words: "**Just as we have been approved by God to be entrusted with the gospel, so we speak, not as pleasing men, but God who examines our hearts**" (1 Thessalonians 2:4).

~

Lord, please give me a teachable spirit so that I may learn from my mistakes. And help me to distinguish worthwhile correction from unhelpful criticism, listening for Your voice above all others.

July 8

Have you ever stopped to think how God could use the sins you've committed, the hurts you've suffered, the rejection you've experienced to minister to others?

All of your past has purpose in God's sovereign plan. However, Satan would have you believe otherwise.

There was a time in my beginning with Jesus when I became depressed over my past. My mind became Satan's hunting ground as I thought about how things could have been different. As these thoughts of what might have been plagued me, I found my emotions careening out of control. I was consumed with regrets over the past.

Can you relate, my friend? Have you worried that you can never be whole, well, healed, set free, or of any value to God? How can we deal with such thoughts?

First of all, we recognize them as lies! Any thought that takes us back to life before Christ is not from God. God always looks at us as the new creatures we are in Christ Jesus.

Satan, however, wants to focus our thoughts on the past so we cannot concentrate on what God has set before us. This is why Paul wrote of "forgetting what lies behind and reaching forward to what lies ahead" (Philippians 3:13). Healing begins with understanding that God is in control and we are part of His sovereign plan.

Then we can prayerfully express our trust to God in the words of Job: **"I know that You can do all things, and that no purpose of Yours can be thwarted"** (42:2).

Sovereign Lord, I believe that You are in control of my past as well as my future and that You can redeem even my worst mistakes for Your glorious purposes.

July 9

God chose you! Can you imagine that? You didn't choose Him. In fact He chose you before the foundation of the world. Nothing you did before you believed on His Son changed His mind. He adopted you as His very own child. He redeemed you through the blood of His only begotten Son so that you became His very own possession. He sealed you with the Holy Spirit (Ephesians 1:3–14). Do you think He's ever going to let you go or turn His back on you? If you think so, you're listening to your flesh or to the enemy, and you cannot trust either one.

Remember, **"He Himself has said, 'I will never desert you, nor will I ever forsake you,' so that we confidently say, 'The LORD is my helper, I will not be afraid. What will man do to me?' "** (Hebrews 13:5–6).

When the adversary parades your guilt, reminds you of your failures, or tells you no one cares about you or wants you, take him to Calvary and remind him that God so loved you that He gave His only begotten Son to die in your place. Tell the devil you are now bone of Jesus' bone, a member of His body, seated with Him in the heavenlies. Then, from your heavenly seat of authority, command him to be gone.

When you feel all alone, look at Calvary and remember the nail prints in His hands; they're His for eternity, and so are you. "I will not forget you. Behold, I have inscribed you on the palms of My hands" (Isaiah 49:15–16).

~

Father, Your love is so amazing that I can hardly comprehend it. Let the assurance of Your presence and commitment wash over me moment by moment today.

July 10

Corrie ten Boom ended up in Hitler's extermination camps because she and her family hid Jews in their home in Holland during World War II. Her miraculous release was followed by another miracle: her worldwide ministry.

At the age of ninety-one, five years before her death, Corrie suffered a stroke that left her speechless. The woman who cared for Corrie in those years wrote of their discussing together why God allowed this illness to take place.

> We wondered, talked, and prayed on the subject, but never came up with a complete answer to the mystery.... What came to us in increasing measure was an assurance of the absolute sovereignty of God. Of vital importance to me was the growing realization that our times were completely in God's hands. He knew the length of Tante Corrie's life. It did not depend on anything except His will.

Corrie's daily prayer was "Lord, keep me close to Your heart so that I see things as it were more and more from Your point of view."[6]

This is my prayer for you and for me as we joyfully surrender in faith to the truth that our times are in His hands. In doing so, I know we'll find Him to be our strength even as He was Corrie's.

Let us meditate today on the words of the psalmist: **"O love the LORD, all you His godly ones! The LORD preserves the faithful... Be strong and let your heart take courage, all you who hope in the LORD"** (Psalm 31:23–24).

Lord, my life is in Your hands—and where could I be safer?

July 11

Oh, friend, have you discovered the vital importance of living daily with praise in your heart and on your lips?

Praise is the spark plug of faith. Praise gets faith airborne where it can soar above the gravitational forces of this world's cares. The secret of faith is continual praise even when your inward parts tremble and your lips quiver. Faith frees you to rejoice in the midst of trouble as you declare, "**The Lord is my strength and song, and He has become my salvation; this is my God, and I will praise Him**" (Exodus 15:2).

When Corrie ten Boom and her sister Betsy were taken to a concentration camp, they were ordered to strip naked and pass before the watching eyes of German soldiers. To these two godly women, this was a horrifying experience. Not only were they enduring great humiliation, there was also the terror of the unknown. They knew they were considered enemies.

How did they endure? How did they keep from losing their inner peace as they stood naked before eyes filled with curiosity, anger, or blatant lust? Betsy reminded Corrie that Jesus, too, had been stripped naked and exposed to the eyes of men at Calvary. She told her sister that they were going to rejoice in the fellowship of His sufferings.

And rejoice they did—time and time again. Oh, humanly there was nothing to rejoice about, but there was Someone in whom they could rejoice! Their fear and doubt were conquered by a faith that enabled them to rejoice—no matter what their circumstances or their future.

~

O Lord, I will bless You at all times. May Your praise be continually in my mouth (Psalm 34:1).

Precious one, if we're going to live in genuine surrender, allowing the Lord to fulfill His purposes in us, we need to know what a righteous lifestyle looks like. So let's spend the next few weeks examining the Beatitudes, in which Jesus tells us exactly how to be blessed by God.

The first beatitude in Christ's Sermon on the Mount is the foundation stone upon which all the others are built. It's the "alpha" of the Christian life and the "omega" to self-achievement. The sum of life is truly hidden in these opening words: **"Blessed are the poor in spirit, for theirs is the kingdom of heaven"** (Matthew 5:3).

What does it mean to be "poor in spirit"?

To be poor in spirit is to realize what state you are in before God. It is to be actively conscious of your total inability to walk with Him, please Him, or serve Him. To be poor in spirit is to abandon all pretense and to acknowledge your *total* dependence upon God for vindication from your sins. To be poor in spirit is to cry out with the apostle Paul, "I know that nothing good dwells in me, that is, in my flesh" (Romans 7:18).

Beloved, will you walk today in complete dependence on your God, forsaking all concern with selfish ambition or achievements?

I need You, Lord. You alone are my help and my deliverer. Be gracious to me, and preserve me through Your lovingkindness and mercy.

July 13

In Matthew 5:3, when Jesus says, "Blessed are the poor in spirit," the word for *poor* means "one who crouches and cowers." It comes from a word that means "to cower down" or to "to hide one's self for fear." It means to be poverty-stricken, powerless, utterly destitute. Destitute of what? Destitute of the Spirit.

Humanity truly is poor in spirit—poor beyond our reckoning. Yet men and women outside of Christ neither acknowledge it nor even recognize it.

Until people see their utter poverty of spirit, they are not ready for the kingdom of heaven. This is what John the Baptist sought to accomplish when he cried out, "Repent, for the kingdom of heaven is at hand" and then told the scribes and Pharisees to bring forth fruit in keeping with repentance (Matthew 3:2, 8). Surely he had seen their unwillingness to leave behind their pride, their self-reliance, and their self-assurance. In all probability they thought God was lucky to have them on His team. Their self-righteousness was like an unyielding stone wall, which kept them from seeing the righteousness that comes by faith.

By contrast, when we recognize that we are utterly powerless and completely destitute, and we throw ourselves on God's mercy, He hears our prayers and transforms our lives. **"He has regarded the prayer of the destitute and has not despised their prayer"** (Psalm 102:17).

God, I praise You for hearing the cry of the poor in spirit, the afflicted, the destitute. I thank You that all the riches of Your glory are available through the Holy Spirit living in me.

July 14

Poverty of spirit is not to be some passing emotional experience or a one-time event in the life of a child of God. Rather, it is a whole way of life, a life of total dependence upon Him. It is continually realizing that in and of yourself you could never please God. You could never meet His standards of righteousness. Only by God's gift of His Spirit and by walking in the Spirit can you please Him.

Can you identify influences or attitudes in your life that might be keeping you from seeing your true poverty of spirit? What are they? Wealth? Worldly wisdom? Strong natural abilities? Your own righteousness? If so, then you must also know that these very things will keep you from the kingdom of heaven. Scripture says only the poor in spirit possess the kingdom of heaven.

As you go before the Lord in prayer, remember, "**The sacrifices of God are a broken spirit; a broken and a contrite heart, O God, You will not despise**" (Psalm 51:17).

Will you pause now to consider what might be keeping you from recognizing your poverty of spirit? Then go before the Lord. Tell Him you choose to surrender these attitudes or things to Him, and acknowledge your complete and utter dependence on Him.

July 15

Of all the Beatitudes, "**Blessed are those who mourn, for they shall be comforted**" (Matthew 5:4) may be the most difficult one for us to understand. What does mourning have to do with "blessedness"? What does grieving have to do with being spiritually prosperous or approved of God? How do tears and sorrow of heart link up with the true and lasting happiness you desire?

In God's economy, it all makes perfect sense, beloved.

The blessedness does not come in the mourning; it comes in the results of the mourning—knowing the comfort of His intimacy, the surety of His arms about you, hearing the beat of His heart as He draws you close to His all-sufficient breast.

The Greek word for *mourn* in the second beatitude means "to mourn for or to lament as a way of life." The way the word is used here means that we are never to be hardened or inoculated to sin or sorrow. We are never to lose our ability to grieve, to weep, to mourn. We are never to become so calloused that we can look at sin or pain and remain unmoved—or even worse, laugh.

Does your heart mourn, precious one? Then turn to your loving Father and find the comfort He has promised.

~

Father, in this world filled with trouble and sin, it would be easy to become hardened to the pain around me. Please keep my heart tender. Help it to beat in rhythm with Your own as I draw close to You and seek Your comfort and peace.

July 16

What do you see as you look around you today? Is it a time for rejoicing in our nation? Is it a time for rejoicing across the world? Look at the condition of men's and women's hearts. Look at the complacency, the apathy within the church. Do you see men and women wholly consecrated to God? Do you see them hungering and thirsting after righteousness? Do you see them pursuing holiness?

Genesis describes a dark period of the earth's history, just before the Flood, when evil ran rampant. I can't help but wonder if this is how God feels about His world today: "Then the LORD saw that the wickedness of man was great on the earth, and that every intent of the thoughts of his heart was only evil continually. **The LORD was sorry that He had made man on the earth, and He was grieved in His heart**" (Genesis 6:5–6).

If Jesus were here again in bodily form, if He were to walk through the inner cities' avenues of entertainment, listen to the conversations in country clubs, peek behind the doors of hotel rooms, sit with us at our tables, and listen to us in our bedrooms, do you think He would be mourning or rejoicing?

Remember that Jesus promised, "Blessed are those who mourn, for they shall be comforted" (Matthew 5:4). What is He calling you to do?

Father, I long to see Your healing in our nation. Show me how to be a part of it. Give me—and many others—a hunger for holiness, a hunger that will be satisfied only as we seek You.

July 17

For the surrendered Christian, the third beatitude—**"Blessed are the meek: for they shall inherit the earth"** (Matthew 5:5, KJV)—serves as an invaluable guide for responding to every difficulty of life. Meekness implies submission to God, choosing to accept God's ways without murmuring or disputing.

I remember when our dear friends Bobby and Diane lost their son Scott in a tragic automobile accident just seven months after his wedding. As Jack and I were ushered into the room where a coffin housed Scott's now-vacant human tent, my eye caught Bobby's. He motioned us over. "I'm all right, Kay," he said. "God has met with me. Everything I've learned from studying the Word of God has held me and prepared me for this moment. His Word is true. God is good, and He is sovereign."

In that moment, I stood face to face with true meekness.

In the years since Scott's death I've never seen Bobby or Diane waver from the certainty that God operated according to His plans for their son. It was God who had knit Scott together in Diane's womb, and it was God who had numbered Scott's days...when as yet there were none.

In Bobby and Diane I've witnessed true meekness, an inward grace of the soul, an acceptance of God's dealings with us as good. Good because they draw us closer to Him. Good because we know we can trust God and rest in His sovereignty even though the situations themselves are not good.

O God, that I would respond to life with such meekness, with an active submission that enables me to walk with grace through every circumstance, no matter how difficult or painful.

July 18

As we saw yesterday, when faced with adversity, meekness bows the knee. Meekness acknowledges that God is eternal.

Meekness looks "not at the things which are seen, but at the things which are not seen; for the things which are seen are temporal, but the things which are not seen are eternal" (2 Corinthians 4:18).

Meekness remembers that man is finite and that God is infinite. The realm of God has no limits or bounds whatsoever.

"Before the mountains were born or You gave birth to the earth and the world, even from everlasting to everlasting, You are God" (Psalm 90:2).

This eternal God who creates prosperity and adversity (Deuteronomy 32:39; Isaiah 45:6–7) has neither beginning nor end. He is not confined to the finiteness of time nor to man's reckoning of time. He is never early, never late, and never in a hurry. And whether we understand our immediate circumstances or not, He views our whole earthly pilgrimage through the eyes of eternity. He knows where we're going. He knows how it all fits together. He knows how to extract maximum good and maximum glory out of every situation, no matter what!

Beloved, let's remember this today so that we'll be able to respond in meekness when we face the unexpected.

God, I trust You. I know You are holy. I know You are righteous. I know You are just. Help me to accept everything that comes into my life without murmuring, without disputing, without retaliation.

Is your heart aching over a broken or disappointing relationship? Do you wonder why God is permitting your pain? Dear friend, the healing of your wounds will come as you trust in God's character and continue in meekness.

Meekness bows the knee and realizes that everything is permitted and used by God for our chastening, our purifying. Meekness says, "Not my will, but Yours be done." Meekness bows before the throne and realizes that the God who sits upon that throne is an all-wise God.

God makes His wise plans on the basis of His righteous character. He has righteous ends in mind and chooses righteous means to achieve those ends.

Meekness knows that the God who sits upon the throne of the universe is a good God. **"For He has satisfied the thirsty soul, and the hungry soul He has filled with what is good"** (Psalm 107:9).

He delights to bless.

He takes holy pleasure in the ultimate welfare and blessing of His people.

He is kind, benevolent, and full of good will.

Therefore, if you are experiencing neither happiness nor fulfillment in your marriage, or any other relationship, and you have done all you should have in light of His Word, rest! God will see to it that even your heartbreak will work together for good. Because He is God, He will satisfy your thirsty soul. He will fill your hungry soul with what is good.

O God, I will trust in Your lovingkindness forever. I will give You thanks, because You have done it, and I will wait on Your name, for it is good (Psalm 52:8–9).

As we continue looking at the Beatitudes and the lifestyle to which God calls us, we come to Jesus' fourth declaration in the Sermon on the Mount: "**Blessed are those who hunger and thirst for righteousness, for they shall be satisfied**" (Matthew 5:6).

So what does it mean to hunger and thirst after righteousness?

Hunger and thirst are bodily cravings that must be satisfied if life is to be sustained. And there, beloved, is the key. The Sermon on the Mount clearly shows us that unless we have a righteousness that surpasses the righteousness of the scribes and Pharisees, we shall in no way attain eternal life. The Sermon on the Mount is all about the righteous lifestyle of those who belong to the kingdom of heaven.

To what degree, then, are we to desire this righteousness? To the same degree that we hunger after food and thirst after water! If we're going to have a righteousness that brings life, then we must crave it with the intensity of hunger and thirst.

Perhaps you're thinking, *That certainly eliminates a lot of people, doesn't it?*

Yes, it does.

Now you can understand why Jesus says that the way is very narrow and the gate is very small (Matthew 7:14)!

~

Give me a longing for righteousness, dear God. Fill me with a hunger and thirst for Your truth, then let me be satisfied solely by Your Word and Your presence in my life.

July 21

Hungering and thirsting for righteousness is not to be a one-time event but a continual habit of life. Just as one meal does not satisfy you for the rest of your life or even for the rest of the week, so one initial hungering and thirsting for righteousness cannot satisfy you for life. It is to be a day-by-day occurrence, just like the cravings for food and drink that are common to all of us.

Is there a hunger and thirst for God within you, a deep craving for righteousness? Can you truly say with the psalmist, **"O God, You are my God; I shall seek You earnestly; my soul thirsts for You, my flesh yearns for You, in a dry and weary land where there is no water"** (Psalm 63:1)?

To hunger and thirst after righteousness is to have a profound inner longing to please God. It is a longing that God Himself plants within our hearts to cause us to seek after Him. To hunger and thirst after righteousness is to desire with all our being to live and walk the way God says to live and walk.

It is to crave God.

It is to crave holiness.

Now, may I ask you again? Do you hunger and thirst after righteousness?

My heart and my flesh cry out for You, O Lord. I love You, and I need You desperately. Fill me with Your righteousness and truth. Help me to walk as You direct through this wilderness, ignoring the world's offers of false hopes and illusions.

July 22

Ours is to be an ever-increasing hunger and thirst for righteousness. The more we get, the more we want; the more we want, the more we get.

Jesus illustrates this ever-increasing hunger and thirst for righteousness in the parable of the sower in Matthew 13: **"For whoever has, to him more shall be given, and he will have an abundance; but whoever does not have, even what he has shall be taken away from him"** (verse 12).

What did He mean? In the parable He had just revealed that only one type of soil—good soil—yielded a crop.

What made the difference? It wasn't the seed, because Jesus tells us in Matthew 13:19 that the seed is the word of the kingdom, the truth of righteous living. It was the soil's receptivity to the seed that made the difference. Mark 4:20 adds clarity here: "And those are the ones on whom seed was sown on the good soil; and they hear the word and accept it and bear fruit, thirty, sixty, and a hundredfold."

Did you notice the words "accept it"? Obviously the more we accept, the greater the crop will be.

Do you want to be righteous? Then receive what God has for you. Be obedient to the revealed will of God, not just with an external obedience, but from the heart. God will give you more and more. But if you neglect His Word, ignore it, or refuse it, you will have a meager harvest.

Lord, I pray You will make my heart a fertile place where You can plant and harvest the fruit of righteousness.

How can we be sure that we have a genuine hunger and thirst for God's righteousness?

First of all, we'll be aware of a longing for God and His Word.

Second, we'll hate sin. Righteousness is incompatible with sin. Therefore, we'll hate wickedness and sin because it keeps us from righteousness. Righteousness loves the things God loves and hates the things God hates.

The third and last evidence of righteousness is a longing to do God's will. If we are genuinely hungering and thirsting after righteousness, we must know and walk in obedience to the will of God. The highest example of hungering and thirsting for righteousness is seen in Jesus when He said, "**My food is to do the will of Him who sent Me and to accomplish His work**" (John 4:34).

What about you, my friend? What is your food? If the Holy Spirit is truly within, you will hunger and thirst for righteousness. You will know He is there, because you will have a longing for God and His Word. You will love righteousness and hate sin. You will long to do His will.

Now, where do you stand? If righteousness is your heart's cry, if you come to God with a genuine hunger and thirst, He will not turn you away empty.

God, I have no righteousness of my own. There is no way I could ever please You in and of myself. Sanctify me through the power of Your Holy Spirit, and fill me with Your righteousness.

Though our culture encourages us to demand "satisfaction"—restitution or punishment—from those who offend or harm us, this is not the attitude we see in Jesus, whose life was a continuous manifestation of the mercy of God.

The Pharisees wanted to stone the woman who was caught in adultery, but Jesus, in mercy, pardoned her. When He saw the multitudes, compassion moved Him to heal them, feed them, and teach them, for He knew that man does not live by bread alone but by every word that proceeds out of the mouth of God.

His mercy prompted Him to call His disciples to plead with the Lord of the harvest to send out workers into His harvest. His life was a constant manifestation of the Father. If you had seen Him, you had seen the Father. And God always acts in mercy, because He is merciful. For this reason, even when Jesus hung on the cross, listening to the taunts of those who had sought His death, in mercy He cried out, "Father, forgive them" (Luke 23:34).

Mercy meets the need of forgiveness.

How vital it is that you see this! Why? Because "**Blessed are the merciful, for they shall receive mercy**" (Matthew 5:7).

Unless you are merciful, you will not receive mercy (Matthew 18:33–35). And if you are going to be merciful, you must forgive others. Mercy and forgiveness are like conjoined twins with one heart. They can't be separated!

Fill me with the mercy and compassion of Christ. Give me a heart that cares for the lost and the needy, a heart that readily offers forgiveness when others offend or harm me.

Because man has transgressed God's holy Law, he stands condemned before God. And yet because God is a God of love and mercy, He took pity on us. He saw our need and sent His Son to shed His blood on Calvary so that God's holiness might be "propitiated" or satisfied.

Have you ever heard of the doctrine of propitiation? In simple language, it means that Jesus' blood, shed at Calvary and applied to God's mercy seat, propitiates or satisfies the demands of holy God. Therefore in Luke 18:13 when the man cries out, "God be merciful to me a sinner" (KJV), it literally means "God be propitious to me a sinner."

Mercy is bonded with love's compassion, which acts on behalf of the needy. So in love and mercy, God sent His Son, Jesus, to die upon the cross: **"By this the love of God was manifested in us, that God has sent His only begotten Son into the world so that we might live through Him"** (1 John 4:9). After His death, Hebrews 9:24, 26 tells us, Jesus entered "into heaven itself, now to appear in the presence of God for us.... [He] put away sin by the sacrifice of Himself." Hallelujah! The righteousness of our holy God was satisfied!

~

Ask God to open the eyes of your understanding so that you will walk in mercy and so receive mercy.

July 26

Have you ever read this greeting in Scripture: "Grace, mercy and peace be unto you"? Grace is the unearned favor that saves us. Mercy is the undeserved favor that forgives us. And peace is the unsought favor that reconciles us.

What a gracious and merciful God we have! And He calls His children to reflect His mercy: **"Be merciful, just as your Father is merciful"** (Luke 6:36).

Oh, beloved, there is a whole world of broken, desperately wounded men, women, and children out there. Yes, many of them may be rude, crude, obnoxious, and self-centered. They're lost! They're despairing!

These are people who in no way deserve mercy…but they need mercy desperately.

They are people who may not even understand they are unforgiven…but they must find forgiveness, or they will perish in their sins.

They need God's mercy and forgiveness. And they need your mercy and forgiveness. Won't you tell God that you want to be merciful—even as He is merciful? that you want to extend the true meaning of the greeting "Grace, mercy and peace be unto you" to them on His behalf?

Mercy, remember, is not for the worthy but the needy.

~

Dear heavenly Father, generous in compassion and forgiveness, I want to be merciful, even as You are merciful. When I am tempted to judge or dismiss others, fill me with Your grace. Help me, through mercy, to be an instrument to bring Your peace into the lives of others.

Do you want to see God, see Him as He really is? Do you want to know Him intimately? Do you want to behold Him face to face someday? Jesus says it's possible…for those whose hearts are in the right condition: "**Blessed are the pure in heart, for they shall see God**" (Matthew 5:8).

The Greek word for *pure* used here does not mean naturally pure; it means "pure as being cleansed." In other words, God is not saying that if I want to see Him, I have to have a heart that has never been dirty or tainted. Rather, it's a purity that comes from having been cleansed. Aren't you thankful? I am! Otherwise, I would never see God! I've been too dirty!

"The heart" can refer to several things. In this instance it refers to the seat of grief or joy, desires or affections, perceptions or thoughts, understanding or reasoning, imagination or conscience, intentions or purpose, will or faith.[7] Therefore, when we speak of purity of heart, it is purity of actions, purity of thoughts, purity of desires and motivations, purity of proper reasoning. If I'm going to have a pure heart, I have to think properly and reason properly. This goes along with the scripture "as [a man] thinketh in his heart, so is he" (Proverbs 23:7, KJV). That is why you have to "watch over your heart with all diligence, for from it flow the springs of life" (Proverbs 4:23).

If you and I are going to see God continuously, then we must keep our hearts cleansed!

~

Lord, I long for intimate, unbroken communion with You, an ongoing sense of Your presence in my life. Show me any impurity that threatens our relationship so that I may seek forgiveness and cleansing and be reconciled to You.

Our hearts are kept cleansed and made pure not only through spending time in the Word but also through confession. The Bible tells us, "**If we confess our sins, He is faithful and righteous to forgive us our sins and to cleanse us from all unrighteousness**" (1 John 1:9).

To confess means to "say the same thing" or to "speak the same word." Therefore, to confess our sins is to agree with God that what we have done is sin. To do that, we name it as sin. We say, "God, I have permitted ________________ to rule me, and that is sin. I confess it as sin right now. I want to turn from that sin."

When we do this, we have a marvelous promise. Because God is faithful and because He is righteous, He forgives our sin. He looks at that blood of Jesus on the mercy seat, the blood that cleanses us from sin.

He also cleanses us from "all unrighteousness." Have you ever wondered where you would stand with God if you hadn't confessed some sin because you couldn't remember it? First John 1:9 promises you that when you confess every *known* sin, then God cleanses you from *all* unrighteousness. Why? Because God sees a heart that wants to be pure, and He moves accordingly.

Isn't it wonderful that God not only calls us to be pure but also makes every provision so that we can be?

~

Thank You, most gracious and merciful God, that You have promised to forgive and cleanse me when I come to You in confession and sincere repentance. Create in me a clean heart, I pray, so I may walk in true fellowship with You.

July 29

If you're going to have a pure heart, you need to keep your heart cleansed by carefully watching what you think about. Every thought needs to meet the qualifications of Philippians 4:8: "Finally, brethren, whatever is true, whatever is honorable, whatever is right, whatever is pure, whatever is lovely, whatever is of good repute, if there is any excellence and if anything worthy of praise, dwell on these things."

The things that you allow to possess your imagination can get you into serious trouble. When you entertain wrong thoughts, they can eventually become footholds or strongholds for Satan.

If you're going to have a pure heart and see God, according to James 4:8 you need to purify your heart and not be double-minded. How do you purify your heart? You "set your mind on the things above, not on the things that are on earth" (Colossians 3:2). **"For out of the heart come evil thoughts, murders, adulteries, fornications, thefts, false witness, slanders. These are the things which defile the man"** (Matthew 15:19–20).

On what is your mind set, my friend—the things of this earth and the flesh or the things of the Spirit from above?

Lord, strengthen me to destroy and discard any thought that is not according to the Spirit. Help me to consistently set my mind on the things above, the things that have eternal value and purpose.

July 30

Jesus, in Matthew 5:9, says, "**Blessed are the peacemakers, for they shall be called sons of God.**" So we need to know, what makes a peacemaker?

First, if you're going to be a peacemaker, you must be at peace with God. Colossians 1:20 tells us that Jesus, the Prince of Peace, has reconciled us to God through His death. He has "made peace through the blood of His cross." You can be at peace with God when you come to Him in poverty of spirit and accept the reconciling sacrifice of His Son.

Second, being a peacemaker means living in peace with our brothers and sisters in Christ. Ephesians 4:1–3 tells us very clearly that if we are to walk "in a manner worthy of the calling with which you have been called," we must be "diligent to preserve the unity of the Spirit in the bond of peace." First Thessalonians 5:13 urges us to "live in peace with one another."

A third thing that makes you a peacemaker is having the ministry of reconciliation: bringing the "good news," the gospel of peace, to other people so they in turn might have peace with God (2 Corinthians 5:18–20). You and I are not only to make peace among ourselves; we are to offer peace to those who are outside of Christ. There is really only one way to do that: introduce them to the Prince of Peace.

Does your life reflect the characteristics of a peacemaker?

Lead me in the way of peace, dear God, that my life will clearly show my position as Your child. I thank You that, through the blood of Christ, I can live at peace with You. Help me to also live in peace with my brothers and sisters in Christ, and show me how to share Your peace with a world in need.

July 31

The Bible sets clear guidelines for how we're to treat others as we go about the business of daily living: **"Love your enemies, and do good, and lend, expecting nothing in return; and your reward will be great, and you will be sons of the Most High; for He Himself is kind to ungrateful and evil men"** (Luke 6:35).

If you and I are to be perfect as our heavenly Father is perfect, we need to remember that "He Himself is kind to ungrateful and evil men." We cannot live as others do. We must live on love's highest plane. "For if you love those who love you, what reward do you have?… If you greet only your brothers, what more are you doing than others?" (Matthew 5:46–47).

Oh, beloved, do you see what is expected of us as sons and daughters of the Most High God? Do you see how high our calling is?

God laid down His life in the person of His Son for all mankind. Some would believe and respond; others would trample on that divine love. It did not matter. Love was willing to be trampled. God is calling us to lay down our lives as well: "Bless those who persecute you; bless and do not curse.… Never pay back evil for evil to anyone.… Never take your own revenge.… If your enemy is hungry, feed him, and if he is thirsty, give him a drink.… Overcome evil with good" (Romans 12:14, 17, 19–21).

Will you live on the highest plane? Do you and I really have a choice?

Lord God, the kind of love You ask of me is impossible in my own strength. Fill me and empower me with Your Holy Spirit so that I can love others in Your name and Your strength.

August 1

If you and I want to have an intimate relationship with God, we need to understand who He is, to be acquainted with His character and attributes.

For example, Elohim is the name for God as Creator. It is used in Genesis 1:1. But of what practical significance is this name to us?

If God is the Creator of all things, who has given us life? Elohim, of course! And why were we created? For Him! You are a unique creation of God, one of a kind, created for His glory. He formed your inward parts. He wove you in your mother's womb. You are fearfully and wonderfully made (Psalm 139:13–14).

Have you ever thought of yourself as being fearfully and wonderfully made? Or do you look at yourself and despise what Elohim has created?

Remember when "Moses said to the LORD, 'Please, Lord, I have never been eloquent, neither recently nor in time past, nor since You have spoken to Your servant; for I am slow of speech and slow of tongue' " (Exodus 4:10)?

What was the Lord's reply? "Who has made man's mouth? Or who makes him mute or deaf, or seeing or blind? Is it not I, the LORD?" (Exodus 4:11).

Will you praise your Creator for making you according to His perfect design? "**For the LORD your God is the God of gods and the Lord of lords, the great, the mighty, and the awesome God**" (Deuteronomy 10:17).

~

"I will give thanks to You, for I am fearfully and wonderfully made; wonderful are Your works, and my soul knows it very well" (Psalm 139:14).

August 2

I had a friend who was probably not more than three feet tall. Her head was normal size, but her body was dwarfed. Julie spent all her days in a sling, much like a baby's walker. In order to move anywhere, her legs had to propel the rolling frame. Julie was lovely, radiant, a delight to all who met her. She knew her Elohim, and she accepted that He created her just the way she was for a purpose. You couldn't tell her God had nothing to do with her physical condition. If she had believed that, she'd have denied His sovereignty, His Word, and His name.

But why would God create people who are different from His normal pattern of creation? Why would He ever permit a sperm to penetrate an egg when it would produce what seems to be a genetic disaster?

Remember when the disciples saw a man blind from birth "and His disciples asked Him, 'Rabbi, who sinned, this man or his parents, that he would be born blind?' " (John 9:2)? How did Jesus answer? "It was neither that this man sinned, nor his parents; but it was so that the works of God might be displayed in him" (John 9:3).

You may not understand how your situation or your loved one's could ever bring Him glory, but you can trust in the name of your Lord. **"Who is among you that fears the LORD, that obeys the voice of His servant, that walks in darkness and has no light? Let him trust in the name of the LORD and rely on his God"** (Isaiah 50:10).

~

Lord, I know that Your thoughts are above mine. I cannot pretend to understand why You have allowed some things in my life, but I will choose to trust in Your good purposes.

August 3

In the midst of our pain, disappointment, or uncertainty, Psalm 139 resounds like the triumphant clash of cymbals. Behold your God. Be awed with His all-encompassing love and care for you: **"O Lord, You have searched me and known me.... You have enclosed me behind and before, and laid Your hand upon me"** (verses 1, 5).

How comforting to know that, because God is omniscient (all-knowing), He is intimately acquainted with all of your ways! Our God who knows it all, who understands everything, has enclosed you behind and before. God is not far away, unconcerned, unaware of the events of your life nor of your secret thoughts. He cares for you in such a way that He, God Himself, has inscribed you on the palms of His hands (Isaiah 49:16). He cannot forget you, beloved! Calvary's nail prints are there forever.

Remember that your Father God knows about everything that has ever been done to you! Remember also that He is the Righteous Judge who will deal with those who have wounded you, His child.

But there's more. Not only does God know all that has happened to you; He was also there, whether you recognized His presence or not. You were never alone. He was there, my friend, when you felt as the psalmist, "Surely the darkness will overwhelm me, and the light around me will be night" (Psalm 139:11). Even then He was there...protecting, keeping, preserving.

~

How precious are Your thoughts to me, O God. I will give thanks to You for all the ways You are present in my life, preserving and protecting me.

August 4

Once you understand and embrace what the Bible teaches about the character and sovereignty of God, you will find calm in the center of life's storms.

Your understanding of the fact that God rules over all—that there are no accidents in life, that no tactic of Satan or man can ever thwart the will of God—should bring divine comfort.

Because God is sovereign, we can believe and embrace the promise of Romans 8:28–30:

> And we know that God causes all things to work together for good to those who love God, to those who are called according to His purpose. For those whom He foreknew, He also predestined to become conformed to the image of His Son, so that He would be the firstborn among many brethren; and these whom He predestined, He also called; and these whom He called, He also justified; and these whom He justified, He also glorified.

When you grasp and bow to the truth of how all things are working together for good to conform you to His image, then in faith you'll be able to rejoice and **"in everything give thanks; for this is God's will for you in Christ Jesus"** (1 Thessalonians 5:18). I know it's possible, beloved, for I'm doing it right now in the greatest trial of my life! It's the obedience of gratitude that sustains me.

Sovereign God of love, I thank You for the ways You are moving in my life, shaping me and conforming me to the image of Your precious Son.

August 5

I do not know your trials or your frustrations, beloved. I can't know what might be troubling you or making you anxious. But God knows those things. What you don't understand, what you feel unable to cope with can be overcome moment by moment if you will live by faith and walk in communion with Him. When you do so, you'll find yourself able to declare with Habakkuk, "**The Lord GOD is my strength, and He has made my feet like hinds' feet, and makes me walk on my high places**" (Habakkuk 3:19).

When you doubt, when iniquity abounds, when you want to question God, there are two things you need to do. First, run immediately into the ever-open arms of your omnipotent, sovereign Father. In faith, fling yourself into all that He is, into all that He has said. Do not attempt to handle life in your own strength. Instead, live by faith.

Second, rejoice in Him. In a sense, rejoicing activates your faith.

When you fling yourself in faith into all that God is and into all His Word says, when you rejoice in Him in the face of every circumstance, then you'll know His strength. It's a strength that will enable you to walk with hinds' feet of faith on high places. Hinds' feet do not slip.

So exult in the Lord, beloved. Rejoice in the God of your salvation. Remember, He is able to deliver you from—and through—any difficulty of life. He will be your strength and give you hinds' feet on high places.

~

Father, You are my strength, the One in whom I trust. Direct my footsteps today. Keep me from slipping or stumbling. Help me to live by faith as I walk in sweet fellowship with You.

August 6

As you walk through the hours ahead, you can expect that the enemy will send a fiery dart to your mind: a lie, a thought of rejection, a wrong doctrine, a deprecating thought, a suggestion to do evil, whatever. How are you to respond?

First, you stop the thought at the door of your mind and test it against Philippians 4:8: "Finally, brethren, whatever is true, whatever is honorable, whatever is right, whatever is pure, whatever is lovely, whatever is of good repute, if there is any excellence and if anything worthy of praise, dwell on these things."

Second, if the thought does not meet the qualifications of Philippians 4:8, refuse to let it linger. Take it captive, reject it, and replace it. If you don't, dear one, it can become a stronghold of wrong thinking, a fortress that will hold you prisoner. The acceptance of a wrong thought can then lead to

an action,
which creates an appetite,
which becomes a weakness,
which becomes a habit,
which brings oppression from the enemy.

To prevent the enemy from building a stronghold in your life, trust in God and maintain a steadfast mind! As the prophet Isaiah declared of God, "**The steadfast of mind You will keep in perfect peace, because he trusts in You**" (26:3).

Let my mind be so filled with the things of You—things that are true, honorable, right, pure, lovely, excellent—that any unworthy thought will immediately be rejected and pushed out.

August 7

When a spouse or child strikes out at us with words, when a co-worker undermines us, when someone has taken advantage of us, righteousness demands that we give our pain and frustration to God. "**For the anger of man does not achieve the righteousness of God**" (James 1:20).

Although God is fully aware of the injustice and cruelty of men, He says, "Be angry, and yet do not sin" (Ephesians 4:26). Anger is never to control us. If we allow anger to stay within, if we don't act in faith and deal with it in God's way, it can destroy us. It can even lead to violence and bloodshed. For that reason Jesus tells us, "Everyone who is angry with his brother shall be guilty" (Matthew 5:22). Anger that simmers within is like committing murder in your heart.

Oh, beloved, others may have committed evil or unrighteous acts against you. Your anger may be righteous anger. But if your soul is going to be right within you, if you're going to live by faith, then you must forgive, give your anger to God, and believe Him when He says it will work together for your good in order to make you more like Jesus (Romans 8:28–29).

Just remember: anger unresolved will bring you only woe.

How is it with your soul today? Is it right within you and before God, or have you stifled your anger?

Lord, I give my anger to You, trusting that as my righteous God, you will come to my defense and vindicate me in Your time and Your way. Through Your Holy Spirit, equip me to put away all bitterness, wrath, and anger, choosing instead to be kind, tender-hearted, and forgiving (Ephesians 4:31–32).

August 8

What is your heart's attitude toward other individuals as you interact in the marketplace, as you move in the business world, as you sit behind the desk as a teacher, as you fulfill the role of a parent, as you live with your mate? How does your heart feel toward those with whom you come into contact?

Matthew 5:48 is a passage in which Jesus describes how God expects us to treat other people: "**Therefore you are to be perfect, as your heavenly Father is perfect.**" If we're to be perfect even as our heavenly Father is perfect, then we must view others in the same way that God does. We must value every person.

How far does this respect for life go? It goes so far that if you know your brother has something against you, you are immediately to seek reconciliation. That is how important relationships are to God. Just before Jesus went to Calvary, He prayed to the Father that we might be one even as He and His Father are one (John 17:20–21). God does not want a schism in the body. Our gifts and our prayers mean nothing to Him if we're not walking in peace with our brothers. God is not interested in external conformity but in internal righteousness.

Do you respect other people as beings created by God in His image, distorted as it may be? Do you value the sanctity of their lives…or do you despise God's creation? What's in your heart?

~

Take a few minutes to take stock of your attitudes toward others. Ask God to search you and see if there is any wicked way in you that you might confess it, turn from it, and embrace a righteous love.

August 9

In a world where people demand to be given what they see as the respect they deserve, it seems ridiculous to consider turning the other cheek. It seems more logical to demand an eye for an eye and a tooth for a tooth, as outlined by the law in Exodus 21:24.

However, if we're to be perfect as our Father in heaven is perfect, we have to reach beyond the legalism of the law to its true intent, which is love. Romans 13:10 says, "**Love does no wrong to a neighbor; therefore love is the fulfillment of the law.**"

The major purpose of that law was twofold: to protect a person against unjust retribution and to cause a man to think twice before committing a crime. For this reason, the law can still be fulfilled by love turning its cheek. This demonstrates before the world the reality of God in us as He was in Christ: "reconciling the world to Himself, not counting their trespasses against them" (2 Corinthians 5:19).

To those who would insult us, seek our possessions, or abuse our privileges, we must demonstrate that, because Christ is in us, we will respond with the grace of God. We're not going to count their trespasses against them, but we'll turn the other cheek, give our coats, go the extra mile, and not turn away from the one who wants to borrow from us.

What will this demonstrate to a watching world? The meekness of Jesus as well as the mercy and kindness of God, which leads men to repentance (Romans 2:4).

~

When I am wounded or insulted by others, lead me to respond with a grace that can come only from You. Help me to think not of my "rights" but of what is right in Your eyes.

August 10

Jesus said to His disciples, "**If anyone wishes to come after Me, he must deny himself, and take up his cross and follow Me**" (Matthew 16:24). May I ask, beloved, whether anyone looking at how you spend your days would see evidence of self-denial, indications that you have taken up your cross to follow Christ?

"We live in a time when many who claim to know Christ undermine the Gospel by short-circuiting the radical implications of a life of discipleship as set forth by Jesus the Christ."[8] When I read this statement in Robert Guelich's commentary on the Sermon on the Mount, I thought, *How true that is!*

We want heaven, life, eternity! Who doesn't? We hear the good news about eternal life through Jesus Christ. It's free, so we take it, tuck it under our arms, and walk away. We're relieved. No hell now; heaven's our home. Then we imagine we can get back to living our lives as we please.

But can we? Does true Christianity allow us to go back to living our own lives?

I would like to switch on a worldwide intercom at this point and shout one loud, resounding *no!* You cannot belong to God and live any way you please! True Christianity is discipleship. It's the willingness to turn around, to leave everything, and to let Jesus Christ be all in all. It's the willingness to follow Him wherever He leads and to do whatever He says. True Christianity is a total commitment of oneself to the lordship of Jesus Christ.

~

Give me the courage, Lord, to pursue You with wholehearted devotion. Lead me into a radical life of dependence on You.

August 11

May I ask, dear one, are you serving God, or are you serving things? You cannot serve both. Listen to the apostle Paul's perspective: **"I count all things to be loss in view of the surpassing value of knowing Christ Jesus my Lord, for whom I have suffered the loss of all things, and count them but rubbish so that I may gain Christ"** (Philippians 3:8).

Paul had fixed his eyes on "the prize of the upward call of God in Christ Jesus" (Philippians 3:14). He served One and One alone, his Lord Jesus Christ. Consequently, he tells us that he learned to be content in whatever circumstances he found himself (Philippians 4:11). That word *learned* is important. It was an acquired skill! He learned how to get along with humble means and how to live in prosperity. In any and every circumstance of life he learned the secret of being filled and of going hungry, of having abundance and of suffering need. Paul would not permit anything to matter to him except that which had eternal value. Now that is something to learn, isn't it?

What about you? To what are you giving yourself, your energies? What do you desire above all else and more than anything else in this life? Is your heart fixed on God…or the temporal things of unrighteous mammon? What possesses you? Is it a passion for God…or a passion for the toys and tinsel of this life?

~

I urge you to ponder these questions, beloved. Let them search your heart. Give God time to speak.

August 12

When life doesn't go our way—when someone cuts us off in traffic, when we miss out on that promotion at work, when our spouse or children drive us to distraction, when someone interrupts our busy schedule with yet another need—how easy it is to respond in the flesh! We know what the Bible says, but will we allow it to guide our responses to life's frustrations?

If you are going to be meek, you will submit to God's authority over your life, even as Jesus submitted to the authority of the Father. You will walk carefully, filled with the Spirit, for the fruit of the Spirit is gentleness, or meekness (Galatians 5:22–23). You will be the good soil that receives God's Word and bears fruit. "**Therefore, putting aside all filthiness and all that remains of wickedness, in humility receive the word implanted, which is able to save your souls**" (James 1:21).

Psalm 25:9 declares, "He leads the humble in justice, and He teaches the humble His way." (The word for *meekness* often is translated *humble* or *afflicted* in the Old Testament.)

Are you willing to be led? Are you teachable? Are you willing to receive with meekness the engrafted Word of God? When you become more than a "hearer of the Word" and begin to walk in obedience as a "doer of the Word," it will show (James 1:22–23)!

~

How does your life measure up to what the Bible teaches about meekness? Think about it and ask God to reveal to you any way in which you have failed to be meek.

August 13

Hypocrisy was as common in Jesus' day as it is today. Jesus frequently referred to hypocrites: **"Woe to you, scribes and Pharisees, hypocrites! For you...outwardly appear righteous to men, but inwardly you are full of hypocrisy and lawlessness"** (Matthew 23:27–28).

It was the religious ones whom Jesus called hypocrites—the ones who claimed to know God—not the prostitutes, drunks, thieves, liars, and adulterers.

Hypocrite was the word used for a stage actor. In Greek and Roman theater, actors customarily wore large masks to indicate a particular mood or emotion. A hypocrite, then, is one who habitually wears a mask.

Pause with me a moment, dear one, and consider. Are you a hypocrite in any way? Do you ever find yourself "acting"? Do you ever slip on a mask to hide how you truly feel? Do you speak words that your life does not back up?

When you pray the Lord's Prayer and say, "Lead us not into temptation, but deliver us from evil...," do you really desire to stay away from temptation? When you pray, "Forgive us our trespasses as we forgive those who trespass against us...," are you really willing to forgive others as God has forgiven you?

Do you behave one way at church and another way at home or in your business? Does your attitude toward your mate or your children change when you get out of the car in the church parking lot?

Remember, God sees your heart. What does it reveal?

~

Lord, reveal to me any hypocrisy, any hidden sin or pride. Make me righteous, inside and out.

August 14

To live in intimacy with God, to truly commune with Him daily, the Bible says we must be pure inside and out:

> **Who may ascend into the hill of the LORD?**
> **And who may stand in His holy place?**
> **He who has clean hands and a pure heart,**
> **Who has not lifted up his soul to falsehood**
> **And has not sworn deceitfully.** (Psalm 24:3–4)

Perhaps you wonder, *Is it possible not to be a hypocrite? Doesn't everyone wear a mask now and then? Is it realistic to think my heart can match what I portray on the outside? Can I truly be righteous—inside and out?*

Yes! Yes, you can!

You can…or Jesus never would have required it of us. Just remember, what He demands, He supplies. How? By coming to live inside you. By giving you His Holy Spirit, who will lead you into all righteousness.

If you will but bow—
if you will yield to Him the throne of your heart—
the kingdom of heaven,
in all its fullness and joy,
will be yours.

It will be yours because God Himself will change you and fit you for the kingdom of heaven. It's the very reason He came among us.

~

I surrender to You, O Lord. Purify my heart. Transform me and use me for Your purposes.

August 15

Some people point to the cross as a testimony of our worth and value. They say that if we did not have worth, God would not have died for us.

Oh, beloved, the cross does not demonstrate our worth to God; it demonstrates God's unconditional love toward us: **"For God so loved the world, that He gave His only begotten Son, that whoever believes in Him shall not perish, but have eternal life"** (John 3:16).

The Bible doesn't say that God so esteemed or saw the value of man that He gave His only begotten Son. Salvation is pure grace; it therefore cannot be based on worth.

It is pure grace that pours out love "that saved a wretch like me," as John Newton, the writer of "Amazing Grace," so well worded it. The apostle Paul notes, "It is a trustworthy statement, deserving full acceptance, that Christ Jesus came into the world to save sinners, among whom I am foremost of all. Yet for this reason I found mercy" (1 Timothy 1:15–16).

Sinners deserve hell. God in love, mercy, and grace offers us heaven, where He will eternally express His love for us and where, at last, we will be able to fully express ours for Him.

Will you not only accept His love, but will you accept your calling—the cross—where you die to self that you might live for God?

I accept my utter unworthiness, God, and my complete dependence on Your grace. Lead me to live daily in the humility that comes from recognizing You as my sole source of worth. And never let me forget the great love with which You have loved me.

August 16

Did you know, beloved, that when we pass through the fires of affliction, suffering, and persecution, our endurance becomes the evidence of our salvation? Consider how Paul responded to suffering:

> **We also exult in our tribulations, knowing that tribulation brings about perseverance; and perseverance, proven character; and proven character, hope; and hope does not disappoint, because the love of God has been poured out within our hearts through the Holy Spirit who was given to us.** (Romans 5:3–5)

Did you notice the progression:

tribulation...

perseverance...

proven character...

hope

As God's children, we can exult in tribulation because of the fruit it produces: perseverance and character. The process of suffering causes us to mature, to become more like our Lord.

The fact that our faith doesn't wither shows that we're made of genuine stuff. We know that we know we are His, because we made it through the testing of our faith. Thus we have a hope that does not disappoint.

Once you pass through a great trial, you'll understand how it's possible to say with confidence, "I've been put to the test, and I have endured. My salvation is genuine!"

~

Thank You, sovereign Lord, for the hope that is mine through the testing of my faith. Help me to see each trial and affliction as an opportunity to mature and grow more like Christ.

August 17

Oh, beloved, what joy it brings me to assure you that whatever trouble comes your way—a broken relationship, the loss of a job, a crisis of health—God's power is enough to carry you through.

In the Garden of Gethsemane Jesus was pressed beyond measure, in such agony of spirit over what lay before Him that He sweat great drops of blood. In His agony He prayed, **"Father, if it is possible, let this cup pass from Me; yet not as I will, but as You will"** (Matthew 26:39).

Of course, anything is possible for God. But to remove Jesus' cup of suffering and death would have meant that His mission would fail. Man would have remained lost. Can you sense Jesus' humanity? And yet with every plea for the removal of the cup, Jesus concluded, "Your will be done."

And His Father's will was done. And through it all Jesus found the Father's grace sufficient to sustain Him!

I'm sure that is why this intimate time with His Father was preserved for us in the Gospels. We need to know and understand that we aren't alone in our suffering or in our service for our Lord.

Paul says of Jesus, "He was crucified because of weakness, yet He lives because of the power of God" (2 Corinthians 13:4).

He lives because of the power of God. That, beloved, is the way we, as followers of Christ, are to live.

~

Lord, I know that whatever comes will be filtered through Your sovereign fingers of love. And I know that You will be with me and will sustain me through Your power and grace. In this I will rest and rejoice.

August 18

When I suffer, it's always a comfort to know I'm not alone and my suffering has a purpose: suffering is one of God's primary means of conforming us to the image of His Son, Jesus Christ. As the God-man, Jesus suffered. As children of God, we will suffer; it's part of the refining process, to purify our hearts so that we reflect the glory of God. **"For You have tried us, O God; You have refined us as silver is refined"** (Psalm 66:10).

Suffering and glory go together. You can't have one without the other. Thus, God likens our suffering to the purifying of silver and gold. Neither metal is pure in its natural state. Both are mixed with all sorts of things that make them impure.

Isn't that the way it is with us? We are born with a sin nature that constantly attracts all sorts of impurities: thoughts, beliefs, destructive actions, and habits. We are influenced by our environment—an environment permeated with sin.

Silver and gold need to be refined before they reveal their beauty. So do we! The process of refining includes the melting down of the metal by fires designed not to destroy the metal but to bring forth its beauty.

Thus we know that our trials serve the purpose of making us shine with the beauty of Christ. Let us hold this truth in our hearts as we walk through this day in meekness and faith.

~

Thank You, Lord, that You are refining me through my circumstances and sufferings, removing my impurities to reveal the beauty of Your glory in me.

August 19

Affliction not only drives us closer to God, but it also gives us a ministry. The comfort we receive enables us to minister to others with the same comfort.

> **Blessed be the God and Father of our Lord Jesus Christ, the Father of mercies and God of all comfort, who comforts us in all our affliction so that we will be able to comfort those who are in any affliction with the comfort with which we ourselves are comforted by God.** (2 Corinthians 1:3–4)

Thus we see an important truth: having received Jesus Christ as our Savior, our lives have a purpose. God has planned good works for us to walk in. Therefore all that you have endured will not only be for your good but also for His glory as you minister to others by telling what you have learned.

In Ephesians 4:16, the apostle Paul describes the body of Christ, noting that "the proper working of each individual part, causes the growth of the body for the building up of itself in love." When you offer comfort drawn from your own relationship with God, He uses you to nurture others. As you live the scriptures you've studied and as you exercise your spiritual gifts, you'll find that your "proper working" will cause the body of Christ to grow and be built up in love.

Being available to take others by the hand and help them live in the light of God's Word is a much-needed and incredibly rewarding ministry. I know of no greater joy.

~

Use me, Lord, to bring comfort and love to others who need the hope You alone can offer. Open my eyes to the people You have set in my path, and give me the words they need to hear.

August 20

Do you know without a shadow of a doubt that you're going to heaven—and how do you know? The apostle John understood how important it is that we be assured of our eternal destiny: "**These things I have written to you who believe in the name of the Son of God, so that you may know that you have eternal life**" (1 John 5:13).

As I've spoken with a variety of individuals in the course of my travels and ministry, it's been interesting to note their varied responses when I ask about their relationship with Jesus. "I know I'm a Christian or going to heaven because

...I'm a good person, and I've lived by the Golden Rule."

...I've been baptized."

...I'm a member of the church."

...I walked the aisle and gave my life to Jesus."

...I've been a Christian ever since I was born."

...God is a God of love, and He wouldn't send anyone to hell."

...I've invited Jesus Christ into my life, I've believed on Him; therefore, I'm saved."

...I've prayed a prayer and asked Christ to come and live inside of me, and I believe He did."

Let's suppose you answered in one of the above ways. Basically all those answers are connected to the past—either something you believed or something you did. So let me ask another question: what present evidence in your life shows you and others that you really are a child of God?

~

Ask the Holy Spirit to examine your heart for present evidence that you belong to God (Romans 8:16–17).

When you and I are living in daily surrender, walking in the Spirit, our lives will look conspicuously different from those who are not saved. We'll have a distinctly Christlike "flavor."

In Matthew 5, Jesus uses salt as a metaphor for the character of a Christian: **"You are the salt of the earth; but if the salt has become tasteless, how can it be made salty again? It is no longer good for anything, except to be thrown out and trampled under foot by men"** (verses 13–14).

The salt of biblical times was not like our pure, refined salt. Instead, it was found in varying degrees of purity. In fact, it could lose its savor altogether and become totally useless. When this happened, it was cast on the ground or used to make paths for men to tread upon.

The Christian's life is to have a distinctive flavor. If it loses this distinction, it becomes worthless. In other words, if you and I are not what we ought to be, if our lives and values are indistinguishable from those who don't claim to follow Christ, then we really have no worth as far as this earth is concerned.

Are you salty salt? Does your presence in the world cause others to thirst after the Fountain of Living Water? Is your life such that it hinders the spread of corruption in your society, in your city, in your schools?

Why don't you spend some time with God in prayer now? In honest objectivity ask Him to show you how salty you really are.

August 22

Why is there so much corruption around us? Is it due in part to us as Christians failing to be the salt of the earth?

In Ephesians 5:11 the Lord through Paul instructs us, **"Do not participate in the unfruitful deeds of darkness, but instead even expose them."**

As evil abounds, as the voices of evil people propagate godlessness, as obscene entertainment invades the media and your community, do you sit in apathy in your salt shaker? Or do you get out of the salt shaker and into the world to stop the spread of corruption? Do you, as Ephesians 5 says, expose the unfruitful deeds of darkness? Do you stand firm against all the attacks of the enemy, Satan, or are you ignorant of his methods and devices? Do you keep abreast of current legislation and how to oppose bills that are in direct opposition to the principles and precepts of God's Word? Or do you sit in your salt shaker, criticizing those who are the salt of the earth?

How I pray that God will speak to you in a very clear way so your life will not be worthless, cast out, and trodden under the foot of men in mockery.

Pastor George Truett once said, "You are either being corrupted by the world or you are salting it." There is no middle ground.

~

Show me, heavenly Father, how to live in this world yet not be tainted by it. Help me to make a difference, to bring Your flavor of righteousness and peace to the world around me.

August 23

Many times we look at people and feel upset that their behavior doesn't conform to our standards of spirituality. Notice I said "our standards," not God's, for we, like the Pharisees, have added our own traditions to the Word of God.

We may acknowledge that the Bible doesn't speak clearly to a particular "issue" yet insist that surely anyone who truly loves God wouldn't be doing what they are doing!

Or if we don't judge the behavior of others, we judge their personalities. We decide that they aren't Christlike because they don't seem sober enough; they joke around too much. Or we determine that nobody could be humble and have such authority, such confidence!

Or maybe it's their style of dress; it's too contemporary. Or maybe it's their...whatever! You name it. It's something we disapprove of, although there is no clear or direct violation of the Word—even in principle. And therefore (we think), surely it could not be spiritual! And so we judge.

When we do this, beloved, we're doing the same thing the Pharisees did in Jesus' day. We're judging on the basis of appearance, forgetting what God said to Samuel: **"God sees not as man sees, for man looks at the outward appearance, but the LORD looks at the heart"** (1 Samuel 16:7).

It's easy to judge according to appearance; it's difficult to judge with righteous judgment! I pray that you and I will remember this in our dealings with others today.

I thank You, Lord, that You see beyond the surface things—beyond my weaknesses and shortcomings and failures—and look at my heart. Help me to do the same with others.

August 24

Have you noticed that many of our conflicts with other believers involve judging one another in the gray area of dos, don'ts, and differences, all depending on our religious upbringing or lack of it? How I pray we will take to heart the words of the apostle Paul: **"Who are you to judge the servant of another? To his own master he stands or falls; and he will stand, for the Lord is able to make him stand"** (Romans 14:4).

We need to remember that when we walk according to love and "pursue the things which make for peace and the building up of one another" (Romans 14:19), then we need not worry about wrongfully passing judgment.

Will you take some time to examine your heart, my friend? Read slowly and give yourself time to freely consider each of the following questions:

Are you sitting as a judge rather than walking in love toward your brother?

Are you seeking to judge the motives of people's hearts when you can only see their outward appearance?

Have you, like the Pharisees, added your traditions to God's Word and then sought to judge another individual's walk with God according to your interpretation of the Law?

Have you confronted errors with humility and gentleness or with a holier-than-thou attitude? Do you need to admit that you are wrong? Do you need to go to anyone and seek forgiveness? Ask God to show you your heart.

Go before the throne of grace right now and ask God to examine your heart. Then whatever the Spirit of God says to do, do it. You won't be sorry.

August 25

If you and I want to stand firm in faith today, we must remain on the alert against the wiles of Satan.

If we take God at His word, it is clear from Ephesians 6 that our enemy is cunning and crafty—out to deceive you, me, and every other child of God. This is why we are warned, **"Put on the full armor of God, so that you will be able to stand firm against the schemes of the devil"** (verse 11).

Sadly, I believe many Christians live in defeat because they don't understand that when they become children of God, they enter into war with the devil himself and all his minions. Not realizing that a war is raging, they don't know victory is theirs for the taking. They simply need to find out what God's Word says and live in the light of it!

My friend, Satan would love to keep you ignorant, misinformed, or fearful of the subject of spiritual warfare. However, in this case the old adage "Ignorance is bliss" has to be the enemy's adage, not God's.

Remember, Jesus said, "You will know the truth, and the truth will make you free" (John 8:32). Truth is always liberating!

~

Omnipotent Father, through Your Holy Spirit living within me, help me to be on the alert against the attacks of the enemy and to respond with the powerful truth of Your Word.

August 26

One of Satan's tactics is to make you feel rejected. Rejection hurts. It isolates. It's destructive.

You can be certain that rejection comes in one form or another to every child of God. Suffering and persecution are a part of the life of those who belong to Jesus Christ. Remember Jesus suffered rejection from His own, for "He came unto his own, and his own received him not" (John 1:11, KJV). And He was perfect. There was no fault in Him. Yet "He was despised, and we did not esteem Him" (Isaiah 53:3). Don't you think Jesus can understand and sympathize with your rejection?

Yet God has promised that He will not leave us nor forsake us. We are accepted in the Beloved. "**Having predestinated us unto the adoption of children by Jesus Christ to himself...he hath made us accepted in the beloved**" (Ephesians 1:5–6, KJV).

Others may—will—reject you. God never guarantees that they won't. They may reject you because of your Christianity. But because you belong to Christ, God has engraved you on the palms of His hands through the covenant of grace. And no one is able to snatch you out of the Father's loving grasp.

Oh, the wonder of being fully accepted, just as I am! Thank You, Father, for freely bestowing on me Your love, for embracing me in Your everlasting arms because of Your Son.

August 27

Have you allowed your past to keep you from serving God? Have you thought because of where you've been, what you did, that you would always be a second-class citizen in the kingdom of God? Are you afraid someone will find out what you were? expose you?

Anyone who did would have to open up a coffin, for that's where the old you lies—dead! Romans 6 tells us that your "old self" died and that a new you has been raised from the dead to walk in newness of life.

"All these things are from God," Paul says (2 Corinthians 5:18), so anyone who comes against you will have to do battle with your Covenant Partner.

And if God is for you, who is against you? "**Who will bring a charge against God's elect? God is the one who justifies; who is the one who condemns?** Christ Jesus is He who died, yes, rather who was raised, who is at the right hand of God, who also intercedes for us" (Romans 8:33–34).

Don't buy the lies of the enemy, beloved, as he uses the tongues of men. Listen to God; believe God. Second Corinthians 5:17—"Therefore if anyone is in Christ, he is a new creature"—is one of the major verses that has given me the freedom to share my past so openly. I know who I am in Christ; I am a new creature. The same is true for you if you're truly His child.

Hallelujah! We aren't what we used to be!

I thank You and praise You for giving me a new life in Christ. Thank You that the past has no hold on me! Please help me to resist the lies of the enemy and simply trust in You.

You can be sure Satan will do everything he can to hinder a believer's search for truth and understanding. This is why Paul warns us, "**See to it that no one takes you captive through philosophy and empty deception, according to the tradition of men, according to the elementary principles of the world, rather than according to Christ**" (Colossians 2:8).

The enemy will set snares in the hope of taking you captive to sin or to false teaching. Remember, he hates truth and will only use it when it's to his advantage, weaving it in with his lies to seduce you or to lead you astray. And if that doesn't work, he'll seek to deceive you with signs and false wonders.

The mind is the devil's primary target, but he doesn't stop there. He also attacks the body. In the Word of God we see that he bound a woman for eighteen years and threw a young boy into convulsions. He put a thorn in Paul's flesh…and God left it there because it served His higher purpose.

The day is soon coming when the devil will no longer have access to the throne of God, where he accuses us night and day. Soon he'll be cast down to earth along with his demons. As that day approaches, his wrath will know no bounds because he'll know his time is extremely short.

But those who follow God won't need to fear. The King is coming—the Kinsman Redeemer who rightly sits as the God-man above all rule, power, authority, and dominion, because He has conquered sin and death.

Lord, You have freed me from the power of sin; help me to walk continually in that freedom, not becoming ensnared by temptation or false doctrine.

August 29

We long for peace, for tranquillity. Yet until Jesus comes, we'll be in a relentless struggle. We are in hand-to-hand combat with the enemy, who has three primary objectives:

First, he wants to destroy our unity with God, with the body of Christ, and with our families.

Second, he wants to entice us to sin so he can gain a foothold in our lives.

Third, he wants to lead us into false teaching. Satan is a liar who doesn't abide in truth. He doesn't want you to either! He knows that the truth will set you free and ground you securely in your relationship with God.

Remember, the devil would either like to keep you blind regarding his existence and activity or take you to the other extreme where he, rather than the Lord Jesus Christ, becomes your focus. He loves it when you see him in everything, when you credit him with all your problems, and when you ascribe to him all your defeats. He wants you to live in fear of him rather than in reverence and awesome respect of God. That's why Jesus told us not to fear the one who is able to kill the body but to fear Him who is able to cast both body and soul into hell (Matthew 10:28).

We're called by God not to cower in a corner but to "**fight the good fight, keeping faith and a good conscience, which some have rejected and suffered shipwreck in regard to their faith**" (1 Timothy 1:18–19).

~

Arm me to fight the good fight, knowing that You are my strength and my shield. Protect my mind and heart from Satan's blinding lies and help me to remain focused on You.

August 30

I've said it before, but it bears repeating: Satan's primary objective is to get us into sin. His target is your mind or, as the Bible often refers to it, your heart.

Sin doesn't originate in your actions; it begins in your mind. This is why Paul urges us, **"Be renewed in the spirit of your mind"** (Ephesians 4:23). If you don't learn to control your thoughts, you'll find yourself ensnared by the devil (2 Corinthians 11:3).

What happens when ungodly thoughts go unchecked? A thought can become an action. If repeated enough, that action becomes a habit. Eventually it can become a stronghold, a base of oppression for the enemy.

Satan wants to ensnare Christians because when God's children are caught in sin, God has to discipline us. A child of God who's involved in sin is not ready to be used of God. "Therefore, if anyone cleanses himself from these things, he will be a vessel for honor, sanctified, useful to the Master, prepared for every good work. Now flee from youthful lusts and pursue righteousness, faith, love and peace, with those who call on the Lord from a pure heart" (2 Timothy 2:21–22).

I encourage you to read that verse again carefully, beloved, noting the *if.* What's a person to do in order to be useful to the Master, prepared for every good work? In your present state, are you useful to the Master? Why or why not?

Holy God, I desire to be a vessel for honor—clean, sanctified, and fit for Your use. Cleanse and renew my mind, purging it of any thoughts that are unworthy of You.

August 31

There's much debate today about what is right and what is wrong. As a society, we have passed from morality to immorality to amorality. Many have abandoned absolutes, claiming truth is relative. As Paul said of the people of his day, **"They exchanged the truth of God for a lie, and worshiped and served the creature rather than the Creator, who is blessed forever"** (Romans 1:25).

What would happen if our society abandoned the wisdom of men and instead adhered to God's commands with respect to our sexuality? God would not have to judge us and other countries that tolerate and protect immorality. Do you realize that what we once condemned we now condone? We have adjusted our standards to cover our unrighteousness, and the flames of hell are licking the earth.

My friend, do you see what can happen even among Christians when we fail to put on our belt of truth and breastplate of righteousness? We'll follow the pack, believe a lie, walk in sin, and be held captive by the devil to do his will (2 Timothy 2:26).

How are you standing? Are you living righteously? If you ask, "What is righteousness?" I would reply, "It's doing what God says is right." And if you ask, "How do we know what God says is right?" I would say, "The Bible tells you what God says is right and wrong. Heed its words carefully, for it will be your judge" (John 12:48).

What will be God's verdict?

Lord of lords, You are blessed forever. Help me to serve You with my whole heart, rejecting the lies of the world. Help me gird myself in truth and righteousness, that I may carefully walk in Your precepts.

September 1

When the apostle Paul urged believers to prove the sincerity of their love through giving, he pointed to Another's example: **"For you know the grace of our Lord Jesus Christ, that though He was rich, yet for your sake He became poor, so that you through His poverty might become rich"** (2 Corinthians 8:9).

The One who spoke and brought the world into existence by the power of His Word,

who knew no limitations of time and space,

who reigned in sovereignty and lived in perfect harmony with His Father—

this One humbled Himself for us,

making Himself of no reputation,

becoming flesh and blood,

taking the form of a servant.

He had no place to lay His head, no home of His own.

He was despised and rejected of men.

He became sin for us—forsaken of the Father.

Because He loved us in all our poverty of spirit, soul, mind, and body,

He willingly became poor

so that through His poverty

we might become rich.

This is the grace of the Lord Jesus Christ, our model of the gracious work, the ministry of giving to which we've been called. Let us follow His example.

How I thank You, Father, for Jesus' sacrifice on my behalf. Lead me to follow Him in giving generously and willingly.

September 2

Everything Jesus did, He did on behalf of others. So as His followers, what does this mean to our relationships? to how we look at others? to how we deal with others? It means that we're to view them as they are in Christ—sins forgiven, brand-new creatures.

> Therefore from now on we recognize no one according to the flesh; even though we have known Christ according to the flesh, yet now we know Him in this way no longer. **Therefore if anyone is in Christ, he is a new creature; the old things passed away; behold, new things have come.** (2 Corinthians 5:16–17)

No person's past is ever to be held against him. A death and a resurrection have taken place. Paul no longer viewed Jesus as a baby in a manger, a son in His mother's arms, a tortured body hanging on a cross, a wrapped body in a tomb. Jesus is raised and seated at the right hand of the Father. His work of redemption, given Him by His father, is complete.

If we see Jesus as complete, then we must see His work of redemption complete in every person who believes on Him. And what are we to see and believe? That every redeemed person in Christ is a new creature; the old things have passed, and the new things have come.

Don't hold a "past" against anyone whom God in His great mercy has redeemed. Would you make yourself greater than God?

Thank You for making me a new creation in Christ. Help me to view others in this same way and to love them wholeheartedly.

September 3

Someone has said, "Show me how a person spends his money, and I'll tell you what his relationship with God is like." It's an interesting statement, isn't it? How true do you think it is?

When Paul brings up the subject of giving, he begins by sharing with the Corinthians how the Macedonian Christians were sending money they really didn't have to spare. Philippi, Thessalonica, and Berea were all cities in Macedonia where the churches were suffering greatly because of persecution from the Jews.

And how were the believers in Macedonia enduring? I love Paul's description:

> **Now, brethren, we wish to make known to you the grace of God which has been given in the churches of Macedonia, that in a great ordeal of affliction their abundance of joy and their deep poverty overflowed in the wealth of their liberality.** (2 Corinthians 8:1–2)

The suffering they were experiencing, their deep poverty, filled them with joy! So much so that when they heard about the collection Paul was taking up, they had to help. They begged to help!

How about you? Do you find great joy in giving generously to the work of the kingdom? Has the Lord laid it upon your heart to share your resources to help another? What will you do with what you've been given?

Lord, I acknowledge that everything I have is a gift from You to be used for Your purposes. Even in difficult times, give me a generous spirit, a willingness to use my resources as You direct.

September 4

Will it be the same for everyone in the kingdom of heaven? Will everything and everyone be "equal"?

Not according to Jesus. Some will be called "least" while others will be called "great." What will make the difference? The degree to which each keeps God's commandments and teaches others respect for them.

> **Whoever then annuls one of the least of these commandments, and teaches others to do the same, shall be called least in the kingdom of heaven; but whoever keeps and teaches them, he shall be called great in the kingdom of heaven.** (Matthew 5:19)

The Bible speaks of a day of accounting—for the lost and for Christians. Second Corinthians 5:10 and Romans 14:10 remind us of the day of accounting for Christians. The Bible also tells us that we can lay up treasures in heaven and that there will be rewards.

When I first heard about the judgment seat of Christ, I didn't like it! I wanted to believe that heaven would be the same for every child of God. As I have studied, however, I've seen that this isn't true. There are those who will be "least" and those who will be "great" in the kingdom of heaven!

Have you ever thought about your accountability to God as a Christian? Have you considered that you could miss certain rewards because you did not walk in obedience? Sobering thoughts, aren't they? How will these truths guide you today?

Help me follow Your precepts carefully, Lord, so that one day I can stand before You unashamed and receive the crown of life, which You have promised to those who love You (James 1:12).

September 5

Sometimes spiritual sayings become popular among Christians. Often these are good reminders of vital truths. But sometimes we carry these phrases to an extreme. Or we negate other truths with these sayings because we forget to consider the whole counsel of God.

For example, some say, "God isn't interested in what you do. He's interested in what you are." Or, "It's not about doing; it's about being."

The truth is, God is interested in who and what we are. He cares about what I am on the inside, and if I serve Him without becoming like Him, something is wrong. However, if we are what we ought to be, our lives will find expression in service for God. Ephesians 2:10 says, "**For we are His workmanship, created in Christ Jesus for good works, which God prepared beforehand so that we would walk in them.**"

One of the ways God's grace is seen in our lives—after salvation—is in our service for Him. Others may not see or recognize our service, but it will be there. Grace may call us to prayer. Grace may be expressed simply in our speech. Or it may be manifested through the gift of helps, mercy, or any of the other gifts listed in the Word of God. But it will be expressed in activity. Why? Grace is active and grace is power. Therefore, it will become active in and through us. Our responsibility is to carry out the work God gives us. He'll be responsible for its impact.

~

Lord, open my eyes to the service You have called me to and prepared me for. Help me to be sensitive to Your leading rather than obsessed with my own to-do list or priorities.

September 6

Are you ever startled by the face in your mirror? Do wrinkles or gray hairs catch you off guard, reminding you that you're not as young as you used to be? Do these indicators of mortality prompt a niggling sense of unease—or turn your mind to matters of eternity?

How can we be sure that when death comes, we'll go home to be with God? How can we declare with Paul, "**We are of good courage, I say, and prefer rather to be absent from the body and to be at home with the Lord**" (2 Corinthians 5:8)?

The indwelling Spirit is our guarantee: "For indeed while we are in this tent, we groan, being burdened, because we do not want to be unclothed but to be clothed, so that what is mortal will be swallowed up by life. Now He who prepared us for this very purpose is God, who gave to us the Spirit as a pledge" (2 Corinthians 5:4–5).

The Greek word for *pledge* means something like a down payment, given in advance as security for the rest. In other words, we can face death with confidence because, through the guarantee of the Spirit's presence, we know that even as we walk through death's door, we'll be at home with our Lord.

So then what should be our ambition? Listen to Paul's heart: "Therefore we also have as our ambition, whether at home or absent, to be pleasing to Him" (2 Corinthians 5:9).

Let those gray hairs remind you of both the privilege of serving God today and the promise of a new life to come.

I thank You for the glorious promise of heaven and for the indwelling presence of Your Holy Spirit here on earth.

September 7

As those who seek to follow God with wholehearted faith, we cannot afford to let our focus stray from the One who is leading us and caring for us along the way.

The Bible records the prayer of Agur, a wise man who wanted to be ever dependent on the Lord. He knew that when things were easy—plentiful and satisfying—he might forget God or that in his need he might not seek God. Thus his caution and his prayer:

> **Give me neither poverty nor riches;**
> **Feed me with the food that is my portion,**
> **That I not be full and deny You and say,**
> **"Who is the LORD?"**
> **Or that I not be in want and steal,**
> **And profane the name of my God.** (Proverbs 30:8–9)

Agur's words remind us not only to assess our weaknesses but also to beware of our strengths, lest in our success we forget to rely on God. Power is the downfall of many, even in Christian circles. Somehow we get the mistaken idea that because we are God's and because what we're doing is so valuable to the kingdom, we can get away with pushing His boundaries. You can't, beloved. I can't. No child of God can, because our Father is a holy God. Pride is tattooed all over Satan, and God will not have His children looking like or imitating His archenemy.

We must be ever so vigilant in our strengths, for it's when we're strong and successful that we're the most vulnerable.

~

Faithful and gracious Lord, I come in humility, asking You to reveal any pride that hinders my complete dependence on You.

September 8

Have you ever wondered how you can survive, let alone succeed in, the tasks that lie ahead of you? I have. At times I think, *How can someone like me succeed?*

Yet these thoughts don't devastate me because I know where success comes from. It's wonderful to be able to evaluate myself honestly and not be thrown by the facts. How do I do it? By looking beyond what I am to what my God is and to what that means to me.

Do you know what I've discovered? It doesn't matter what I am. It only matters who He is, because He is all I need! He is my Jehovah-raah, the Lord my Shepherd. And because the Lord is my Shepherd, I shall not want (Psalm 23:1). Oh, what a marvelous revelation the Spirit of God gave us as He breathed those words through the pen of David!

It's much better to cling to the precepts of God than to positive thinking. Can you see the difference? Subtle though it may be, there is a difference between the natural and the spiritual, between our ways and God's ways. Though positive thinking may give lip service to God, it still puts man at the center. It says, "Believe in yourself; you can do it."

God's Word, however, says, "Apart from Me you can do nothing" (John 15:5). From this perspective, I see my poverty and turn to His precepts. With my faith firmly planted in God and all He is, I say, "**I can do all things through Him who strengthens me**" (Philippians 4:13). This is biblical thinking.

Lord, I confess that apart from You, I can do nothing of true worth or value. Help me to walk through this day in faith, strengthened with Your power and glorious might.

September 9

Do you realize that your sexual conduct serves as a barometer of your relationship with God?

Recently I spoke with a grieving young man who told me a story that is repeated endlessly in homes across America. His mother had left his dad for another man. That man had left his wife, entangling two families in the web of adultery.

The action itself was bad enough. But the mother's response made it even worse.

"Mom says I'm living under legalism when I tell her that she's not doing right," the young man told me. "She says that she's 'under grace' and not to worry about her."

The young man's mother has been enticed by sin. She lurked at her neighbor's doorway. She committed a lustful crime that would consume her and uproot and destroy the blessing of life that God had intended for her. According to Jude, she's an ungodly person who has turned the grace of our God into licentiousness. She has denied her Master and Lord, Jesus Christ: **"For certain persons have crept in unnoticed, those who were long beforehand marked out for this condemnation, ungodly persons who turn the grace of our God into licentiousness and deny our only Master and Lord, Jesus Christ"** (Jude 4).

Remember, beloved, Jesus will tell those who call Him 'Lord, Lord' but have practiced lawlessness to depart from Him (Matthew 7:21–23).

How I pray that you and I will never use grace as an excuse for our sin.

Dear Father, let me never disgrace Your name by pursuing my own lusts and claiming that my sin is acceptable to You.

September 10

As we go through our daily routines, we need to remember that all around us an unseen, but very real, spiritual battle rages. First John 5:19 says, "**We know that we are of God, and that the whole world lies in the power of the evil one.**" You've perhaps heard that we have three enemies: the world, the flesh, and the devil. And this is true. However, the three form a coalition, and Satan is the mastermind.

This coalition was formed when Adam and Eve disobeyed in the Garden of Eden. The kingdoms of this world and their glory were handed over to Satan. The world became our enemy—an enemy that wants to squeeze us into its mold. Remember that you deal with the world by knowing God's Word and refusing to conform to the world's pressures.

And what about the flesh? The minute Adam bit the fruit, the flesh became Satan's cohort. Before we were saved, we walked according to our flesh, indulging its desires (Ephesians 2:1–3). However, when the Holy Spirit takes up residence within us, the battle begins.

How is the battle won? Galatians 5:16 says if we walk by the Spirit, we will not carry out the desires of the flesh. Please note that it does not say that the flesh will not lust. However, when the Holy Spirit is in control, He enables us to override the desires of our flesh.

As I said, the brain behind this coalition is Satan. He governs the world and, as the tempter, appeals to the desires of our flesh. When you meet the devil, you must resist him.

~

Help me to walk by the Spirit, resisting the flesh, Satan, and the enticements of the world. Give me the wisdom to conquer the natural appetites and pursue true spiritual satisfaction.

September 11

Because we find ourselves living in the midst of a violent, destructive, sinful, unstable society, it's critical that we carefully build our lives on the Rock, who is God, and take refuge in Him. If we'll live in this manner, we'll find ourselves able to live stable, consistent lives, unmoved by all the problems around us.

How often the psalmist referred to God as his Rock! In fact, in David's last words he referred to God as the Rock of Israel (2 Samuel 23:3). Why? Because in his conflicts with Saul and his enemies, David ran to the Rock which was higher than he. Delivered again and again, he would sing:

> **The LORD is my rock and my fortress and my**
> **deliverer;**
> **My God, my rock, in whom I take refuge. . . .**
> The LORD lives, and blessed be my rock;
> And exalted be God, the rock of my salvation. . . .
> Therefore I will give thanks to You, O LORD, among
> the nations,
> And I will sing praises to Your name.
> He is a tower of deliverance to His king,
> And shows lovingkindness to His anointed,
> To David and his descendants forever.
> (2 Samuel 22:2–3, 47, 50–51)

Will you join David in praising God as your Rock of refuge and turn to Him throughout your day?

Lord, You only are my rock and my salvation, my stronghold; I shall not be shaken. On You my salvation and my glory rest; the rock of my strength, my refuge is in You (Psalm 62:6–7).

September 12

So often we forget that the same grace that saves us is the grace that keeps us, enabling us to survive day in and day out, no matter what.

The grace of God goes beyond the ordinary course of what we expect from a holy God. That's why it is hard for us to accept it in our daily living. Consider this statement of James Orr in his explanation of grace: "Grace...is an attitude on God's part that proceeds entirely from within Himself, and that is conditioned in no way by anything in the objects of His favor."[9]

We simply don't expect God to deal with us on the basis of grace. Rather, we expect Him to react as we would react, to respond as we would respond. We forget that He is God and that we are man. We forget to think as He would think. We forget that we must learn to live by His words and not by man's reasoning and philosophies.

Grace is one of the hardest truths for us to comprehend and to live by—and yet its power to transform our lives is undeniable. "**Therefore let us draw near with confidence to the throne of grace, so that we may receive mercy and find grace to help in time of need**" (Hebrews 4:16).

Oh, beloved, won't you live this day in the confidence of God's unfailing grace?

Lord God, engrave the truth of Your grace on my mind and heart so that I will be freed from any attitudes, misconceptions, or independence that would keep me from appropriating Your grace in all its sufficiency.

September 13

It is one thing to have access to God's grace; it is another thing to appropriate it.

In the opening of his first epistle, Peter wrote, "**May grace and peace be yours in the fullest measure**" (1:2). He was writing to people who, in the midst of their suffering, needed to remember how to relate to others—to those outside the faith, to those in positions of political power, to the elders of the church, to those within their households. Appropriating the grace of God in its fullest measure would enable them to serve God in an acceptable way—and it will do the same for you.

Are you in a difficult relationship? Are you living with an unsaved or difficult spouse? God's grace is there. You have access to it. Allow Him to control you rather than your being controlled by the circumstances of that relationship.

Are you being mistreated by others because of your Christianity? There is grace to enable you to endure without returning insult for insult, evil for evil (1 Peter 3:8–4:19).

Is spiritual warfare wearing you down? There is grace to enable you to resist. "After you have suffered for a little while, the God of all grace, who called you to His eternal glory in Christ, will Himself perfect, confirm, strengthen and establish you" (1 Peter 5:10).

Acceptable service unto God involves manifesting His grace by the way we live. Therefore, let us keep in mind this principle: the child of God always has access to the grace of God, but we must choose to appropriate it.

~

Amid today's difficult encounters, please help me appropriate Your grace so I will honor You in all my relationships and conversations.

September 14

Are you willing to love the people God brings into your life today—even the difficult, annoying, or rude ones?

When you accept God's love, you will allow God to love others through you. This is why 1 John 4:7 exhorts us, **"Beloved, let us love one another, for love is from God; and everyone who loves is born of God and knows God."**

Having believed and received the love of God and, thus, having His love poured out within our hearts, we then become channels for His love (Romans 5:5). "We love, because He first loved us" (1 John 4:19).

How different from what we're hearing! So many are saying that self-love is the prerequisite for loving others. They say our ability to love God and to love our neighbor is proportionate to our ability to love ourselves. In other words, if you can't love yourself, you can't love your neighbor or God.

The way to love others is not through love of self. In order to really love God and others, we must die to self. Death to self causes us to take up our cross, deny ourselves, and follow Him.

As you and I learn to live the crucified life, we'll continually be concerned with death to self rather than love of self. And in doing so, we'll be filled with an abundance of love for others.

~

Fill me with Your love, dear God. I don't want to buy into some weak substitute; I want to be a vessel for Your life-giving, life-changing love, to be poured out into the lives of others.

September 15

Have you considered how your dealings with others indicate your spiritual state?

A righteous walk with God will always manifest itself in our relationships with our fellow man. The two are inseparable, for our righteousness is demonstrated in our treatment of one another.

Jesus calls us to walk as He walked. As He fulfilled the Law, so are we to fulfill it. And how do we do this? The answer is in Matthew 7:12: "**In everything, therefore, treat people the same way you want them to treat you, for this is the Law and the Prophets.**"

This is the "Golden Rule"—the great rule of life so many say they try to live by. "Do unto others as you would have them do unto you."

Don't we all need and want love—unconditional love, love that desires our highest good? Then we are to treat other people in precisely the same way we want to be treated! This is the Law and the Prophets. This is fulfilling the Law.

If we want to follow Jesus, we must continually keep the highest good of others before us, doing unto them as we would have them do unto us.

Can you imagine what a difference it would make in our world if every child of God lived this way?

I want to walk in love, as Jesus has called me to do. Help me, God, to treat others with kindness, mercy, and grace—even when I don't feel like it!

September 16

Life may seem so frustrating, overwhelming, and futile right now that you're tempted to check out.

Maybe you've thought of walking away, leaving it all—maybe having an affair or getting a divorce. Maybe you've been tempted to compromise your convictions because it doesn't seem to do you any good to live righteously. Maybe you're thinking of selling out to the pressure and saying yes.

Do maybes like these ever plague your thoughts? The Bible calls these "imaginations" or "speculations," and they can devastate or destroy you. Your best defense, as the apostle Paul knew, is to destroy them first: **"We are destroying speculations and every lofty thing raised up against the knowledge of God, and we are taking every thought captive to the obedience of Christ"** (2 Corinthians 10:5).

You're in a war, and the enemy is targeting your mind with his poison arrows. Satan wants to persuade you to act independently of God, to walk according to the flesh rather than the Spirit.

Maybes are lies. They are Satan's alternatives to total obedience to God's Word. They are shortcuts to happiness that bring only misery—a living hell.

The cure for maybes is to focus on the certainties of the character of your God and, in faith, to embrace all that He is—His holiness, His faithfulness, His sufficiency. As you bring every thought captive to the obedience of Jesus Christ, the lies of the enemy will lose their power.

Lord, please reveal to me any areas in which I have given the devil a place of opportunity by believing his lies (Ephesians 4:27). By the power of the Holy Spirit, free my mind of worthless thoughts.

September 17

When heartache, disappointment, persecution, or suffering mark our path, Jesus is our example, according to 1 Peter 2:21–25. **"For you have been called for this purpose, since Christ also suffered for you, leaving you an example for you to follow in His steps"** (verse 21).

First, when Jesus suffered, He "committed no sin" (verse 22). Many times suffering tempts us to react in a fleshly way. To resist this temptation, we need to cry out to God in the midst of our pain and cast ourselves upon Him. He will help us to hold our fleshly reflexes in check.

Second, we see that Jesus kept His mouth shut. He uttered no threats. No deceit was found in His mouth. He didn't revile when they reviled Him (verses 22–23).

Third, Jesus prayed. He stayed in communion with God. He "kept entrusting Himself to Him who judges righteously" (verse 23). Jesus trusted in His Father, the One who would righteously judge His tormentors.

Last of all, Jesus endured the persecution. He "bore our sins in His body on the cross" (verse 24). He didn't run away but accepted it as the Father's will so that we might be healed.

When you follow our Lord's example, you have no need to fear, no matter what persecution or suffering comes into your life. God holds you in His hand (John 10:28–29), and God is love. You can bear whatever comes your way—or He never would have permitted it. And in the bearing of it, you will testify to the reality of your faith in Jesus Christ.

When trials and suffering come, I will cast myself on You, the God of all mercy and grace and comfort. Help me respond to persecution in a way that testifies to Your glory and power.

September 18

Failure can be overwhelming, especially if you desire to please God. You may wonder, *Can God ever use me again? Does He even want me? Will things ever be the same again with us?*

Have you destroyed your opportunity for a meaningful and joyous life? Are you to live forever in the shack of your failure, barely surviving rather than experiencing joy, satisfaction, peace, fulfillment?

Are you frightened by the knowledge that God is in control? Do you wonder how He will deal with you?

Do you want to run but don't know where?

Don't you know that you belong to the God of all grace?

Grace is God's heart laid bare. Grace is there to preserve you in the darkest night of your failures. Do not let His grace be in vain. His grace—sufficient for all sin, for all failure, for all your inadequacy, for all your powerlessness—is yours to claim: "**My little children, I am writing these things to you so that you may not sin. And if anyone sins, we have an Advocate with the Father, Jesus Christ the righteous**" (1 John 2:1).

Remember, Jesus stands at the right hand of the Father, where He lives to make intercession for you. Draw near with confidence to the throne of grace!

~

I so long to serve You in faithfulness, and yet I am so often weak. God of glory and grace, I claim all that You have promised to me as Your child—forgiveness, mercy, strength, and hope.

September 19

The battleground for our spiritual health and growth is the mind, our thought life. As you read the following verses, let me remind you that for the Jews, to whom Jesus was speaking, the mind and heart were the same.

> **But the things that proceed out of the mouth come from the heart, and those defile the man.** For out of the heart come evil thoughts, murders, adulteries, fornications, thefts, false witness, slanders. These are the things which defile the man. (Matthew 15:18–20)

Can you see why God says, "Do not be conformed to this world, but be transformed by the renewing of your mind, so that you may prove what the will of God is, that which is good and acceptable and perfect" (Romans 12:2)? If it is our minds that defile us or are the source of our actions and responses, it is vital that our minds be renewed.

The Christian life is to be a whole new way of thinking. When we know God's Word, we gain a new perspective—God's perspective—on everything we face, including pain and suffering. We see why we can give thanks in everything, for we have God's mind, not man's.

As you submit to God, placing your all on the altar, and as you are transformed by the renewing of your mind, then, precious friend, you will know the will of God. You will find it acceptable, good, and perfect.

Transform me, Lord, from the inside out. Let my mind be renewed and my heart be undefiled. Give me Your perspective so I can respond to life's challenges with eternity's values in view.

September 20

What will our daily lives look like when we give ourselves fully to God? Our words, our actions, our thoughts will reflect the heart and likeness of our holy God. Listen to Paul's instructions to the believers in Ephesus:

> Walk no longer just as the Gentiles also walk, in the futility of their mind.... Lay aside the old self, which is being corrupted in accordance with the lusts of deceit,...and **put on the new self, which in the likeness of God has been created in righteousness and holiness of the truth.** (Ephesians 4:17, 22, 24)

Paul wants us to understand that the old self is laid aside and that the new self is put on. The old self is all you were before you were saved. The new self is what you become once you are indwelt by the Holy Spirit of God.

As new creations, children of God, we are expected to live righteously day in and day out. When we don't choose to live in this way, we must confess our sins so the devil has no opportunity to wound us in our vital organs.

Sin in a believer can become an open door to the enemy.

Take heed, my friend. If you tolerate sin in your life, you'll open the door to the one who has sinned from the beginning. And you'll find that sin will not only take you farther than you wanted to go; it will keep you longer than you intended to stay, and it will cost you more than you ever thought you'd pay.

~

Thank You, God, for putting a new heart and a new spirit within me. Lead me to lay aside the old, corrupt self daily and walk in the new self, practicing righteousness and holiness.

September 21

As we step forth into a new day, we need to be alert to the spiritual war going on within us.

What is the greatest enemy of the child of God? What is the first enemy a Christian has to deal with after he is saved? Who attacks from the rear when we are faint and weary? Isn't it your flesh? Isn't this why Paul wrote of groaning to get rid of this mortal body and "longing to be clothed with our dwelling from heaven" (2 Corinthians 5:2)?

He wrote, "For I joyfully concur with the law of God in the inner man, but **I see a different law in the members of my body, waging war against the law of my mind and making me a prisoner of the law of sin which is in my members**" (Romans 7:22–23).

A perpetual warfare is waging in our bodies: "For the flesh sets its desire against the Spirit, and the Spirit against the flesh; for these are in opposition to one another, so that you may not do the things that you please" (Galatians 5:17). We can't do the things we please. Rather, we must constantly be on the alert, ever cognizant of the promise that if we walk by the Spirit, we "will not carry out the desire of the flesh" (Galatians 5:16).

The flesh must constantly be put to death. It can't be tolerated, catered to, or spared in any way. If it is, it will devastate us.

Lord, strengthen me today through Your Spirit dwelling within me so that I will make no provision for the flesh and its lusts (Romans 13:14). Instead, may I do only those things that please You.

September 22

Yesterday I said that the flesh cannot be tolerated, catered to, or spared in any way. Death to the flesh is to be the battle cry of every child of God. As Paul wrote, "**Now those who belong to Christ Jesus have crucified the flesh with its passions and desires**" (Galatians 5:24).

"But how?" you ask. And "Why?" Because if you don't declare the flesh, with its passions and lusts, dead, it can kill you. This truth is depicted in the life of King Saul. God told Saul through Samuel the prophet to "strike Amalek and utterly destroy all that he has, and do not spare him" (1 Samuel 15:3). Not one vestige of the Amalekites was to be spared, including livestock and possessions.

The flesh got the best of Saul. He did not fully obey God. Instead of destroying every one of the Amalekites and their possessions as God had commanded, he saved the best to sacrifice to God (1 Samuel 15:15). Instead of destroying Agag, king of the Amalekites, Saul brought him back captive, only to become the captive of an Amalekite himself one day and die by his hand. In 2 Samuel 1:6–10 you can read about the Amalekite who dealt Saul his final deathblow.

Oh, beloved, this is what I hear is happening all throughout Christendom these days because the flesh was not crucified—constantly reckoned dead.

When will we agree with God and say, "For I know that nothing good dwells in me, that is, in my flesh" (Romans 7:18)? When will we determine that we will walk by the Spirit, who dwells within every believer?

Holy Lord, when temptation comes, enable me to stand firm in the strength of Your might rather than relying on my unworthy flesh.

September 23

As we deal with people in our daily lives—people who are flawed and sinful yet created in the image of God—we find in Ephesians 5:1–2 a challenge to allow God's love to permeate our every interaction: **"Be imitators of God, as beloved children; and walk in love, just as Christ also loved you and gave Himself up for us, an offering and a sacrifice to God as a fragrant aroma"** (Ephesians 5:1–2).

Will you choose to walk in obedience and forgive, "just as God in Christ also has forgiven you" (Ephesians 4:32)? To refuse to forgive is to sin. To obey and forgive is to say, "God, I love You, and I am willing to sacrifice self and its desires." To that, Jesus says, "If anyone loves Me, he will keep My word; and My Father will love him, and We will come to him, and make Our abode with him" (John 14:23). What fellowship, what intimacy obedience brings!

Remember that forgiveness is a matter of your will, a choice to obey God regardless of your emotions. However, the more you comprehend the greatness of God's forgiveness of you, the more you will love. And the more you love, the easier it will be to forgive.

Use the next few moments to ask the Lord to convict you of any unforgiveness toward someone who has wronged you or a loved one. Then tell your heavenly Father that you choose to forgive, out of obedience to His clear command and because of His great love for you. And ask Him to show you how.

September 24

True forgiveness of another will bring love for that person. As I speak of love, I'm not speaking of a sentiment. I'm speaking of an action. As you see when you read through the Bible, love is an action verb. Therefore, if you say you have forgiven a person, yet you don't want to have anything to do with him, you need to go back to God and ask Him what is keeping you from loving the person.

> If someone says, "I love God," and hates his brother, he is a liar; for the one who does not love his brother whom he has seen, cannot love God whom he has not seen. **And this commandment we have from Him, that the one who loves God should love his brother also.** (1 John 4:20–21)

Forgiveness and love cannot be separated. Stop and think of love's associations. Love is part of the ninefold fruit of the Spirit—love, joy, peace… As "imitators of God," you are to "walk in love, just as Christ also loved you and gave Himself up for us, an offering and a sacrifice to God as a fragrant aroma" (Ephesians 5:1–2).

You may have a difficult time loving someone you have forgiven, but true forgiveness will make the sacrifice. Jesus didn't forgive you and then refuse to love you. He forgives and treats you as if you never sinned against Him. That's God's forgiveness. And your forgiveness is to be like God's.

Will you make the sacrifice of genuine forgiveness today?

God, out of sheer obedience, I want to forgive. Help me. Show me how to let go of my bitterness and resentment and allow Your love and grace to fill that space in my heart.

September 25

As you enter the challenges and opportunities of a new day, you can walk with bold confidence, knowing that you're not alone on that battlefield; look to the Lord. It is also His battle. Under His banner, victory is always assured.

> Hear, O Israel, you are approaching the battle against your enemies today. **Do not be fainthearted. Do not be afraid, or panic, or tremble before them, for the LORD your God is the one who goes with you, to fight for you against your enemies, to save you.** (Deuteronomy 20:3–4)

Do you remember what happened in Israel's battle against Amalek? When Moses' hands were up, Israel prevailed. When they came down, Amalek prevailed. (See Exodus 17.) And what was in Moses' hand? The rod of God that became a serpent and swallowed Pharaoh's rods that had turned into serpents. The rod that turned water into blood and brought plagues upon the land of Egypt. The rod that parted the Red Sea. The rod of the One who brought the worlds into existence and who is able to subdue all that He has created.

Under the banner of God, victory is always assured; but apart from it, defeat is a certainty. Apart from God you can do nothing (John 15:5).

Only by abiding under the power, the standard, the banner, the ensign of Jehovah-nissi, can you have victory over the flesh, the world, and the devil, your enemies and God's.

All-powerful, Almighty God, I'm so thankful that You not only walk with me into battle, but You offer the guarantee of victory when I trust only in You. You are my banner and my shield.

September 26

Beloved, I'm sure you've seen, as have I, how anger ensnares and consumes and destroys. "**An angry man stirs up strife, and a hot-tempered man abounds in transgression**" (Proverbs 29:22). A child of God doesn't have to live this way! We can be set free from anger and bitterness through forgiveness, faith, and obedience. God has made every provision—we're without excuse.

Healing begins when we are willing to forgive. This is why Paul urges us, "Let all bitterness and wrath and anger and clamor and slander be put away from you, along with all malice. Be kind to one another, tender-hearted, forgiving each other, just as God in Christ also has forgiven you" (Ephesians 4:31–32).

If you and I are unwilling to put away bitterness, anger, wrath, and malice, if we are unwilling to forgive, we'll find ourselves immobilized, worthless for the cause of Christ. To be unwilling to forgive anyone is sin, and sin gives your adversary the advantage. Is that what you want?

When Paul tells us to put away our bitterness and anger and to forgive as Christ forgave us, we must realize that it is possible to do so because the old man has been put off, and we've put on the new. Therefore, if these things are not put away, if we don't forgive, we're to blame!

God has done everything necessary for you and me to have victory over our flesh and over the devil.

Dear Lord, free me from any root of bitterness or anger that lies within my heart. Teach me to forgive willingly, generously, just as You have forgiven me.

September 27

Do you feel caught in a web of sin woven out of the threads of rejection, anger, fear, and bitterness? Have you been told that you'll never be free—that it's impossible to recover?

Have you been told that you'll be maimed for life? that you'll always be an emotional cripple, never completely well, never completely whole?

Do not listen to the finite wisdom of man, beloved. Man is but man—limited by his humanity. What man does will always fall pitifully short of what God can do.

Remember what He has said:

> **Behold, I am the LORD, the God of all flesh; is anything too difficult for Me?** (Jeremiah 32:27)

> Call to Me, and I will...tell you great and mighty things, which you do not know. (Jeremiah 33:3)

> Turn to Me and be saved, all the ends of the earth. (Isaiah 45:22)

Turn to your God. Nothing is too difficult for Him to accomplish.

~

Take a few minutes to write out a prayer to your God. Pour out your heart to Him. Are you afraid to trust in Him, to call to Him? Are you afraid that He will fail you? Tell Him. Or if you want to trust Him, to learn to run to Him first, if you want your heart to be fully His, tell Him this. Put it in black and white. When you finish, read your prayer aloud to God. It doesn't have to be fancy or eloquent, simply from your heart.

September 28

I never thought I would go through a divorce. There had always been only one thing I wanted in life, and that was to be happily married for ever and ever...just like my mom and dad.

But after six years of marriage, the dream was over. I had failed.

Oh, how it hurt! But one day I would cry out, "**Heal me, O LORD, and I will be healed; save me and I will be saved, for You are my praise**" (Jeremiah 17:14). I would discover that there was a balm in Gilead that could heal the sin-sick soul.

All my hurt would be healed by this same balm and by my Great Physician, whom I would come to know as Abba, Father.

I have a message for you, a message of hope, of life, of peace: whatever your wound, your hurt—whether it is mostly a self-inflicted wound like mine or whether it is a wound inflicted by others—God's Word says that there is a balm in Gilead, that there is a Great Physician there. And because that is true, you can cry out, "Heal me, O LORD, and I will be healed."

~

Lord of all, I believe that You have the power to heal the wounds of my soul. I will praise You for what You have done, for what You are doing, and for what You will do in my life.

September 29

No matter what you are suffering through, dear child of God, the Bible promises that God's grace and strength are sufficient. Through the centuries, that promise has buoyed up Christian after Christian in trial after trial. And God has given us another wonderful promise for times of difficulty: "God is faithful, who will not allow you to be tempted beyond what you are able, but with the temptation [trial, testing] will provide the way of escape also, that you will be able to endure it" (1 Corinthians 10:13).

Therefore, when you suffer, you must remember the following:

First, it is not more than you can bear.

Second, God has provided a way of escape. The way of escape is not to run from the trial or circumstance. God uses trials to bring us to Christlike maturity. Everywhere trials are discussed—from Romans to James to 1 Peter—you see this message. So when you look for "the way of escape," make sure that it is God's way of escape, not your way or your rationalization of His way. He will hold you accountable.

And remember, it is one thing to grit your teeth, to bear your trials and say, "Well, I guess His grace will be sufficient." It's another thing to say with Paul, **"I have learned to be content in whatever circumstances I am.… I can do all things through Him who strengthens me"** (Philippians 4:11, 13). When you say the latter, you prove that you know His grace is sufficient.

~

Whatever lies ahead, I know that You are with me, Father, offering Your all-sufficient strength.

September 30

Nothing, beloved—absolutely nothing—brings greater peace in the midst of suffering than to know you're where God would have you to be.

I love God's words to Paul in Acts 18:9–10: "**Do not be afraid any longer, but go on speaking and do not be silent; for I am with you,** and no man will attack you in order to harm you, for I have many people in this city."

Have you ever thought of the great apostle Paul being fearful? We forget, don't we, that the heroes of the faith were people just like us, people who battled the same emotions and dealt with the same fears. The fear of shame. The fear of suffering. The fear of rejection.

Paul was afraid! Thus he was given the Lord's imperative, His command: do not be afraid. The Lord was telling Paul, "Stop being afraid—it's all right. Go on speaking. Don't let fear silence you. I am with you."

That's all Paul had to hear. Listen to the next words: "And he settled there a year and six months, teaching the word of God among them" (Acts 18:11).

Just to know that you're in God's will brings peace—and the ability to continue to do what He has called you to do. Without that knowledge, there's either a confusion that can immobilize you or a harried scurrying about as you try to do more than God ever intended.

Nothing is more valuable than knowing "This is the way, walk in it" (Isaiah 30:21). It gives you the strength and confidence to settle in and persevere.

~

Am I where You want me, Lord? Please speak peace to my heart and confirm what You have called me to do today.

October 1

Is it possible that you are committing idolatry, beloved? Before you answer, listen to what God says: "**Consider the members of your earthly body as dead to immorality, impurity, passion, evil desire, and greed, which amounts to idolatry**" (Colossians 3:5).

When we think of idolatry, we usually think of people worshiping images fashioned by their own hands. But do we consider greed to be idolatry? Probably not, unless we recognize an idol as anything that takes God's rightful place in our allegiance, devotion, time, or energies.

If a Christian doesn't have time for Bible study but has time for television, would you call that idolatry? Or what if a child of God finds time to exercise but is too busy to pray; is that idolatry? Or if a Christian chooses to work longer hours or take on a second job to have more money for more things but doesn't have time for the Lord, would you call that idolatry?

You may say, "But I need to earn extra money just in case something happens." Or you may argue, "All my life I've wanted such and such, and I'm going after it—I deserve it."

Let's look at what God says about our pursuit of treasures: "Do not store up for yourselves treasures on earth, where moth and rust destroy, and where thieves break in and steal. But store up for yourselves treasures in heaven,...for where your treasure is, there your heart will be also" (Matthew 6:19–21).

Where is your treasure, my friend?

God, please reveal to me any area in which I have allowed something or someone else to assume Your rightful place in my life.

October 2

If you're a believer, a true child of God in covenant with Jesus Christ, does this mean you'll never sin again? No! It means that because you have believed in Him, you will have forgiveness of sins and eternal life. That is the covenant of grace. Not grace that gives you license to live in sin, but grace that enables you by the gift of the Holy Spirit to overcome the law of sin and death.

When you sin, God will have to discipline you, but that doesn't mean He has forsaken you. God is simply acting according to His character and fulfilling His purpose. "When we are judged, we are disciplined by the Lord so that we will not be condemned along with the world" (1 Corinthians 11:32).

Oh, beloved, don't despair over your sin, but confess it, knowing that God could never fail to forgive one of His children who repents (1 John 1:9). For Him not to forgive would be to go against His covenant! He loves us with an everlasting love, and His words to Israel remain true for us: **"For I know the plans that I have for you," declares the LORD, "plans for welfare and not for calamity to give you a future and a hope"** (Jeremiah 29:11).

I thank You, Lord, that You are a covenant-keeping God who has promised to never leave nor forsake me. Thank You for Your gift of forgiveness, which frees me to trust in Your plans for my life.

God loves you, precious one, with an everlasting, unconditional love. Can you accept that truth and cling to it, no matter what?

When you don't like who you are or what you've done, or when the enemy comes whispering in your ear, knocking at the door of your mind, telling you that you are nothing, agree with your adversary. Then give him the truth. Tell him that apart from Jesus Christ you are nothing and you can do nothing that has eternal worth or value.

Also tell Satan that God loves you when you are nothing, accepts you just the way you are, and loves you with an everlasting, unconditional love that is transforming you into His image. Tell the devil that you are secure in God's love, that the love of God has been poured out within your heart "through the Holy Spirit who was given to us" (Romans 5:5), and nothing "will be able to separate [you] from the love of God, which is in Christ Jesus our Lord" (Romans 8:39).

Martin Luther had it right when he said, "God does not love us because we are valuable, but we are valuable because God loves us."

If ever you're tempted to doubt God's love for you, think of what He's already done to demonstrate His commitment. First John makes it clear: **"In this is love, not that we loved God, but that He loved us and sent His Son to be the propitiation for our sins"** (4:10).

Loving Father, when the enemy whispers in my ear, when I am discouraged and defeated by my own weaknesses and failures, let the Holy Spirit bring to mind the truth about Your unconditional, everlasting love.

October 4

As you decide how to respond in the various situations that will arise today, I urge you to remember that you are in a war. Satan's strategy is to besiege your mind until he wears down your resistance and captures your thoughts. You can expect a barrage of thoughts to constantly hammer away at your defenses. It is spiritual warfare.

From the beginning, Satan has cast doubt on the Word of God. He wants you to question, doubt, distort, alter, embellish, discredit, or ignore the Word of God. Disguised as an angel of light, he will do anything and everything he can to undermine God's Word.

The devil's tactic is not only to cause you to doubt, ignore, and disobey God's Word. It is also to get you to doubt God's love. To doubt God's love is to doubt His character. Once the enemy casts doubt in your mind on God's love, he cuts you off from the only true and sure source of healing—your Jehovah-rapha and the Word of God.

Know your God. Know His Word. And live accordingly. **"Submit therefore to God. Resist the devil and he will flee from you"** (James 4:7).

Remember, the Word of God is all you need in order to be perfect, thoroughly adequate for every work of life (2 Timothy 3:16–17). Victory is assured as long as you let Jesus be your captain and do what He says.

Thank You for Your Word, in which You so clearly reveal Your character, Your love, and Your directions for holy living. Let me live in the knowledge of its glorious truths.

October 5

After I was saved, at times I would find my mind roaming back into my sin-filled past. Depression frequently set in as I questioned why I had done what I had, as I let my thoughts dwell on my mistakes, my failures, my weaknesses, my sins, my…

When our thoughts dwell on the depressing circumstances of our past, we need to remember that person died with Christ (Romans 6:6). Everything that happened to you before you came to know Jesus Christ belongs to a dead man or woman.

> For the death that He died, He died to sin once for all; but the life that He lives, He lives to God. **Even so consider yourselves to be dead to sin, but alive to God in Christ Jesus.** (Romans 6:10–11)

Keep the nails in the coffin. Don't sit on the old man's tombstone and reminisce or weep about your past. That behavior is not what God wants.

When your thoughts want to wander over the past, go to God in prayer.

~

O Father, I'm so thankful that person no longer lives; that part of me is dead, never to be resurrected. Thank You that those old things have passed away. Thank You for making me new, brand-new. Thank You for forgiving all my sins, for remembering them no more, for putting them behind Your back, for removing them as far as the east is from the west. O Father, forgive me for even beginning to remember, to recall, what You have so adequately taken care of, forgiven, and forgotten. Lord, I will focus my thoughts on those things You say are true of me now.

October 6

If you and I are to pursue righteous living, we need to know that God's grace not only delivers us from the penalty of sin, but it is also sufficient to deliver us from the power of sin. There's grace to cover our sins, but there's also grace to keep us from sin. It's this aspect of living in the power of grace that many of us forget.

How much better off we will be if we learn to appropriate God's grace every time temptation gives its siren call. We must not neglect the means that God gives us for knowing and maintaining a life lived in the grace of God. "Are you so foolish? Having begun by the Spirit, are you now being perfected by the flesh?" (Galatians 3:3).

Christianity is the only religion in the world wherein man becomes totally dependent upon God and remains dependent upon Him for all of life. To the Christian, independence is sin. It is the taproot of all our failures. By contrast, the key to success in daily living is complete dependence on God. **"Cast your burden upon the LORD and He will sustain you; He will never allow the righteous to be shaken"** (Psalm 55:22).

Deliverance from the power of sin comes as we cease our striving in the flesh and cast ourselves in dependence upon Him. When we're dependent upon Him, we'll find His grace is always sufficient.

~

Lord of all grace, You have made every provision for me to live this day in righteousness. I choose to live in dependence on You, trusting Your Spirit to strengthen me against temptation.

October 7

Dear one, we need to realize that when anyone unwraps the gift of salvation, he or she will find suffering tucked in with it. The two are inseparable. Paul wrote to the church he founded in Philippi, "For to you it has been granted for Christ's sake, not only to believe in Him, but also to suffer for His sake, experiencing the same conflict which you saw in me, and now hear to be in me" (Philippians 1:29–30).

At the very end of his life, as Paul prepared to die for his faith, he wrote his final letter to Timothy, his son in the faith. Paul reminded Timothy that "**all who desire to live godly in Christ Jesus will be persecuted**" (2 Timothy 3:12). This is something you and I need to understand and remember as we give each day to the Lord.

Strange as it seems, suffering is a precious gift when viewed from an eternal perspective, because suffering not only proves our faith but is used of God to make us more like Jesus. And believe me, when we stand someday at the judgment seat of Christ, that's all that will matter.

O God, please give me the courage to suffer for Your sake and yet remain faithful in all things. I give You this day, Lord, and trust You with whatever may come.

October 8

When we trust God's purposes during trials, others see the reality of Christ and His sufficiency in us.

Have you ever seen your trials and suffering from this perspective? As you appropriate His all-sufficient grace, afflictions become your platform for sharing the reality of Christ. Thus Paul wrote:

> **We who live are constantly being delivered over to death for Jesus' sake, so that the life of Jesus also may be manifested in our mortal flesh.... For all things are for your sakes, so that the grace which is spreading to more and more people may cause the giving of thanks to abound to the glory of God.** (2 Corinthians 4:11, 15)

Paul viewed his sufferings as God's means of spreading His grace to others. Our suffering will do the same if we stand firm in His grace.

When the saints suffer, it is never in vain. Why? Because those without Christ realize that if they were in our shoes, they would probably behave differently. As we appropriate God's grace, they see us "in no way alarmed by [our] opponents" (Philippians 1:28).

Remember, we are afflicted, "but not crushed; perplexed, but not despairing; persecuted, but not forsaken; struck down, but not destroyed" (2 Corinthians 4:8–9). The way we suffer shows the difference between us and the lost. The difference is the grace of God—grace that not only saves us but sustains us, sufficient for every need, every trial.

May my response to suffering bring glory to You, precious Lord, and prompt others to turn to You.

October 9

When God does not seem to answer you or move on your behalf, when you cannot seem to go on, what do you do?

Oh, beloved, let me encourage you to meditate on Psalm 31:14–15, which says: "**But as for me, I trust in You, O LORD, I say, 'You are my God.' My times are in Your hand.**"

Your times are in His hands! This truth will sustain you when there seems no relief in sight and when you are weak and weary of fighting the good fight, of running the race with endurance.

Habakkuk 3:17–18 reveals magnificent faith as God's prophet contented himself with God's timetable and plan:

> Though the fig tree should not blossom
> And there be no fruit on the vines,
> Though the yield of the olive should fail
> And the fields produce no food,
> Though the flock should be cut off from the fold
> And there be no cattle in the stalls,
> Yet I will exult in the LORD,
> I will rejoice in the God of my salvation.

God does not want compliant resignation. When life is difficult, God wants us to have a faith that trusts and waits. He wants us to have a faith that doesn't complain while waiting but rejoices because we know our times are in His hands—nail-scarred hands that labor for our highest good.

I thank You that I can bring You my worries and concerns and leave them in Your hands. Sustain me as I rejoice in You, O Lord.

October 10

When you give to people or to a ministry with needs, do you give with the hope of getting your name on a plaque or printed in the bulletin? Will you give only if your giving is going to be recognized in some way?

If so, then Matthew 6:2 says you already have your reward in full. There's no more reward coming. But look at what happens when you follow Jesus' instructions: "**When you give to the poor, do not let your left hand know what your right hand is doing, so that your giving will be in secret; and your Father who sees what is done in secret will reward you**" (Matthew 6:3–4).

When do you want your reward, beloved? Now or later?

There is something about our unredeemed flesh that wants to be seen…applauded…praised…appreciated. Jesus knows this. He knows what a stumbling block it can become to us. Therefore, He warns us in Matthew 6:1: "Beware of practicing your righteousness before men to be noticed by them."

God wants His children to be aware of the flesh "putting on a show" in order to be seen and applauded by others. This is the way the hypocrites live, and we're not to live that way.

~

Go to the Lord and examine your habits of giving to the needs of the kingdom and your motives for doing so. Ask God to search your heart and your checkbook. Many times you can tell the condition of your heart by looking at how you handle your finances!

October 11

Many Christians are stumbling through life, unable to see clearly the path of purpose because their spiritual vision is blurred or obstructed by the things of this world. John's first letter warns, **"For all that is in the world, the lust of the flesh and the lust of the eyes and the boastful pride of life, is not from the Father, but is from the world"** (1 John 2:16).

Because our eyes can be an instrument of lust—because they can lead us into the sin of covetousness—it is vital that we keep our eyes healthy. But how? We live in a world filled with all sorts of alluring things. Books, magazines, television, movies, billboards, and computers constantly display treasures belonging to this life and this life only. How then can a child of God keep his vision clear?

Focus!

As the author of Hebrews says, we need to fix our eyes on Jesus, the Author and Perfecter of our faith. Or as Paul says in 2 Corinthians 4:18, we need to look "not at the things which are seen, but at the things which are not seen; for the things which are seen are temporal, but the things which are not seen are eternal."

It's all a matter of perspective—eternal perspective. Where is your focus? Is it upon the things of this world? Is it riveted to the treasures of this life that can be consumed by moths and rust and stolen by thieves? Or is it upon heavenly treasures, which have eternal value?

Help me, dear God, to keep my eyes on You and on the things that matter to You. Don't let me be distracted or drawn away from You by worldly things.

October 12

Who sets the standard of how you should conduct yourself? How do you measure up to our culture's standards socially, intellectually, physically, culturally, sociologically? Once you settle these questions with the right answers, you'll find yourself gloriously free from having to seek the approval of others rather than of God.

The apostle Paul dealt with the issue of being wrongfully judged. Like many today, the Corinthians judged him according to his physical appearance and the way he presented himself publicly. They measured Paul against the standard of their day. "You are looking at things as they are outwardly," he wrote in 2 Corinthians 10:7, which means they were looking at what was right in front of their faces. But Paul didn't let their criticism defeat him. He was secure in who he was and had a sober assessment of himself: "He who boasts is to boast in the Lord," he continued. "**For it is not he who commends himself that is approved, but he whom the Lord commends**" (2 Corinthians 10:17–18).

Although the Corinthians were on Paul's heart and he desired their love and affection, he would not allow them or any man to set his standards. Paul didn't have to commend himself to anyone. He knew that he met the standard of Jesus Christ and had His approval.

Can you say the same?

Forgive me, Father, for seeking the approval of others rather than looking only to You for my standards of life. May my words and actions today spring from a heart that is fully Yours.

October 13

Do you feel bitterness over a broken relationship or a past event? Are you finding it hard to let go of your anger and disappointment and move on? If so, beloved, I'm sure you don't have peace. And, in all probability, you're angry and bitter with God.

You're probably thinking that if God is sovereign, He should have done something to stop whatever it was that made you bitter. Maybe your parents didn't love you or raise you as you think they should have. Maybe your children didn't turn out the way you'd hoped, even though you did your best. Maybe it's your mate, your employer, or_______________; you fill in the blank.

Whatever the reason, if you're bitter, peace will continue to elude you until you submit to God. Meekness is the cure for bitterness. Meekness is accepting everything without murmuring or complaining because you realize that it was permitted by God and that it will serve an eternal purpose. Therefore, "**Let all bitterness and wrath and anger and clamor and slander be put away from you, along with all malice**" (Ephesians 4:31).

Remember, God is sovereign; He rules over all. Nothing can happen without His permission. And even though the circumstance or event in and of itself is not good, God promises that it will work together for your good and that He'll use it to make you into the image of His Son. Isn't it time to put away your bitterness and discover God's peace?

~

Almighty God, let Your peace that surpasses all understanding reign in my heart. Help me to let go of any form of bitterness, regret, or resentment that keeps me from intimacy with You.

October 14

My friend, have you lately looked around at what is condoned in America, even in our churches? Abortion used to be considered murder; today it's a common means of birth control. Even many churches will not take a strong stand against abortion. At one time homosexuality and lesbianism were against the law; now some churches have even established homosexual congregations.

Why are we in such a state? I believe it's because we've lost the Word of God. Think about it. What place does the Bible have in the lives of the majority of pastors, let alone churchgoers? Has your church lost the Word of God? Have you lost it? Could it be that, like the people of Judah, we've mislaid God's Word in our pursuit of worldly priorities and idols? Perhaps it's time for us to heed the words of King Josiah:

> **Go, inquire of the LORD for me and for those who are left in Israel and in Judah, concerning the words of the book which has been found;** for great is the wrath of the LORD which is poured out on us because our fathers have not observed the word of the LORD, to do according to all that is written in this book. (2 Chronicles 34:21)

Beloved, let's ask God to search our hearts and show us what, if anything, has taken priority over His Word. Then let's renew our commitment to give the Bible its rightful place so that in all things God will have preeminence.

Forgive us, dear Lord, for neglecting Your Word. I pray that across the nation and around the world You will bring into leadership those who study, live by, and proclaim the truths of Your Word in the hearing of Your people.

October 15

Christians need to learn how to deal with their sin once they have failed God. Many worry that one day God will have had enough and walk away, that the forgiveness available through His grace will eventually dry up.

This kind of thinking is understandable, because this is the way we often respond to one another. We allow people to push us so far, and then we walk away, no longer wanting to have anything to do with them. And we think God will do the same. The cure for this misconception about God is a renewed mind whereby we measure God by what He says about Himself rather than by man's concept of Him.

What do you need to remember when you sin? "**Therefore there is now no condemnation for those who are in Christ Jesus**" (Romans 8:1). You are under grace alone, not grace and law. You are not to look at what you see or what you feel; instead, look at the promises of God. He promises you cleansing and forgiveness, and what God promises, He is able to perform.

So if you feel condemned, if you feel you must do something to make amends for your sin, remember that feelings have nothing to do with faith. Faith is taking God at His word, no matter how you feel or what you see or think.

Don't struggle in your own strength to be better. Don't determine that you're going to try harder. Simply confess your sin to God, acknowledge your need of His all-sufficient grace, and then go forward, trusting in His grace.

~

How thankful I am that Your ways are above our ways, O Lord. Thank You that Your mercies and compassion do not fail but are new every morning!

October 16

How important it is that you and I take great care in what we put into our minds. When Satan has access to the mind, he has an inroad to the flesh. Remember that he already has the world. Satan wants what he doesn't have—you! And he's deployed his forces to that end.

The "spiritual forces of wickedness" described in Ephesians 6:12 are just that—spirit beings with malign influence. From MTV to pornography to horror movies. From crime to brutality to sexual perversion. When you see wickedness in operation, know that evil spiritual forces are behind it.

Part of our problem is that many who acknowledge the existence of the devil only think of him as the source of evil when he boldly identifies himself or when something is clearly satanic. Remember that even though he and his angels belong to the pit of darkness, "**Satan disguises himself as an angel of light**" (2 Corinthians 11:14).

Vulgar television shows, provocative music, and sleazy Web sites may seem to be more flesh than demonic. We know, however, that Satan's rulership is over the sons of disobedience, who indulge the desires of the flesh and of the mind (Ephesians 2:2–3).

Thus Paul's sharp command: "Take up the full armor of God" (Ephesians 6:13). With this command comes the assurance "so that you will be able to resist." When you take up God's armor, you'll be able to quell the enemy and hold your position. Obedience guarantees victory.

Lord, I pray You will keep me alert at all times so that I will not be drawn to the false light of Satan through the enticements of the world or of the flesh. Help me resist and stand firm.

October 17

President Ronald Reagan once spoke about America being "a city on a hill" in a dark world. But we are now far removed from that description. Many who call themselves "Christian" in our country have failed in their dual functions of salt and light. Their testimonies no longer stop the spread of corruption; their lifestyles no longer dispel the darkness so men can see their good works and glorify their Father in heaven.

How about you, my friend? Do you order your life according to the dictates of God, the statutes of life? Or do you merely quote the Ten Commandments?

Jesus urged His disciples, "Strive to enter through the narrow door; for many, I tell you, will seek to enter and will not be able" (Luke 13:24). He didn't want them deceived. He didn't want them lured into a false security that would land them in the eternal lake of fire. He wanted them to understand the narrowness of the way that leads to life, the gravity of not just hearing what He said but living accordingly.

Christianity is not a religion—merely adhering to an external set of rules. It is, rather, hungering and thirsting for righteousness—a righteousness that is an inside-out reality. It is a righteousness of the heart. "**The path of the righteous is like the light of dawn, that shines brighter and brighter until the full day**" (Proverbs 4:18).

What does your life reveal about the state of your heart? Are you shining His light of righteousness into a dark world?

Father of light, I pray that Your holy life would shine from inside me so all that I do will illumine the darkness around me and bring praise and glory to Your Son, who is the Light of the world.

October 18

The Word of God clearly states that Jesus Christ is coming to the earth "a second time...to those who eagerly await Him" (Hebrews 9:28). And when He comes to earth the second time, He will thoroughly deal with all the ungodly.

Listen to what God spoke through the apostle Paul: "The Lord Jesus will be revealed from heaven with His mighty angels in flaming fire, dealing out retribution to those who do not know God and to those who do not obey the gospel of our Lord Jesus" (2 Thessalonians 1:7–8).

You and I are to proclaim and to live in the light of His coming and of His judgment of the wicked. We are responsible to read and know the Word of God, and then we are responsible to proclaim it (2 Timothy 4:1–4). In Ezekiel 3, God warns, "**When I say to the wicked, 'You will surely die,' and you do not warn him or speak out to warn the wicked from his wicked way that he may live, that wicked man shall die in his iniquity, but his blood I will require at your hand**" (verse 18).

We need to share that although God seemingly allows the wicked to prosper and destruction and violence to parade like conquerors through the cities of our land, there will come a day of reckoning. We need to clearly communicate that if men do not turn from their iniquity, they will experience the fierce wrath of Almighty God.

"Near is the great day of the LORD, near and coming very quickly" (Zephaniah 1:14).

God, please give me the courage and strength to live righteously in light of Jesus' return and to share the truths of Your Word so others may come to know You and escape the wrath of judgment.

October 19

In our conversations and interactions with other people, we need to continually bring to mind these words of Jesus: **"Do not judge so that you will not be judged.... How can you say to your brother, 'Let me take the speck out of your eye,' and behold, the log is in your own eye?"** (Matthew 7:1, 4).

The judgment that Jesus forbids in Matthew 7 is the judgment of hypocrites who concern themselves with a speck in their brother's eye even while they are stumbling around with beams under their own eyelids. They expect perfection from others but are far from perfect themselves. They have an attitude that can only be described as judgmental.

Did you notice the blatant contrast? A log compared to a speck! And remember, Scripture says we will be judged according to the way we judge. The standard of measure we use will be the measure by which we are measured. That's a sobering thought. Do I expect the same thing from myself that I consistently expect from others? Am I willing to give the kind of mercy I would like to receive? Am I willing to extend the sort of love that grants grace and covers imperfections?

The judging that Jesus calls hypocritical is that which notices specks in the eyes of others and misses our own logs and beams. This is why we need to spend time with God daily, allowing Him to clear our vision.

Reveal to me any form of hypocrisy that leads me to sinful judgment of others. Make me aware of the logs that blur my vision and help me to view others through a lens of righteous love.

October 20

Why do we think we can disobey God and get away with it? Do we think God will exempt us from wholehearted obedience and fidelity to Him because we are His people? Do we think He would never allow the wicked to triumph over us because we profess Him and they don't?

Apparently that is what Judah thought. " 'For the house of Israel and the house of Judah have dealt very treacherously with Me,' declares the LORD. **They have lied about the LORD and said, 'Not He; misfortune will not come on us, and we will not see sword or famine'** " (Jeremiah 5:11–12).

Rather than turning in shame from their sin, they chose to believe that God would not punish them. God said of their false prophets, "They have healed the brokenness of My people superficially, saying, 'Peace, peace,' but there is no peace" (Jeremiah 6:14). The people loved what the prophets said and believed their message. Lulled into complacency, they did not turn to God with all of their heart.

You may be hearing, "Peace, peace," but is there peace deep within your heart? a peace that is not dependent upon your circumstances? If you want peace that the world cannot take from you, make sure your relationship with God is what it ought to be. God must be your priority. Get rid of anything that hinders you from Him.

Lord, reveal to me the areas of my heart that need to be broken up like fallow ground (Jeremiah 4:3), the things that need to be circumcised or cut away so that my heart can beat unreservedly for You.

October 21

His name is Adonai, Lord, Master. Down through the ages His servants have known that well! "'**And if I am a master, where is My respect?' says the LORD of hosts to you**" (Malachi 1:6).

Do you see the need to bow before Him and say, "My Lord"? With submission comes all we need for the task He puts before us. But as Adonai, God has a right to expect obedience. When God called Moses to go before Pharaoh and tell him to let His people go, Moses argued with God:

> Then Moses said to the LORD, "Please, Lord, I have never been eloquent, neither recently nor in time past, nor since You have spoken to Your servant; for I am slow of speech and slow of tongue." The LORD said to him, "Who has made man's mouth? Or who makes him mute or deaf, or seeing or blind? Is it not I, the LORD? Now then go, and I, even I, will be with your mouth, and teach you what you are to say." But he said, "Please, Lord, now send the message by whomever You will." Then the anger of the LORD burned against Moses. (Exodus 4:10–14)

Why was God angry? Because Moses was calling Him Lord but not trusting and submitting to Him.

Our Lord—our Adonai—is to be obeyed. He is God; we are man. He is the Creator; we are the created. Therefore, every knee should bow now. All will bow eventually!

Master, Savior, Lord—You are all these things to me. You deserve my complete faith and obedience. Use me today as You will. I am at Your service.

If you were to analyze the people of your nation as a whole, who or what would you say has mastered them? It is what masters a people—what captures their minds, their wills, and their bodies—that makes them what they are and determines how they live.

Take a good look around you. Think about your friends and associates. Consider the lifestyles of the so-called rich and famous. Watch the down-and-outers, the alcoholics, drug addicts, and amoral celebrities. What is the dominating factor of their lives? Where are they headed as a result of what or who has gained mastery over them? It is a wise person who considers these pathways—and their ultimate destinations—before choosing to follow a hero or role model. Where do these lifestyles lead? What is their end result?

Remember, Jesus has said, **"No servant can serve two masters; for either he will hate the one and love the other, or else he will be devoted to one and despise the other. You cannot serve God and wealth"** (Luke 16:13).

Ultimately, it is not what we know that determines our destiny but what we do, what we allow to rule our lives.

Lord, I want to serve You with all my heart, soul, mind, and strength. I want Your righteousness and will to rule my life. Help me to walk as one who is faithful and wise.

October 23

Whenever I teach 2 Corinthians 5:10—**"For we must all appear before the judgment seat of Christ, so that each one may be recompensed for his deeds in the body, according to what he has done, whether good or bad"**—one of the first things my students ask is, "What about our sins? Are we going to be judged for our sins?"

My answer to this question is no.

Jesus was judged for our sins when God "made Him who knew no sin to be sin on our behalf" (2 Corinthians 5:21). Since Jesus purged us from our sins, "having offered one sacrifice for sins for all time," there is therefore "no condemnation for those who are in Christ Jesus" (Hebrews 1:3; 10:12; Romans 8:1). We cannot be judged for what Jesus has already paid for!

However, when a Christian walks in sin for a period of time, that time is lost as far as being profitable for the glory of God and His kingdom. It is wasted, for "apart from [Him] you can do nothing" (John 15:5). This, I believe, brings a resulting loss of reward.

When you appear before the judgment seat, don't you want to hear the words, "Well done, good and faithful servant"? Then let that ambition guide your steps today.

Let me not waste a single day, not a single moment that could be used in communion with You and service for You, dear God. I want to serve You faithfully with all that I am and all that I have.

The essential character of the believer is obedience. Faith and obedience are irrevocably linked. They cannot be separated. This is why Jesus says in Matthew 7:24–25:

> **Everyone who hears these words of Mine and acts on them, may be compared to a wise man who built his house on the rock.** And the rain fell, and the floods came, and the winds blew and slammed against that house; and yet it did not fall, for it had been founded on the rock.

Jesus makes it clear that faith isn't just hearing but also acting. Those who hear and act are like the man who built his house on the rock. No matter what circumstances raged all around him, his house did not fall because it was founded on the rock. But those who hear Christ's words and do not act upon them are like the man who built his house upon the sand—and great was its fall.

Oh, beloved, is there evidence that Christ is in you? Is there a hunger and thirst for righteousness within you, and is it being satisfied? And what about your conduct? Are you becoming more and more like your heavenly Father?

If you cannot answer these questions in the affirmative, then I invite you to go to God and tell Him you want Jesus to be your Master and Lord in the fullest sense of the words.

~

If you know that your house of faith is solid and sure, thank God for the gift of the Holy Spirit within you, helping you live in obedience. If you aren't certain, I urge you to take that step of faith today and enter into the righteousness that God offers through the shed blood of His Son, Jesus Christ.

October 25

So many times we're tempted to blend into the world, to simply surrender to cravings of the flesh. Paul understood the need to conquer such dangerous temptations: **"But I discipline my body and make it my slave, so that, after I have preached to others, I myself will not be disqualified"** (1 Corinthians 9:27).

Essentially he was saying, "Listen, if my body, rather than God's Spirit, is going to dominate me, then God's going to have to disqualify me. I'm out of the running, out of the race. Why? Because I am not what I ought to be as a child of God. I have lost my true use and value."

The Christian life is not just a matter of doing; it's a matter of being. It's a matter of living out a God-ordained life, fulfilling God's ordained functions. If you neglect or refuse to do this, then you have no value to the kingdom of God.

Perhaps you would reply, "Wow, Kay, that's kind of harsh teaching, isn't it? It seems pretty narrow."

Yes, it is. And a lot of people don't like that. They want an easy believism, a gospel that makes no demands and doesn't call for a wholehearted commitment. They want to short-circuit the radical implications of a life of discipleship. They want their own "lite" brand of Christianity.

But we're not the ones who are calling the shots! God is.

I truly want my life to count for You, God. Don't let me lose my value to You by compromising my standards or seeking friendship with the world. Help my every choice to be made with Your kingdom and eternal values in view.

Does the righteousness of God seem an impossible attainment, a goal never to be reached? Do you shudder at your own inability to be holy? On what basis do you try to make yourself acceptable to God?

Righteousness comes only from God. It can never be attained by the flesh or by your self-righteous efforts. "**He saved us, not on the basis of deeds which we have done in righteousness, but according to His mercy, by the washing of regeneration and renewing by the Holy Spirit**" (Titus 3:5).

To be declared righteous means to be put in right standing with God because your sins have been taken care of. When Christ hung on the cross, it was for your sins. There God "made Him who knew no sin to be sin on our behalf, so that we might become the righteousness of God in Him" (2 Corinthians 5:21).

At the moment of faith, the moment of trusting in Christ's substitutionary death for your sins, you are declared righteous. But that is just the beginning! The righteous man or woman is to live righteously. This is done by faith!

No matter what the trial, no matter what the circumstances, you and I are to live by every word that proceeds out of the mouth of God—without compromise. We are to know His Word and obey it. There is literally no other way to please Him.

This, beloved, is holiness, the righteousness of faith.

O Father, if I am to be righteous, I must know Your Word. Help me to discipline myself for the purpose of godliness, to honor You by doing what You say is right.

Beloved child of God, every trial—past, present, and future—is part of God's refining process to make you like Jesus.

The question that confronts you is this: how will you respond to suffering? Not only the suffering that awaits you but also the suffering you have endured in the past. Will you let it embitter you—or transform you? Will you hold on to the dross—or will you be made like Jesus?

> **Beloved, do not be surprised at the fiery ordeal among you, which comes upon you for your testing, as though some strange thing were happening to you; but to the degree that you share the sufferings of Christ, keep on rejoicing, so that also at the revelation of His glory you may rejoice with exultation.** (1 Peter 4:12–13)

Every trial of life is a test of your faith, because with each trial you are called upon to make a decision: Will you believe God and, thus, respond in the way He says to respond, or will you cling to the dross of independent disobedience and, therefore, sin in the unbelief of the flesh?

Guide my thoughts, words, attitudes, and actions today, holy God. Teach me to respond to disappointments, pain, and trouble in a way that brings praise and glory and honor to You.

October 28

"All I want is to be happy!" You've heard those words before, haven't you? You've probably said those words...if not out loud, then at least in the quiet corners of your heart. Let me assure you, dear friend, that what you desire is not an elusive dream, though it may seem that way. What you crave is actually not temporal happiness, which depends upon circumstances, but true blessedness, which takes you through every circumstance.

What we want when we say we want to be happy is disguised under the term *blessed* or *blessedness.* In the Scriptures *blessedness* means "a sense of God's approval."

What you and I seek comes from being right with God. Psalm 128:1 says, **"How blessed is everyone who fears the LORD, who walks in His ways."**

The contentment we desire comes from doing what is right in His sight.

This, then, is true happiness. It is an enduring, flowering plant that draws its life and beauty and fragrance not from the shifting ground of circumstances but from being solidly, deeply rooted in a right relationship with God Himself. True happiness—the genuine article—will sustain you with peace, quietness, and confidence through all the years of your life, no matter your circumstances.

~

Holy and righteous God, let me not be deceived by the world's cheap imitations of happiness. Instead, lead me to true blessing and lasting peace as I walk beside You in sweet communion.

October 29

Bitterness comes when we don't respond to the difficult circumstances of life from a biblical perspective. Such bitterness can lead to an angry and resentful state of mind that causes us to despise God's blessings. Bitterness can also manifest itself as an angry and hostile outlook on life expressed in resentment and outbursts toward others.

If bitterness is not released and forsaken, it will cause trouble not only in our own hearts and lives but in the lives of those around us.

So if you are worn-out with the burden of hurt, anger, frustration, and bitterness, listen to God: "**Pursue peace with all men, and the sanctification without which no one will see the Lord.** See to it that no one comes short of the grace of God; that no root of bitterness springing up causes trouble, and by it many be defiled" (Hebrews 12:14–15).

Now then, let's reason together. What has to change within if you obey God and pursue peace with others and sanctification, holiness? And how can you bring about such change? Appropriate God's grace and uproot the bitterness—it's a weed! It will take over the garden.

Peace and bitterness cannot grow together. Which do you want? The choice is yours.

~

Bow your knees in prayer. Tell God you will accept His dealings with you as good, and, therefore, you will stop murmuring and disputing with Him over why certain things have happened in your life. Ask to exchange your anger and bitterness for His meekness. Tell Him that you will trust Him to use the circumstances of your life—past, present, and future—to make you into the image of His Son.

October 30

If you're being held captive in a cell of bitterness, meekness—or humility—is the key that will swing open the door of your self-imposed prison. Meekness will bring a peace and freedom like you have never experienced before.

Meekness is an attitude of submission and trust that accepts all of God's ways with us as good, and therefore it does not murmur, dispute, or retaliate. It realizes that what comes to us from man is permitted and used by God for our discipline and thus for purifying us. Meekness is a trusting attitude that looks beyond circumstances and beyond man to the sovereign God and, bowing the knee, says, "Lord, what pleases Thee pleases me."

From that description, it's obvious that meekness is not the natural disposition of sinful man, nor is true meekness possible apart from the Spirit of God. Because meekness is an inwrought grace of the soul, it is only possible when Jesus Christ lives within. It is our Lord who is meek and lowly in heart (Matthew 11:29, KJV).

Will you surrender this day, and all it holds, to God in meekness and humility, trusting Him to take care of the rest? **"Humble yourselves under the mighty hand of God, that He may exalt you at the proper time"** (1 Peter 5:6).

Lord, help me to seek Your eternal perspective when life isn't going the way I think it should. Give me a spirit of meekness and trust and a heart that is pleased by whatever pleases You.

October 31

When God made the earth, He intended for man to rule as His vice-regent over creation. All man had to do was walk in submission to God, in total dependence upon his Creator. For that submission to be authentic, however, it had to be voluntary. So God gave man a free will.

Would he choose to walk with God, or would he choose to turn his back and walk an independent path? It had to be put to the test. And strangely enough, the test was embodied in a tree. The tree of the knowledge of good and evil.

God's instructions were very clear: "**From any tree of the garden you may eat freely; but from the tree of the knowledge of good and evil you shall not eat, for in the day that you eat from it you will surely die**" (Genesis 2:16–17). Man was not blind to the consequences of his sin. God tells us very clearly in 1 Timothy 2:14 that Adam was not deceived. Eve was, but not Adam. He knew exactly what he was doing when he listened to the voice of his wife rather than the voice of God. He ate of the fruit of the tree in willful disobedience. In so doing, Adam chose to walk independently of God and lost the right to rule as God's vice-regent on earth.

Man lost the earth because he wasn't willing to submit to God. Only meekness will regain what was lost in the garden: "Blessed are the meek: for they shall inherit the earth" (Matthew 5:5, KJV).

What will you inherit, my friend: the reward of sin or of meekness?

~

Forgive me, Lord, for the times I've chosen to walk independently of You. Grant me the meekness, the humility, to submit fully to Your leadership and rule in all things.

November 1

Do you realize that our interactions with other people—how we speak to and behave toward those we encounter each day—are rooted in our relationship with God?

When you consider the Ten Commandments in Exodus 20, you may notice that they first describe the relationship between God and man. The commandments begin with loving God, having no idols before Him, not taking His name in vain, and keeping the Sabbath holy. Then the commandments go on to speak of the relationships between people. We are told to honor father and mother and not to murder, commit adultery, steal, bear false witness, or covet another's possessions.

We see the same pattern in the Beatitudes and in Jesus' response when asked about the greatest commandment:

> **"You shall love the LORD your God with all your heart, and with all your soul, and with all your mind." This is the great and foremost commandment. The second is like it, "You shall love your neighbor as yourself."** On these two commandments depend the whole Law and the Prophets. (Matthew 22:37–40)

What truth is hidden in this order of priority? I believe it's the truth of being rather than just doing. Doing always finds limits when it functions out of its own strength or according to its own moral code. Doing is limited by what we are. But if we honor God as God and are inhabited by God, then we can love others as we want to be loved, because the One who lives and loves through us is God.

~

Help me to live in Your strength and love rather than operating out of my own limited resources.

November 2

Does your treatment of others reflect the humility that characterizes a disciple of Jesus? Or do you view the people you encounter at work, in the grocery store, at home, at the gym as just so many interruptions to your agenda?

Beloved, we're called to follow Jesus' example of a life given in service to others: "Have this attitude in yourselves which was also in Christ Jesus, who, although He existed in the form of God, did not regard equality with God a thing to be grasped, but emptied Himself, taking the form of a bond-servant" (Philippians 2:5–7).

Just before our Lord was betrayed, He gathered His disciples in the upper room. In those days slaves washed the feet of all who entered a house. But since the upper room had been rented by the disciples, there was no slave to wash their feet. Then Jesus "got up from supper…poured water…and began to wash the disciples' feet and to wipe them with the towel with which He was girded" (John 13:4–5). When He finished, He said, **"I gave you an example that you also should do as I did to you"** (John 13:15).

This is the example of the One whom they called Teacher and Lord. And He would give them yet an even greater example when He laid down His life for them.

Are there any aspects of your attitude toward or your relationships with others in which you've resisted following the example of Jesus? Allow the Lord to search your heart. He'll do it in love. He simply wants a clean temple.

"Examine me, O LORD, and try me; test my mind and my heart" (Psalm 26:2). Convict me of any pride or anger that stands in the way of my following Christ's example.

November 3

The world tells us to demand our rights, to look out for number one, to distance ourselves when disagreements arise with our neighbors, co-workers, family members.

Jesus, however, calls us to demonstrate love. And love does not seek personal justice. This is why Jesus told His disciples, **"If anyone wants to sue you and take your shirt, let him have your coat also"** (Matthew 5:40).

Love will give up its rights in order to demonstrate the character of God. Why? Because love lives on a higher plane.

It's not easy up there on that higher plane, is it? It lets people take advantage of you. But then…what's new? Don't people take advantage of God? Yet it never alters His character. And, like Him, our character is never to be altered by the behavior of others. No matter what anyone else does, we are to walk in love.

Love does not cling to its personal possessions. Therefore, love gives to him who asks and does not turn away the one who wants to borrow. Love expands itself. Love gives the ultimate and in its giving disarms the receiver. Love even loves its enemies and in compassion prays for those who persecute it. Love cannot restrain its affection—not if it's God's love!

Love lives on a higher plane.

My human nature rebels against the thought of allowing someone to take advantage of me. Help me to remember, Father, that You are molding me into the image of Your Son, who humbled Himself in obedience, even to the point of death on the cross (Philippians 2:8).

November 4

The love that marks the life of a Christian isn't a sweet, mushy feeling; it's a compelling force, a deliberate choice to be guided by God in the practical, everyday encounters of life.

During the time Jesus walked on earth, a Roman soldier could compel a civilian to carry his burden the distance of one mile but no more. The law was designed to keep the soldier from taking advantage of the civilian. Jesus addressed the situation of His day, and in doing so gave all of us a practical illustration of righteous love: "**Whoever forces you to go one mile, go with him two**" (Matthew 5:41).

Love goes beyond what it is compelled to do. Love lives on a higher plane than the Law.

If you're going to turn the other cheek, give away your coat, go the second mile, give to him who asks, and love your enemies, then it logically follows that you cannot be occupied or concerned with self. This is meekness (or gentleness, as some translate it) personified.

God is telling us, in essence, that love does not demand its rights. It does not ask for a just reward. Love is merciful. It looks beyond the immediate to another's eternal good.

Whenever you turn the other cheek, or give away your coat, or walk an extra mile, or give to the one who wants to borrow, you must remember that you are doing it out of love. Love is the true intent of our Lord's words.

I pray that my life—my words, my responses, my relationships—will be controlled by the love of Christ expressed through me. Help me to walk in meekness, offering mercy and grace rather than demanding justice.

November 5

"You are the light of the world," Jesus declared to His followers in Matthew 5:14. And we know that light has one purpose: to dispel darkness. Light serves its purpose only when it shines forth, to be seen of men. If a lamp or candle doesn't give light, what good is it?

Therefore Jesus admonishes us: "**Let your light shine before men in such a way that they may see your good works, and glorify your Father who is in heaven**" (Matthew 5:16).

I want you to notice something important here: our good works cause the light to shine. But those good works are to be done in such a way that they do not glorify us but our Father. If they do not point men beyond us to the Father, then something is wrong with the way we are letting our lights shine.

I'm not saying that it's wrong for people to love and appreciate you. This is obviously going to happen if you're used of God in a significant way in somebody's life. That love and appreciation, however, should never stop with you. It should rather be primarily directed toward the Source of all Light, Jesus Christ. The lampstand is not significant, but the light that comes from the lampstand is. The lampstand is merely a vessel to bring light to those who are in its presence.

Just as the moon reflects the sun's light, so we are to reflect the Son's light!

Your Word says that "the path of the righteous is like the light of dawn, that shines brighter and brighter until the full day" (Proverbs 4:18). I pray that this will be true of my life, that it will shine with good works, lighting a pathway to You.

November 6

When you receive the late-night phone call announcing a tragedy, when you witness the failure of a project dear to your heart, when your doctor delivers a devastating diagnosis, when you're passed over for the promotion at work, when you're misunderstood by someone you love—please know, beloved, that every heartache serves a purpose.

It will help to remember that your sufferings are for your Lord's sake, endured by His grace! Suffering is never wasted—it is used to make us more like Christ and, as a result, causes the grace of God to spread, and God is glorified. Thus, Paul explains our suffering: **"For Your sake we are being put to death all day long; we were considered as sheep to be slaughtered"** (Romans 8:36).

I believe it will also help you to endure life's disappointments with unwavering trust if you'll look at the Author and Finisher of your faith and remember "the grace of our Lord Jesus Christ, that though He was rich, yet for your sake He became poor, so that you through His poverty might become rich" (2 Corinthians 8:9).

Oh, beloved, remember that no matter what your sufferings or the cost of Christlikeness, the grace of God has made you rich in Jesus. It serves an eternal purpose, bringing with it eternal value and reward.

~

Lord my God, I pray that You may count me worthy of my calling, that the name of the Lord Jesus may be glorified in me, and I in Him, according to Your grace, O God, and that of the Lord Jesus Christ (2 Thessalonians 1:11–12).

November 7

When unexpected events interrupt our plans, why do we not rest at peace in the unchangeable character of Jehovah God?

Jehovah (YHWH or Yahweh) is the self-existent One—"I AM WHO I AM." The eternal I AM, the Alpha and the Omega, the same yesterday, today, and forever (Hebrews 13:8).

At the burning bush, Moses said to God:

> "Behold, I am going to the sons of Israel, and I will say to them, 'The God of your fathers has sent me to you.' Now they may say to me, 'What is His name?' What shall I say to them?" **God said to Moses, "I AM WHO I AM"**; and He said, "Thus you shall say to the sons of Israel, 'I AM has sent me to you.' . . . This is My name forever, and this is My memorial-name to all generations." (Exodus 3:13–15)

Through this statement, God revealed Himself to His covenant people as the unchanging God who remains faithful to His word throughout all generations.

When you need assurance that God is there, that He will keep His promises without changing—even though you have wavered in your promises to Him—run to your Jehovah. Trust in His name. It can't change because He can't change. He is "I AM"—everything you and I will ever need.

Jehovah God, You are eternal and You are faithful. I praise You for being a God who keeps Your promises, and I choose to trust in Your name.

November 8

We're so accustomed to living in an instant world that it's difficult to wait for anything. Our society has promoted and provided instant gratification to such an extent that to deny ourselves or wait for anything seems almost cruel.

Man is the center of his own world. When he wants something, he goes after it. Self will be satisfied!

In a world like this, a man or woman who lives by faith is a rarity. Living by faith requires patience because the one who lives by faith becomes dependent upon God. You no longer call the shots. You no longer operate on your timetable. You don't just rush out to get, to do, to have, to satisfy.

You pray. You ask. You seek His will, His counsel. Then you wait for God's leadership—His insight, His wisdom, His provision, His answer.

Faith recognizes that God is in control, not man.

Faith does it God's way, in God's timing—according to His good pleasure.

Faith does not take life into its own hands but in respect and trust places itself in God's hands.

This is the contrast we see in Habakkuk 2:4: "**Behold, as for the proud one, his soul is not right within him; but the righteous will live by his faith.**" Pride moves according to its own desires, its own will, its own timing. Pride does what it wants to do, when it wants to do it, and the way it wants to do it! Faith waits and trusts, taking God at His word.

How are you living, my friend—in faith or in pride?

Lord, please help me to live today recognizing that You are in control. When I'm tempted to follow my own desires, help me instead to place my life in Your hands.

November 9

On what are you basing your faith? Your words, your desires, your beliefs? Are you one of the many who are saying, "I claim that by faith"? If so, on what basis are you claiming it?

I become so distressed when I receive letters from people who think God has forsaken them because they haven't received what they claimed by faith. And how I grieve over those who write to me and request a book, CD, or even a personal letter giving them counsel from God's Word and then say that they can't send me any "seed faith money" because they're broke. But they assure me that they will when they can, if I'll only help them. I just want to cup their faces in my hands and say, "Read my lips carefully: God is not like that. You don't have to give to God's servants in order to get from God."

Proverbs 16:20 reveals the secret to receiving God's blessing: **"He who gives attention to the word will find good, and blessed is he who trusts in the LORD."**

He's a God of grace. Remember that, my friend, and trust in His Word. When you trust in His Word, He will honor your faith.

~

If you're confused by preachers and others who tell you to "name it and claim it," ask God to reveal His truth to you as you study His Word. If this is not an issue for you, pray that God will raise up trustworthy, faithful men and women to teach His Word to those hungry for truth.

November 10

When your spirit is wounded, when you can't seem to shake the pain or regrets of the past, when you feel trapped by your emotions, you will find healing and wholeness at the throne of God.

God's name is Jehovah-rapha, the God who heals. And that is what God does: He heals. And He can heal you. God's name is as good as God's person. His name stands because He never changes. God is the same yesterday, today, and forever (Hebrews 13:8). He has always been, and He always will be, Jehovah-rapha: **"I, the LORD, am your healer"** (Exodus 15:26).

Like the people of Jeremiah's day who in vain sought healing from sources other than God, so many today try to find healing for their wounded souls in the things the world has to offer. They should instead be seeking God's counsel and cure for their hurts.

Beloved, to whom have you run for healing? Make sure you get godly counsel—that which has its very foundation in the Word of God, that which points you to God and all that He is—rather than counsel that is apart from Him and His precepts of life. The eternal God is not only your Creator; He is also your Sustainer. Won't you trust Him to care tenderly for every aspect of you—body, soul, and spirit?

~

I thank You for being a God who can heal and make new. I choose to seek Your wisdom from above rather than earthly knowledge. Please reveal any counsel that is not according to Your Word so that I might not be deceived.

November 11

Today there are many voices in the world, and even in Christendom, telling us that the root source of our problems is a lack of self-love and self-esteem. It sounds good, especially when it comes from the so-called experts. It may even sound more plausible when it comes from active Christians. It also seems more credible when we see it in print—discussed, explained, and substantiated by "experts" in magazines and books. But what does the Word of God say about self-esteem, self-worth, our self-image? Nothing, except that apart from Jesus we are nothing.

Nowhere does the Word of God tell us that our problem is a lack of self-esteem or a lack of self-love or a poor self-image. Instead, the Bible tells us that from the very beginning of the Garden of Eden, man's problem was unbelief. Unbelief caused man to sin. Sin separated man from God, and God is love. When man cuts himself off from love, he then begins the search to find a substitute. In this search, many hurts are incurred, many wounds inflicted. Self-love is that poor, but very deluding, substitute for God's love that deceptively puts man instead of God at the center.

Don't worry about self-love, my friend; simply let God's love do its work in you. "**The love of God has been poured out within our hearts through the Holy Spirit who was given to us**" (Romans 5:5).

~

Precious Lord, through the Holy Spirit and Your love poured out within my heart, help me to walk as Jesus walked. Let me live with You at the center of my world so that Your love will be perfected in me.

November 12

I know, beloved, that it's not easy to rejoice when we find ourselves in the midst of devastating circumstances. It seems like insanity to be "always giving thanks for all things" (Ephesians 5:20). However, we are not to rejoice in the circumstances but in the God who is in charge of the circumstances!

With the apostle Paul, we can say:

> Not that I speak from want, for I have learned to be content in whatever circumstances I am. I know how to get along with humble means, and I also know how to live in prosperity; in any and every circumstance I have learned the secret of being filled and going hungry, both of having abundance and suffering need. I can do all things through Him who strengthens me. (Philippians 4:11–13)

God is fully adequate! We can rejoice in our circumstances because we're not looking at them but at Him.

Our faith will become airborne when we follow the urging of James 1:2–3: **"Consider it all joy, my brethren, when you encounter various trials, knowing that the testing of your faith produces endurance."**

~

Loving Father, what joy it is to know that You are shaping me into the image of Your Son. Thank You for offering me Your strength and for giving me joy unspeakable and full of glory.

November 13

As you prepare your heart for the day ahead, seeking God's provision for your every need, remember that grace is activated by faith.

It is one thing to stand in the grace of God and to be gifted by God for the work of ministry. It is another thing to live in the light of these facts. This is where faith comes in. Faith activates or releases the grace of God. **"For by grace you have been saved through faith"** (Ephesians 2:8).

Grace strips us of our need for anything but humility. Then it gives to the humble a vault of all the treasures and resources of God. However, that vault is only unlocked with the key of faith. That's why so many of God's children are powerless.

First, they have not humbled themselves under the mighty hand of God. Instead, they've been seduced into a pseudo-faith that centers on what we believe about ourselves and our human potential and abilities.

Second, they don't understand biblical faith. Their faith is placed in what they believe about God rather than on the whole counsel of the Word of God. However, the certainty of faith is found not in the believer but in who and what is believed. If we believe in what we say, our faith rests in ourselves. If we believe what God says—in the context of the whole Bible—our faith rests in the infallible Word of God and in the character of God.

On what is your faith resting?

Lord, I choose to place my faith wholly in You. Please open my eyes to any ways in which I am trusting in the wisdom of man rather than in Your Word and character.

November 14

Yesterday we saw that grace strips us of our need for anything but humility, and grace opens to the humble a vault of all the treasures and resources of God, which we unlock with the key of faith. Grace and faith cannot be separated. We cannot lay hold of grace apart from faith.

By faith we rely totally on God, rejecting confidence in ourselves and placing our confidence in who God is and in what He says. This is how we are to live in every situation of life. "**So that your faith would not rest on the wisdom of men, but on the power of God**" (1 Corinthians 2:5).

When you encounter trials that you feel will overwhelm or destroy you, how can you survive without losing your faith or your mind? You must believe that His grace is sufficient for any and every circumstance of life. The minute you believe that, the power of grace is released.

Grace can never be earned or merited. It can only be believed, appropriated by faith. "The righteousness of God is revealed from faith to faith; as it is written, 'But the righteous man shall live by faith'" (Romans 1:17). The Christian life begins with faith, is lived by faith, and is maintained by faith. It is all of faith.

~

Please strengthen my faith, Lord, so that I will trust solely in Your all-sufficient grace to meet my every need, to cover my every weakness, to heal my every wound, to equip me for every good work.

November 15

Oh, beloved, what will you give to pay for your sins? What can you do to pay back the exorbitant debt you owe our righteous and holy God? Work a lifetime? Keep all His commandments at all times, never faltering once? Always be everything you are supposed to be? Always be totally, unfailingly like Jesus? Can you do that? Of course not! Then what will you do to compensate for the times when you have been less than perfect? What will you do to make up for the times you've willfully, knowingly disobeyed the will of God?

Whether your sin has been gross and blatant or delicate and disguised, there is only one way to receive God's forgiveness. It is through the blood of the Lord Jesus Christ—Jesus, the sinless One who was made sin for you that you might be made His righteousness. **"He made Him who knew no sin to be sin on our behalf, so that we might become the righteousness of God in Him"** (2 Corinthians 5:21).

God's forgiveness is always an act of grace. It is appropriated simply by acknowledging your sin against God and receiving full pardon from Him. It is written in God's infallible Word: "It is a trustworthy statement, deserving full acceptance, that Christ Jesus came into the world to save sinners" (1 Timothy 1:15).

~

I humbly acknowledge that I can do nothing to earn Your forgiveness and mercy. Thank You for Your marvelous gift of grace and for making me righteous through Your precious Son.

November 16

Beloved, is it possible that you're preoccupied with external requirements, perhaps even becoming caught up in a self-righteousness that has blinded you to the true, heart-transforming righteousness that is based on faith alone?

Self-righteousness is always man's interpretation or addition to the clear-cut teaching of God's Word. It's a process of tacking on extra laws, requirements, and expectations and then saying that if you're really going to be righteous, you must keep all these rules. It is judging others by your standards rather than God's.

True righteousness—God's righteousness—begins with a dissatisfaction, a yearning. When sin's presence within is finally realized, an inner longing is kindled—a longing to be righteous. With every glimpse of God's shining holiness and purity comes an accompanying awareness of self as described in Isaiah 64: "**But we are all as an unclean thing, and all our righteousnesses are as filthy rags; and we all do fade as a leaf; and our iniquities, like the wind, have taken us away**" (verse 6, KJV). I'm unclean! I've fallen short of God's standard of perfection! All my righteousness is as filthy rags in God's sight.

Finally the realization comes: "God, You alone are righteous." A hunger and thirst for righteousness awakens and grows—a hunger and thirst that can be satisfied only when we run to the Fountain of Living Waters and receive the gift of the indwelling Holy Spirit. He alone can lead us into a life of righteousness, by leading us into the truth.

O God, open my eyes to any ways in which I've redefined righteousness by my standards rather than Yours alone. I want to experience the life-transforming righteousness that comes only by the Spirit.

November 17

After we've been cleansed by the blood of Jesus Christ from an evil conscience (Hebrews 10:22), how do we stay pure? How do we keep our hearts from being stained all over again?

Listen to the answer from Psalm 119:9: "**How can a young man keep his way pure? By keeping it according to Your word.**" We keep our hearts cleansed through the Word of God. When the Word cleanses us, it cleanses from wrong thinking, wrong doctrine, and wrong behavior. This is why Jesus prayed to the Father on behalf of His followers, "Sanctify them in the truth; Your word is truth" (John 17:17).

How often do you think such sanctification, such cleansing by the Word, is necessary? How much do you think it takes to make or keep you clean?

I've heard some people say, "Just spend three minutes a day alone with God."

I can understand where they're coming from. Some believers go through their days without spending any time with the Lord. And three minutes with God is better than none!

But the question is, are we selling God short? Are we selling God's Word short? Is Deuteronomy 8:3 true when it says that "man does not live by bread alone, but man lives by everything that proceeds out of the mouth of the LORD"? In three minutes a day can I really present myself "approved to God as a workman who does not need to be ashamed, accurately handling the word of truth" (2 Timothy 2:15)?

~

Prayerfully evaluate how much time you are spending in God's Word. If you've been shortchanging God, ask Him to show you how to reprioritize your schedule.

November 18

It seems odd to think of ourselves as idol worshipers in our modern culture, doesn't it? And yet so many of us are. The idols that tend to attract our attentions are not as easy to spot as the icons of Old Testament times or the fetishes of superstitious people who still worship other gods. But they are just as real. They are just as damning. And God's warning remains just as true: **"Do not go after other gods to serve them and to worship them, and do not provoke Me to anger with the work of your hands"** (Jeremiah 25:6).

Why is God against idolatry? Because its focus is on what man creates rather than on the Creator. God loves us and desires our highest good. He made us for Himself. Nothing—no person, no object—is to take His rightful place in our affections or our attention.

Think about it. Does He have the preeminence in your affections? Do you desire Him above all else and everyone else? Or have others—idols—crowded Him out so that you live for others, seeking to please them above your God? And what priority do you give Him? How much of your attention does He receive? Do you talk with Him daily? weekly? monthly? annually? Do you take vacations from God or with God?

I urge you, beloved, to take a moment and think about these things. If you have idols in your life, you must realize they are as great a sin as adultery or murder. Hear, oh, hear the word of the Lord in Exodus 20:3: "You shall have no other gods before Me." Have you?

O Lord my God, You alone are worthy of my worship, my affection, my praise. I give this day to You. Show me how to use my time, my words, my life for Your glory.

November 19

Have you noticed that the most miserable and wretched people are those who live for themselves? Not only are they never satisfied and terribly discontented, but they also usually make everyone else that way simply by their presence. And what is their problem? They need to be reconciled to God and walk in the fullness of that reconciliation.

But how can this happen? That, dear one, is where we come in.

Despite the differences in our spiritual gifts, our talents, our personalities, and our denominations, every child of God has one ministry in common: the ministry of reconciliation. Not reconciliation between two parties living here on earth, but between One who resides in heaven and another who resides on earth.

"All these things are from God, who reconciled us to Himself through Christ and gave us the ministry of reconciliation" (2 Corinthians 5:18).

If we belong to the King, we're ambassadors of the King. Whenever, wherever, we always have an ongoing ministry. The ministry of reconciliation. We have the message that every man, woman, child, and teenager needs: they must be reconciled to God, or they will perish.

God has done all that will ever be done on their behalf. They just don't know it, and it is your calling and mine to let them know the truth.

~

Dear Lord, how I pray that You will open my eyes and my heart to those who need to be reconciled to You. Give me the words, dear Lord, to lead them to Your truth.

November 20

When we do not fix our eyes upon Jesus and things of eternity, we will eventually find ourselves no longer serving God but serving material possessions.

A friend of mine told me of an occasion when she happened into a small convenience store. The magazines on the rack in that store were so perverted and distressing that my friend felt compelled to speak to the owner. As she did, she confessed Jesus Christ as her Savior.

The man replied, "I'm a Christian also, ma'am, but God is God and business is business."

Is that true? Can God be kept in a Sunday box, served and worshiped one or two days of the week, while we devote the other days to "business"? Jesus said, **"No one can serve two masters; for either he will hate the one and love the other, or else he will be loyal to the one and despise the other. You cannot serve God and mammon"** (Matthew 6:24, NKJV).

What did Jesus mean by the word *mammon*? What is God's chief rival in our society today? I believe it is "things," material possessions. I'm reluctant to use the word *riches* here because you might think, *But I'm not rich! I just want enough to get by on. All I want are the necessities of life. That can't be wrong, can it?* Yes, it can be wrong—if you are anxious about them or if your necessity list doesn't match God's!

The only way we can be sure of serving God wholeheartedly is to fix our eyes on Him and trust Him to take care of our needs.

Precious Lord, let my love for You guide my daily decisions. Help me resist the temptation to value earthly wealth and possessions above the work of Your kingdom.

November 21

If you and I want to experience the abundant life, if we want to serve God wholeheartedly, undistracted by the worries and pleasures of this world, then our hearts and actions must reflect God's priorities:

> **Instruct those who are rich in this present world...to do good, to be rich in good works, to be generous and ready to share, storing up for themselves the treasure of a good foundation for the future, so that they may take hold of that which is life indeed.** (1 Timothy 6:17–19)

Any riches we might gain will be for others, to share with those who have less. Every gift we have comes down from the Father above (James 1:17), and the gifts are ours so that we may genuinely bless those in need. If we don't have the possessions, the heirlooms of the generations—houses, land, and stocks—it matters not. We are heirs of God and joint-heirs with Jesus Christ (Romans 8:17, KJV). And if we do have such riches, they're to be held with an open hand, for we won't allow them to possess us.

We belong to One: Jesus Christ. We live for One: Jesus Christ. Our passion is to exhibit the high calling of a faithful servant of God.

Oh, beloved, how are you doing? Are there any changes you need to make, any new attitudes you need to develop, any new disciplines you need to institute? If so, ask God to show you how. Seize the day while it is yet day.

Thank You, heavenly Father, for the rich blessings You've given me. Help me to hold the things of this world loosely, using them as You direct, for the comfort and encouragement of others.

November 22

How easily we take offense at the words or actions of others, allowing anger to steep in our hearts and brew bitter thoughts and attitudes. But Jesus warned about the dangers of allowing anger to mar our relationships:

> **Whosoever is angry with his brother without a cause shall be in danger of the judgment: and whosoever shall say to his brother, Raca, shall be in danger of the council: but whosoever shall say, Thou fool, shall be in danger of hell fire.** (Matthew 5:22, KJV)

Jesus declared that anyone who is angry with his brother should be guilty before the court. Anyone who calls his brother "Raca" should be guilty before the supreme court, the Sanhedrin. And anyone who would refer to a brother as a fool would be guilty enough to go to Gehenna, the lake of fire.

What is Jesus trying to show us? I think He wants us to see the value of a person. *Raca* is an Aramaic word for *empty-headed* or *good-for-nothing.* How can I use such a term to describe a man or woman made in God's image, created to glorify Him? Who am I to ascribe that kind of label to one given life by the Creator? Who am I, another human being, to sit in the seat of God and tell another person that he or she is not worth anything? Isn't that a form of murder—saying that his life has no value, that there's no reason for his existence?

It's not wrong to be indignant over sin, but it is wrong to harbor anger that would destroy a person made in God's image.

In moments of frustration and anger, dear Lord, give me a spirit of grace and forgiveness. Help me to remember that the other person is made in Your image, just as I am.

November 23

Do you feel you've missed your opportunity for service? You made a choice—the wrong one—and now you're imprisoned in the consequences.

Or maybe you have taken account of who you are and what you have to offer, and you are firmly convinced that your life has little, if any, purpose in the kingdom of God—let alone in the world. You wonder, *Why try? What's the point?*

Or perhaps you have settled into a routine Christianity in a routine daily existence. *Considering who I am,* you think, *there isn't much more I could expect anyway.*

No, there really isn't much more to expect, except for the grace of God. "For the grace of God that brings salvation has appeared to all men" (Titus 2:11, NKJV). As a matter of fact, if it weren't for the grace of God, we would all face defeat and despair.

If anyone has ever understood that grace covers our past and equips us for God's future, it was the apostle Paul, who had persecuted and murdered Christians prior to his conversion. Listen to his words: "**By the grace of God I am what I am, and His grace toward me did not prove vain; but I labored even more than all of them, yet not I, but the grace of God with me**" (1 Corinthians 15:10).

In Paul's writing of those God-breathed words, we see that the whole of life is to be lived in the understanding and appropriation of the grace of God. Oh, how I pray that God will grant you this understanding and that He will anoint this writing to your good and His eternal glory.

~

Reveal to me, Lord, how You want to use me. Let Your grace flow in and through me so I can experience the abundant life Jesus offers.

November 24

Mercy. The word has been uttered as a whisper and a shout, as a question and a plea. But each utterance holds one meaning: "Meet my need. Give me what I need, not what I deserve."

And our God, "being rich in mercy" (Ephesians 2:4), hears our cries. God is so different from us that it's hard to comprehend His grace and His mercy.

Although the enemy cannot separate you from the love of God in Christ Jesus, once you are saved, Satan delights in deceiving you so you don't appropriate what is yours. The enemy wants to heap guilt and condemnation on you. His strategy is to convince you that whatever you need from God you don't deserve. He wants to convince you that you shouldn't ask Him for it or expect Him to give it to you.

Don't listen to the devil's lies. Mercy is an attribute of God.

> **Blessed be the God and Father of our Lord Jesus Christ, who according to His great mercy has caused us to be born again to a living hope through the resurrection of Jesus Christ from the dead, to obtain an inheritance which is imperishable and undefiled and will not fade away, reserved in heaven for you.** (1 Peter 1:3–4)

God is your very present help in the time of trouble. He longs to be merciful. So run to—not from—His throne of grace. There you'll find mercy and grace to help.

~

Almighty, loving God and Father, if not for Your mercy, I would be desperately lost. Thank You that I am free from condemnation and guilt, free to claim my inheritance as Your beloved child.

November 25

Do you long to live a life that is pleasing to God? Faith is the key that unlocks the door to the unmerited favor of God. And once that door is unlocked, we forever stand in the grace of God. "**Therefore, having been justified by faith, we have peace with God through our Lord Jesus Christ, through whom also we have obtained our introduction by faith into this grace in which we stand**" (Romans 5:1–2).

Oh, beloved, these truths are absolutely vital to a life of peace and victory! Many are living defeated lives because they do not realize what it means to live by grace—by grace alone.

I am not speaking of a perversion of grace that would lead to licentiousness. I am speaking of an understanding of grace that releases the power of God in our lives, a comprehension that brings great peace and places us in the undisturbed eye of the hurricane as we live more and more in the knowledge and experience of the grace of God.

Grace is more than unmerited favor. It is reality. By grace you live, by grace you please God, and by grace you are freed from religion and released into a relationship with your heavenly Father. Grace is always based on who He is and what He has done. Grace is never based on who you are apart from Him or on what you can do.

Take a few minutes to examine how you relate to your heavenly Father. What is the basis of your relationship with Him? Ask Him to reveal any area in which you're relying on something other than His grace.

November 26

Do you tend to excuse or justify sin in your life, believing it's simply an unavoidable consequence of being human? What about the grace you received through salvation, beloved? Salvation is not merely salvation from hell and eternal condemnation. When one is saved, one is saved from the power of sin.

Yet people are told they need to get saved so they won't go to hell. It's true that if they are saved, they'll never taste eternal death. However, the reason people who are saved don't go to hell is because hell and eternal condemnation are the consequences of sin.

The "benefit" of salvation lies not only in being freed from sin's penalty or consequences in the future but also in being freed from sin's power and sin's presence in our lives now—resulting in sanctification. And the outcome of that sanctification, Romans tells us, is eternal life: "**But now having been freed from sin and enslaved to God, you derive your benefit, resulting in sanctification, and the outcome, eternal life**" (6:22).

Do you see my point? When we view salvation as merely an escape from eternal judgment, we have a tendency to deal lightly with the issue of sin. And when we deal lightly with sin, we diminish the grace of God—the unearned, undeserved, unmerited favor of God—which delivers us from sin's penalty *and* sin's reigning power.

I thank You that You have saved me not only from judgment in the life to come but from the power of sin in my life today. Help me to live in the knowledge of this truth and to share it with others who need to hear the good news of freedom from sin's power.

November 27

When the world looks at the life of a Christian, they should see a clear contrast to their own lifestyle and values. Sadly, this isn't always so.

The book of James addressed this problem in the early church, offering a call to repentance to people who were caught up in a friendship with the world—a friendship that had made them proud, had led them into spiritual harlotry, and had broken the heart of God. This reminds me of how many Christians today make light of the world's sin, even laughing along at the innuendos and vulgarities portrayed in the media.

What is the solution? How can we draw near to God once more? What is God's word to us?

Stop laughing at sin.

James wrote, "**Cleanse your hands, you sinners; and purify your hearts, you double-minded. Be miserable and mourn and weep; let your laughter be turned into mourning and your joy to gloom**" (4:8–9).

Is that the sort of attitude toward sin you see as you look around today? Hardly!

Yet how can we laugh over sin when sin nailed Jesus to the cross?

Do you have God's heart when it comes to the matter of sin? Do you shrug it off—or even laugh along? Or do you find your heart broken, your spirit mourning at how far those around you have descended into degradation?

~

Honestly before God determine what your attitude toward sin is. Are you willing to be changed? Talk to Him about it.

November 28

Have you been trying to straighten out yourself? Have you been trying to shape up? Are you totally frustrated? Let me assure you, beloved, you're not the first to feel this way.

The writer of Ecclesiastes declared, "**Indeed, there is not a righteous man on earth who continually does good and who never sins**" (7:20). Man cannot straighten out himself. Humanity cannot untie the knots of sin and sorrow in which it has entangled itself. But what is impossible with man is possible with God!

Has God shown you that you need a new heart? Has He shown you your need for salvation? Then come and let Him straighten you out. Tell Him that you repent. Tell Him that you've had a change of mind, that you believe Jesus Christ is God in the flesh and He has the right to be your Lord, your Master. Tell Him you want no other master but Jesus Christ. Thank Him for sending His Son to take the penalty for your sins so that you, through believing in Him, might have His righteousness. Ask God to give you His Holy Spirit. Thank Him for freeing you from sin's dominion and enabling you to walk in newness of life as a brand-new creature in Christ Jesus. Thank Him for the gift of eternal life.

Now, record this most important day of your spiritual birth in your Bible. Welcome, beloved, to God's forever family!

~

If you know that you have already received a new heart from God, take this opportunity to pray for someone else who needs to be set free from slavery to sin.

November 29

As followers of Christ, we're called to a vital role within God's kingdom. He has ordained us as ambassadors for Christ, committing to us the word, or the message, of reconciliation: "**God was in Christ reconciling the world to Himself, not counting their trespasses against them, and He has committed to us the word of reconciliation**" (2 Corinthians 5:19).

As new creatures in Christ Jesus, we are called, commissioned, and endued with power from on high by the Holy Spirit, who indwells every believer. We stand in the lavish grace of God that supplies our every need. We're not to fear the threats of men. Nor are we to fear death. We're to move wisely, fearlessly, prayerfully into the nations and kingdoms of this world with the word of reconciliation, laying down our lives for the sake of the gospel of Jesus Christ.

The grave will never contain our souls, for we'll be immediately absent from the body and present with the Lord. The tears will quickly be wiped away by the finger of our God as He says, "Welcome home! Well done, My good and faithful servant!"

And who will be our joy, our crown of rejoicing? It will be those to whom we took the word of reconciliation.

What higher calling could we have than to be ambassadors for Christ? To reconcile men to God is to have a heart like His. This is why He sent His Son into the world and why His Son sends you into the world!

Send me, Lord. Use me in whatever way You see fit to reconcile others to You. Make my heart sensitive to those who are hungry for Your truth, and fill my mouth with Your life-giving words.

November 30

Have you ever found yourself in a dark place, cast there by someone who wounded you deeply? You feel rejected, and discouragement threatens to overwhelm you.

"Where is God?" you ask. "Where is this sovereign God who promises that all things work together for good? Does He know what's going on? Does He see?"

Yes, He is El Roi, the God who sees. The omnipresent God is there, and His eyes are not shut. There is no hiding the facts from Him, as the psalmist so eloquently noted: **"Where can I go from Your Spirit? Or where can I flee from Your presence?… Even the darkness is not dark to You, and the night is as bright as the day. Darkness and light are alike to You"** (Psalm 139:7, 12).

God isn't asleep. He knows the sin that was committed against you. And someday He will vindicate you. There is forgiveness, but to those who refuse to receive the Lamb of God, who takes away the sins of the world, there is also a day of judgment. And it will be a righteous judgment, for God sees it all (2 Thessalonians 1:5–10).

After you realize that He is the God who sees, you need to know that in His sovereignty He permitted it. Therefore, as horrible and as destructive as it seems, in God's economy, it will be used for good. You must know Him, believe Him, and put your trust in His name, for He does not forsake those who seek Him (Psalm 9:10).

Today run into the strong tower of His name and rest!

Your eyes are open, Lord, and You take notice of every detail of my life. When pain and discouragement well up within me, help me to remember that You have not forsaken me.

December 1

Christmas is just twenty-four days away. The holiday season brings so many demands for our time and attention, doesn't it? As you prepare to celebrate Christmas—and celebrate it you should!—may I urge you to intentionally quiet yourself at some point each day and spend some priceless time contemplating the wonders of the birth of our Lord Jesus Christ.

The essence of Christmas is found in John 3:16, where we read that God loved us so very much that He gave His only Son, Jesus, to be the payment for our sins.

Oh, beloved, do you realize that if this season is not centered on God and all that His gift of His Son means to you and to the world, then Christmas will leave you spiritually hollow? However, if you'll focus on grasping, savoring, and relishing the meaning of this season and the awesomeness of His unearned favor, then you'll find yourself joyfully declaring with the apostle Paul, "**Thanks be to God for His indescribable gift!**" (2 Corinthians 9:15).

Won't you resolve before God to spend time alone with Him each day leading up to Christmas? Read through one of the Gospels or the book of Hebrews. Ask Him to take you to new depths of understanding and intimacy as you explore the wonder of Christmas. Let this be your gift to your heavenly Father: time alone with Him, appreciating and giving thanks for "His indescribable gift."

Father, thank You for this season and the opportunity to rejoice anew in the gift of Jesus. Help me to center my thoughts and celebration on You and on all that Christmas signifies.

December 2

On December 25 you and I and Christians around the world will celebrate the birth of Jesus Christ. In reality, we do not know precisely when Jesus was born; nothing in the Scriptures tells us, nor do the annual feasts celebrated by Israel foreshadow His birth, only His death and resurrection. Therefore, the exact *when*—the day of Christmas—is not the issue; what matters is the time. Galatians 4:4–5 tells us that "**when the fullness of the time came, God sent forth His Son, born of a woman, born under the Law, so that He might redeem those who were under the Law, that we might receive the adoption as sons.**"

Christmas came in God's time—the fullness of time.

The One first promised in Genesis 3:15 to Adam and Eve after they sinned—the One who would bruise the head of Satan, the serpent of old—was finally born. All the writings of Moses and the prophets pointed to this time. "God, after He spoke long ago to the fathers in the prophets in many portions and in many ways, in these last days"—in the fullness of time—"has spoken to us in His Son" (Hebrews 1:1–2). The problem is, many are not listening so as to truly hear, and many are not believing—really believing—so as to live according to the truth of what Jesus came to accomplish. Instead they're entangled with the affairs of this world.

Oh, beloved, in this twelfth month of the year we're spending together, my desire for you and for me is to hear and believe what we've heard from the Father and the Son so that we might celebrate and live out His birth in a way that truly glorifies our God in these last days.

~

Talk to God about your heart's desire for this month.

December 3

Have you waited and watched year after year for something to happen at Christmas? something to fill the void? When I was a child, Christmas seemed wonderful, exciting! The holiday season was filled with family and friends, goodies to eat, songs to sing, presents to give and receive. But with adulthood came a void. An elusive something was missing. I didn't realize the *something* was a Someone.

The amazing thing is that Jesus was there all the time. But I didn't know Him. I knew His name. I had a Bible in my house. Church was part of my life. I thought I was a Christian. In the fullness of time Jesus had arrived, but I simply hadn't moved from a religion to a relationship. Then it finally happened. At age twenty-nine I had my first real Christmas!

All through the Old Testament, God shouts, "Christmas is coming! The Promised One is coming. The One who will fill the void in your life, He is coming." In Isaiah 7:14, God gave a prophecy to His people: "**Therefore the Lord Himself will give you a sign: Behold, a virgin will be with child and bear a son, and she will call His name Immanuel.**"

Immanuel means "God with us," and that's exactly what Christmas is all about: letting Jesus fill that God-shaped void inside. The joy of Christmas is knowing that if you've received the gift of His Son—truly received Him as your Savior and Lord—you'll never be alone. It's knowing Jesus will never leave you, never forsake you (Hebrews 13:5).

If your Christmas season seems empty, could it be that you've missed the Someone of Christmas?

~

O God, You know all things. You know what I've done with Jesus. Show me as I wait quietly before You.

December 4

I'll never forget my first Christmas as a Christian. All I could think of was, *Born to die... Jesus was born to die.* Born to die that I, who was dead in my sins, might have life. What wonder this knowledge brought.

As you think about that truth, have you ever wondered, *When did God conceive Christmas in His heart?* The answer brings awe!

In Revelation 13:8 Jesus is described as "the Lamb slain from the foundation of the world" (NKJV). Why from the foundation of the world? Because an all-knowing God knew what man would do. Before He ever created man, God knew that Adam and Eve would believe a lie and disobey Him. So He planned our redemption and proceeded to create us in His image.

Ephesians 1:4 tells us He chose us in Christ before the foundation of the world. Awesome! In Matthew 25:34 Jesus reminds us that when He comes again, **"the King will say to those on His right, 'Come, you who are blessed of My Father, inherit the kingdom prepared for you from the foundation of the world.'"** From the foundation of the world!

When God spoke and brought the world into existence, Christmas was on His heart! Christmas is all about Jesus, the Lamb of God slain *from* the foundation of the world! It's about Jesus, God's gift of redemption, born to die in your place, for your sins, because the wages of sin is death.

Write it down. Post it on the refrigerator or the bathroom mirror: "Jesus—born to die that I might live!"

~

Heavenly Father, I stand in awe. May I think about this every day right up to Christmas morning, basking in Your love.

December 5

What do you know about this Christ of Christmas, dear one? Knowledge is vital. It frees us from error, from misconceptions and acts of ignorance that oftentimes bring great pain.

In his final epistle Peter wrote, **"Grace and peace be multiplied to you in the knowledge of God and of Jesus our Lord; seeing that His divine power has granted to us everything pertaining to life and godliness, through the true knowledge of Him who called us by His own glory and excellence"** (2 Peter 1:2–3). So, too, it is my desire that grace and peace will be multiplied in your life as together we delve into key truths about Jesus in the next several days. I pray that you will grow in your knowledge of the Christ of Christmas and therefore better understand the surpassing riches of the greatness of knowing Jesus Christ—of possessing Him and being indwelt by Him.

Who is this Christ of Christmas, who has come to take up residence within you? Who is this One who lived in total dependence upon the Father and became the "grain of wheat" (John 12:24) that fell into the earth and died so that you might be forgiven of all your sins and never experience the second death, the lake of fire?

My friend, have you "unwrapped" the Christ of Christmas? How well do you know Him? How well do you *want* to know Him? In Jeremiah 29:13, God promises, "You will seek Me and find Me when you search for Me with all your heart." How earnestly are you searching?

~

Won't you spend some time in prayer, asking God to give you a true knowledge of the Christ of Christmas?

December 6

"In the beginning"—what incredible truth these three words reveal about the nature of Christ! Under the inspiration of the Holy Spirit, John began his gospel with the same words that Moses, moved by the same Spirit millenniums before, opened the Bible with: "In the beginning"!

If you'll read the Bible from cover to cover, you'll see clearly that the Spirit of God wants us to know that the Christ of Christmas is more than just a baby; He's also the Creator. "For by Him all things were created, both in the heavens and on earth…all things have been created through Him and for Him" (Colossians 1:16).

The Christ of Christmas is part of that Holy Trinity first revealed in Genesis 1. When we read that "in the beginning God created," the word for God is *Elohim* in the Hebrew, with the *im* indicating a plurality. And if you let the text speak for itself—if you read it in faith as the very words of God—then it becomes evident that when God spoke, the Spirit of God, the third member of the triune Godhead, was moving over the surface of the waters (Genesis 1:2).

On the sixth day of creation, God said, "Let Us make man in Our image, according to Our likeness" (Genesis 1:26). Once again it's clear that Jesus, the Word who was God, was there with God in the beginning. **"All things came into being through Him, and apart from Him nothing came into being that has come into being. In Him was life"** (John 1:3–4).

This, beloved, is the Christ of Christmas: the One who from the very beginning has been the sole Source of life.

~

Thank You, dear God, for the gift of a new beginning and true life available only through Your Son.

December 7

Who is this One whose birth we celebrate at Christmas? Why does He bear the titles "Son of Man" and "Son of God"?

As we saw yesterday, John opened his gospel with a description of Jesus: **"In the beginning was the Word, and the Word was with God, and the Word was God. He was in the beginning with God"** (John 1:1–2). Read it aloud once more, you who have so wisely determined to know Him. Do you see the truth revealed here? John tells us that the Word—Jesus—was with God *and* the Word was God. Jesus is a member of the triune Godhead!

But John has more to tell us about the Word: "And the Word became flesh, and dwelt among us, and we saw His glory, glory as of the only begotten from the Father, full of grace and truth" (1:14). The Word begotten—born of God—became the Son of Man. Because you and I are flesh and blood, Jesus became the same: a human being. Yet He remained God. It's the mystery of the incarnation. The Christ of Christmas was—is—God in the flesh. Every bit God and every bit man.

And what was the purpose of His becoming flesh? Hebrews 2:17 tells us that "He had to be made like His brethren in all things, so that He might…make propitiation for the sins of the people." The Word became flesh to die in your place, because even when you were yet a sinner, you were beloved of God!

~

Read the first chapter of John and underline the words that describe the Christ of Christmas. Don't miss the last three words. Then worship the Father and the Son.

December 8

Every Christmas Eve my husband, Jack, reads the Christmas story, as told in the gospel of Luke, to the family, and we hear once more the angels' joyous declaration of "good news of great joy" to the shepherds: **"Today in the city of David there has been born for you a Savior, who is Christ the Lord"** (2:10–11).

If we're not careful, those words can become so familiar that we miss their significance. A Savior has been born for us! There is salvation for me, for you, for mankind. Jesus is the Savior for all who believe.

This baby whom the shepherds would find "wrapped in cloths and lying in a manger" (Luke 2:12) is "the radiance of His [God the Father's] glory and the exact representation of His nature" (Hebrews 1:3). To put it simply, the Son is just like His Father! Thus, when Philip asked Jesus to show him the Father, Jesus said to him, "He who has seen Me has seen the Father" (John 14:9).

The Savior born in the city of David, Bethlehem, is the Christ, the Anointed One sent by God. His words and His works were accomplished by the Father. And because Jesus, the sinless Son of God, willingly paid for our sins with His life, we can have forgiveness of sins and, with forgiveness, eternal life. What greater gift could we be given?

When you and I receive Jesus as Savior, God rescues us "from the domain of darkness" and transfers us into "the kingdom of His beloved Son" (Colossians 1:13). That's the joyous gift wrapped within the Christmas story!

~

O God, thank You for the day of our Savior's birth. May the story never grow old, only sweeter.

December 9

Christmas is about reconciliation. It is God's move on the chessboard of time to keep us from being checkmated by the devil.

Listen to what God tells us through the apostle Paul in 2 Corinthians 5:18–19: "Now all these things are from God, who reconciled us to Himself through Christ and gave us the ministry of reconciliation, namely, that God was in Christ reconciling the world to Himself, not counting their trespasses against them, and He has committed to us the word of reconciliation."

Read it again and underline *reconciliation.* Do you see that God first reconciles us to Himself through Jesus Christ and then gives us the ministry, the word, of reconciliation?

To reconcile is to put away the enmity between two parties, to make peace. Although man is the one who moved away to become God's enemy, it is God who moves toward man. "**While we were enemies we were reconciled to God through the death of His Son**" (Romans 5:10). Awesome, isn't it!

Therefore, Paul tells us, "we are ambassadors for Christ, as though God were making an appeal through us" (2 Corinthians 5:20). You and I have a mission, a purpose, a calling, an obligation to declare this message of reconciliation to others! It's the message of Christmas, the greatest gift you can give.

O Father, help me to remember this Christmas and, for as long as I have breath, to fulfill my purpose as Your ambassador, sharing Your message of reconciliation. I know this is the greatest gift I can give anyone, for it prepares them for eternity.

December 10

I was in New York City one November for a speaking engagement at Calvary Church right in downtown Manhattan. All the stores were dressed in their finest for Christmas, creating a veritable wonderland, and I had the day off to wander around and gather ideas for decorating our home.

As I walked with my friend through Bergdorf Goodman, looking at the treasures of this world—and reminding myself that these are the things moths eat and rust destroys and thieves steal—suddenly I was arrested by the words of the Christmas carol being played throughout the store.

> God rest ye merry, gentlemen, let nothing you dismay,
> Remember Christ our Savior was born on Christmas Day;
> To save us all from Satan's power when we were gone
> astray.
> O tidings of comfort and joy, comfort and joy;
> O tidings of comfort and joy.

There it was, the glorious gospel: "**Christ died for our sins**" (1 Corinthians 15:3). These precious words of reminder truly were "tidings of comfort and joy." Tears came to my eyes in that blessed moment. I rejoiced anew that God, in His grace, had unwrapped the Christ of Christmas for me in 1963. I was overwhelmed with gratitude.

Yet all around me people hurried on, apparently untouched by the carol and by the glorious truth of Christmas. What about you, beloved? Are you missing the tidings of comfort and joy amid the holiday rush?

~

O Father, amid the clamor of the world's version of the holiday season, let me hear Your message and share it with others.

December 11

Have you ever wondered how the focus of Christmas shifted from Christ our Savior wrapped in swaddling cloths in a Bethlehem manger to jolly ol' Saint Nick dressed in a bright red suit with white fur in a North Pole workshop?

It started out quite innocently. The man who came to be known as Saint Nicholas was born around AD 280 in what is now Turkey. As a follower of Christ, this dear man gave away his inherited wealth to help the poor. Centuries later, the day of his death, December 6, became a feast day that included the giving of gifts to children and the poor.

By the time of the Renaissance, Saint Nicholas was the most popular saint in Europe. In the Netherlands, Sinterklaas, as he was called, brought presents to good children. In Germany and elsewhere, Saint Nicholas was believed to be accompanied in his gift giving by the Christ Child or "Christkindl," from whom we get the name "Kriss Kringle." Eventually immigrants brought their various traditions to America, where writers and illustrators added new details to the character of Saint Nicholas until our modern Santa Claus gradually emerged in the late 1800s. Then it happened: the marketing of Christmas without the Christ.

"**The god of this world has blinded the minds of the unbelieving so that they might not see the light of the gospel of the glory of Christ**" (2 Corinthians 4:4). The shift came subtly, as often happens when we don't evaluate everything against the plumb line of God's Word. We veer slightly off center, and we soon lose track of the center altogether.

~

Ask God to reveal any place where you have veered from the truth of His Word.

December 12

Yesterday we saw how the focus of Christmas gradually shifted from celebrating the miracle of God made flesh to anticipating the arrival of Santa Claus with his bag of goodies. In 1822, Clement C. Moore, a clever and caring father, wrote his three daughters a frivolous and delightful poem: "An Account of a Visit from Saint Nicholas," better known as "'Twas the Night Before Christmas." The poem quickly gained popularity, as did the concept of Saint Nick as a jolly old elf, with a miniature sleigh and eight flying reindeer, who slid down chimneys and delighted children with gifts.

And, of course, all those highly anticipated gifts had to come from somewhere, so Santa Claus became the ideal mascot for the Christmas buying season. His image, as popularized by Thomas Nast's illustrations in *Harper's Weekly* during the mid-1800s, soon featured large in advertising campaigns. How ironic that today so many people spend most of their time shopping for the "perfect" gift for that special someone rather than rejoicing in the one Perfect Gift who arrived that very first Christmas for everyone.

It all reminds me of Romans 1:22–23: **"Professing to be wise, they became fools, and exchanged the glory of the incorruptible God for an image in the form of corruptible man."**

Oh, beloved, have you in any way gone off center from the real meaning of Christmas? Have you become more enthralled with the world's celebration of Christmas than with worshiping the Christ of Christmas?

Dear Lord, show me anything about my Christmas celebration that displeases You or keeps Jesus from being the centerpiece.

December 13

After Madison Avenue seized hold of Christmas, it became the most advertised of holidays and, subsequently, the most expensive and the most hectic. For countless people, the most anticipated day of the year is packaged with disappointment and hurt. The season conjures up painful memories and emotions for many. Others experience a more palpable sense of loneliness at this time of year. Some are crushed by unattainable expectations. Many allow the emphasis on material things to drive them into debt and desperation.

All this unhappiness points to one thing: someone has taken Christ out of Christmas!

"The whole world lies in the power of the evil one" (1 John 5:19), and his children—sons of disobedience, children of wrath (Ephesians 2:1–3)—have gone to war for the sole purpose of capturing Christmas.

Because of this, in many places it's illegal to erect a manger scene, and schools have banned traditional Christmas carols. Even saying "Merry Christmas" has become socially unacceptable; in the name of tolerance and inclusivity, we're urged to restrict our greetings to "Happy Holidays."

"The god of this world has blinded the minds of the unbelieving so that they might not see the light of the gospel of the glory of Christ," but **"God, who said, 'Light shall shine out of darkness,' is the One who has shone in our hearts to give the Light of the knowledge of the glory of God in the face of Christ"** (2 Corinthians 4:4, 6).

Oh, beloved, may your light shine bright so those in darkness will see Christ in you and come to the Light of salvation.

Father, help me shine brilliantly bright for You.

December 14

If you want to shine "brilliantly bright," as we prayed together yesterday, then you'll have to walk as Jesus walked. Now don't tell me that it's impossible! God doesn't command us to do the impossible.

If you're a child of God, if you've unwrapped the Christ of Christmas, truly believing He is the Son of God, then you have all you need to obey God's command: **"Therefore as you have received Christ Jesus the Lord, so walk in Him"** (Colossians 2:6).

If you're going to walk as Jesus walked, then you must "walk no longer just as the Gentiles also walk, in the futility of their mind, being darkened in their understanding" (Ephesians 4:17–18). Rather you are to "be kind to one another, tender-hearted, forgiving each other, just as God in Christ also has forgiven you" (Ephesians 4:32). You must "walk in love, just as Christ also loved you and gave Himself up for us, an offering and a sacrifice to God as a fragrant aroma" (Ephesians 5:2).

Read those verses again and underline the phrase "just as," which is used three times. Who are we to walk "just as," and what will this look like in contrast to how the rest of the world is walking?

Think about this in light of your relationships and recent conversations, my friend. Are you shining brightly? Or is unkindness, unforgiveness, pride, or selfishness darkening your heart like black soot on a window?

How appropriate, Lord, that I deliberately choose to love and forgive at this season of the year. Please make my life shine as I walk just as You did.

December 15

As you picture the original nativity scene, place two spikes in the baby's soft pink fists and lay another at His squirming feet. Jarring though it may be, that's the message of God's gift to the world, a message to all who long for healing of the spirit, healing from the ravages of sin.

The Promised One from God became a human being like you and me so He might not only die for us but also represent us before God. He experienced all the flesh-and-blood realities of life, including temptation and suffering, so that as our high priest He could sympathize with our weaknesses.

Isaiah 53:4–5 says, "**Surely our griefs He Himself bore, and our sorrows He carried; yet we ourselves esteemed Him stricken, smitten of God, and afflicted.** But He was pierced through for our transgressions, He was crushed for our iniquities; the chastening for our well-being fell upon Him, and by His scourging we are healed."

Healed of what? Of the consequences of sin, which is death. "And He Himself bore our sins in His body on the cross, so that we might die to sin and live to righteousness; for by His wounds you were healed" (1 Peter 2:24).

What is Christmas? Christmas is God's sending His Son to become flesh and blood, to experience our sufferings, and to be "tempted in all things as we are, yet without sin" (Hebrews 4:15). Christmas is Jesus' being nailed to a cross where He paid for your sins and mine once for all!

Christmas is the promise of healing from sin for all who believe.

~

Help me, precious God, to walk in wholeness, knowing that Jesus already has endured all that is necessary for healing my inner man.

December 16

Hope, joy, anticipation, peace. These are the themes of the songs that permeate our homes, stores, and parties this time of year. The same themes crop up in Christmas specials on television, in magazine articles, and on Internet sites. Yet do you realize how many people are without joy, without peace, without hope? For many, perhaps even for you, Christmas simply means an extra day off work…an extra burden of things to do amid an already-packed schedule… incredible loneliness…disappointment.

Oh, precious one, let's change that. Let's abandon the world's version of Christmas. It's a fairy tale gone sour, centered on fleeting pleasures that cannot satisfy. Instead, let's embrace a Christmas centered on the hope that does not disappoint (Romans 5:5). The hope of peace with God. The hope of forgiveness of sins. The hope of relationship with One who will never forsake us. The hope of eternal life.

God sent His Son so that you and I might be washed, sanctified, declared righteous, set free of the despair that sin and iniquity bring, and become part of the body of Jesus Christ, the eternal family of God. "**He saved us, not on the basis of deeds which we have done in righteousness, but according to His mercy, by the washing of regeneration and renewing by the Holy Spirit, whom He poured out upon us richly through Jesus Christ our Savior, so that being justified by His grace we would be made heirs according to the hope of eternal life**" (Titus 3:5–7).

Did you notice the word *eternal*? This Christmas let's celebrate the things that last forever!

~

O Father, remind me to turn from the temporal to the eternal!

December 17

What a wonderful season this is supposed to be—but is it?

When you look around as you shop at the mall, talk with your colleagues at work, walk the halls of schools or the streets of your city, what do you see? What is the countenance on the faces you encounter? When you peer into the eyes of those around you, are those eyes bright and peaceful? Or are they dark with despair, pain, anger, or bitterness?

What do these dear souls need? They need Jesus. They need to know Him experientially. They need to understand who He is, why He came, where this Christmas holiday came from, and what it's really about. They need truth, not a lie. Reality, not a phantom substitute.

And who's going to help them? Who will offer what they need? What about you, my friend?

Mark 10:45 tells us Jesus' purpose in coming to earth: **"The Son of Man did not come to be served, but to serve, and to give His life a ransom for many."** The celebration of Christmas ought to serve as a reminder of our purpose as well, to do the works that He did—only greater (John 14:12).

Think of Christmas as the calling to be His witness to the people He puts in your path. Ask God to lead you to lost or wounded sheep in desperate need of the Shepherd of their souls. Lavishly show love in the name of Jesus, and serve the needs of others generously and willingly, without expecting anything in return. Fulfill your purpose, dear one.

~

Open my eyes and my heart, Lord, to those around me who need to be touched with the peace and joy of Christ. Lead me to serve them in the truth and power of Jesus' love.

December 18

Has Christmas—a holiday touted as a time of family and friends, of joy and hope, of singing and rejoicing—become instead a remembrance of your failures, of broken relationships? Oh, precious one, it can be changed from a season of pain to a season of new beginnings.

Christmas isn't just a holiday to be celebrated; it's an event to be experienced in a way that transforms our lives.

Jesus was born to die on the cross and to do away with the ineffective sacrifices we offer for our sins. These include the ways we try to appease God, the promises we make, the bargains we propose, our efforts to be good and to do good—none of which can ever take away our sins or the consciousness of our failures. All the New Year's resolutions in the world cannot cleanse our guilt or make us perfect.

Only Christ, the Promised One of Christmas, could provide the sacrifice that takes away our sins for all time. "**For by one offering He has perfected for all time those who are sanctified**" (Hebrews 10:14). The minute you are sanctified—set apart for God "through the offering of the body of Jesus Christ once for all" (Hebrews 10:10)—your sins are forgiven, your past is blotted out, and you have a brand-new beginning.

So what will you do this Christmas? Put away the pain, the failure, and mend the broken relationships as best you can. Say, "I'm sorry for the hurt that I've brought you. I've asked God to forgive me, and He has. Now I want you to forgive me. And if there's restitution to be made, I'll make it to the best of my ability." Restitution is the proof of repentance.

Gracious Lord, thank You for the opportunity to begin anew.

December 19

Are you having a hard time this Christmas season because you're missing a loved one? Are you overwhelmed by bittersweet memories of a happier time? Let's consider together the hope of reunion that Christmas brings.

Remember, Jesus came that we might have life and have it abundantly (John 10:10). God has given us eternal life—life that lasts forever and ever—in His Son (1 John 5:11).

Salvation is not just about this life; it's about the resurrection unto eternal life for every believer—a life without tears, pain, separation, or death. Jesus' victory over sin and death (Acts 2:24) means that we have the promise of resurrection from the dead if we have received Jesus Christ. In addition, 1 Thessalonians tells us that Jesus is coming again and He'll bring with Him all our loved ones who died in faith:

> **For if we believe that Jesus died and rose again, even so God will bring with Him those who have fallen asleep in Jesus....** For the Lord Himself will descend from heaven with a shout, with the voice of the archangel and with the trumpet of God, and the dead in Christ will rise first. Then we who are alive and remain will be caught up together with them in the clouds to meet the Lord in the air, and so we shall always be with the Lord. (4:14, 16–17)

In other words, one day you'll be reunited with every loved one who believed on the Lord Jesus Christ. This is the hope you have this Christmas, the hope of being with your loved one in the presence of God. Cling to it, beloved.

Thank You, God, for the comfort and hope of the resurrection.

December 20

Christmas is only five days away. Now things really get busy! Last-minute shopping is crowded in among parties, programs at church, decorating, giftwrapping, cooking, and cleaning. It's so very easy for the many urgent activities on our to-do lists to crowd out the truly important things.

But do you remember what it was like to be a child at Christmas? The tree, lights, gifts, and traditions, all leading to the anticipated culmination of opening presents with family gathered around? Do you remember the simple joy the Christmas season used to bring, the delight of considering that precious baby in the manger and hearing the captivating story of His birth? Shepherds and sheep gathering round, angels singing in the heavens, wise men following a star. What wonders to capture a child's heart and imagination!

Sadly, as adults we so often miss the wonder of the Christmas season. Yet Jesus said in Luke 18:17, **"Whoever does not receive the kingdom of God like a child will not enter it at all."** This Christmas, won't you allow the richness of the story to light your heart once more? Invite the Holy Spirit to rekindle that joy, that childlike faith and belief, as you come to Jesus anew and experience the excitement of truly knowing the One whose birth we celebrate.

May I suggest you put aside the to-do list for a while and focus on the priceless gift of that first Christmas?

~

Ask God to help you experience Christmas as a joyous time, a holy time, a time for awe-filled wonder.

December 21

In Isaiah 9:6 God gave His people a wonderful promise, the promise of Christmas: "**For a child will be born to us, a son will be given to us; and the government will rest on His shoulders; and His name will be called Wonderful Counselor, Mighty God, Eternal Father, Prince of Peace.**"

Jesus is our Jehovah-shalom, the Prince of Peace, the One who reconciles us to God, who enables us to stand in His grace before Him, face to face without fear. "Therefore, having been justified by faith, we have peace with God through our Lord Jesus Christ" (Romans 5:1).

He gives us a peace that does not alter, regardless of circumstances, because it resides always in the One who promised, " 'I will never desert you, nor will I ever forsake you,' so that we confidently say, 'The LORD is my helper, I will not be afraid. What will man do to me?' " (Hebrews 13:5–6).

Therefore, when others about us are fainting in fear, we can "exult in our tribulations, knowing that tribulation brings about perseverance; and perseverance, proven character; and proven character, hope; and hope does not disappoint" (Romans 5:3–5).

Remember, peace is found only in Jehovah-shalom. In the joyous yet busy Christmas season and in the trials of earthly life, He will keep you in perfect peace when your mind is stayed upon Him (Isaiah 26:3, KJV). So abide in Him, being filled with the Holy Spirit, whose fruit is peace.

~

Jehovah God, I thank You for the gift of peace that surpasses all comprehension (Philippians 4:7). When trials and temptations come, fill my mind and heart with the truth of Your protective, loving presence.

December 22

What's the most precious Christmas gift you could receive this year? I believe it would be God's awesome gift of hope.

We all need hope, and that's what Christmas is all about. Isaiah 9:2, anticipating the arrival of the Messiah, says, **"The people who walk in darkness will see a great light; those who live in a dark land, the light will shine on them."**

Christmas assures us that there's hope, beloved! Hope for those who are walking in darkness. Hope for the oppressed. Because of the events set in motion that first Christmas, we have the hope of forgiveness of sins, the hope of the resurrection, the hope of eternal life, the hope of reunion with loved ones, the hope of a helper for every situation of life, the hope of help in times of trial.

Because of Christmas, you have a counselor who cares, listens, and has the answers. Because of Christmas, you can roll your burdens onto the shoulders of the Mighty God, the ruler over all. Because of Christmas, you have an eternal Father, the ideal Father you've always desired. Because of Christmas, you have access to peace through the Prince of all Peace (Isaiah 9:6).

Precious one, where can you find hope this Christmas season? You'll find hope in understanding that the moment you received God's Christmas gift of Jesus Christ, He began to shine light into your life. The light of truth. And as you daily surrender to Him—totally, completely, and absolutely—you'll gain ever greater peace and hope.

~

Thank You for the hope that is mine because of the Christ of Christmas. O Father God, help me live today in His light.

December 23

What difference does Christmas make in you, beloved? Do you feel as if you're still a prisoner in a dungeon of your own making? shackled to your past or chained to your unrelenting passions, emotions, worries? Maybe you're angry, frustrated by the seeming injustices and disappointments of life. Maybe you've celebrated Christmas, dear one, but you've never really experienced it.

Luke 2 relates the story that so many of us traditionally read on Christmas Eve or Christmas Day. Let's look together at verses 6 and 7, which describe so simply and yet so memorably that scene in the stable in Bethlehem, where Mary and Joseph had traveled to register for the census: "While they were there, the days were completed for her to give birth. **And she gave birth to her firstborn son; and she wrapped Him in cloths, and laid Him in a manger, because there was no room for them in the inn.**"

The divine imagery is awesome. Did you know that *Bethlehem* means "house of bread"? And a manger is a feeding trough for animals? God laid our Christmas present—His own precious Son—in a feeding trough! Why? Because Jesus is the Bread of Life. Those who eat of Him live forever; they will never perish (John 6:50–51). Jesus nourishes and satisfies the longings of our souls.

Beloved, whatever the secret desires of your heart, whatever your circumstances, the Bread of Life offers you lasting satisfaction. Won't you let Him feed your soul this Christmas? You'll find in Him all you could ever want or need.

Lord, let my soul be filled with the presence of Jesus, who alone can satisfy my heart with gladness.

December 24

Christmas Eve! The wonder and splendor of the season comes to a crescendo tonight. All around the world Christians are gathering to recall the birth of our Lord.

Images come to mind: Mary and Joseph being turned away from one guesthouse after another; the pains of a woman about to give birth; Joseph trying to prepare a comfortable and clean setting in the midst of a dank stable.

Our pretty crèches with their clean straw and sweet animal figurines likely romanticize the events of that first Christmas. The manger where the newborn Jesus slept was probably made of stone; the stable, a cave. As you picture the scene, let your thoughts fast-forward thirty-three years to another cave, another place where Jesus was laid on stone, this time by Joseph of Arimathea: "Joseph took the body and wrapped it in a clean linen cloth, and laid it in his own new tomb, which he had hewn out in the rock; and he rolled a large stone against the entrance of the tomb and went away" (Matthew 27:59–60). The Lamb of God, sacrificed for your sins and mine, crucified and laid to rest in a borrowed tomb. That's the reason He was born, to die for your sins.

But—hallelujah!—just three days later His followers found that stone rolled away. Once again angels heralded the news: "**Do not be afraid; for I know that you are looking for Jesus who has been crucified. He is not here, for He has risen, just as He said**" (Matthew 28:5–6).

~

Prayerfully reflect on the full and wondrous meaning of Jesus' birth: God came in the form of man, born to die so you might live in the fullness of life.

December 25

My friend, I hope you've grasped the truth that Christmas is not just another holiday. It's not just remembering that a baby was born in a stable two millenniums ago.

Christmas is all about a baby who was laid in a manger with the shadow of a cross looming over it.

The baby laid in that manger is the Lamb of God who died to take care of your sins and mine. The Lamb of God who would hang on Calvary's cross. The Lamb of God whose blood would be a ransom, a payment to redeem you out of the slave market of sin. The Lamb of God who would die, be buried, and be raised again on the third day, never to die again. The Lamb of God who would say, "He who believes in Me will live even if he dies" (John 11:25).

Christmas is not found in presents or Santa Claus, beloved. It's not found in the tinsel of the world or the parties. Christmas is found in the Gift of gifts: the Lord Jesus Christ.

Is He the centerpiece of this day? Oh, beloved, slip away from everything and everyone for a few minutes and look in wonder at your gift—the Christ of Christmas—and then give thanks to God for the great love with which He has loved you: "**See how great a love the Father has bestowed on us, that we would be called children of God**" (1 John 3:1).

~

Joy to the world, the Lord is come! Thank You, holy God, that Jesus was born, that He willingly became flesh and blood to die for my sins. And thank You for the presence of the Holy Spirit and for the hope of eternal life—all the joys that I can experience because of the Christ of Christmas!

A Christmas Prayer

Lord, in Your wisdom
and loving concern
You sent Your Son
to become one with us,
to be born poor
and without shelter
to parents far away from home.
Bless all people this Christmas,
especially those in need.

Amen.

2014 December

21 Sunday

22 Monday

23 Tuesday

24 Wednesday

A Christmas Prayer

Lord, giver of all
good gifts,
at Christmas
we thank You
for the living gift
of Jesus, Your Son —
in darkness, a light,
a shining lamp at night —
who dwells in our hearts
and our homes. Amen.

2015 December

20 Sunday

21 Monday

22 Tuesday

23 Wednesday

December 26

They say the day after Christmas is the greatest shopping day of the year. You would think we'd had enough of the things of this life! Yet we always seem to want something more, something new.

The word *new* carries an element of hope, doesn't it? Well, New Year's is coming. How about making this a year of lasting newness, of continual hope? What might happen, beloved, if your life, beginning today, centered not on the world's newest or latest great thing but on reveling in all that is new to us because we belong to Christ?

There's the new self—what you became when you received the Christ of Christmas. "**[You] have put on the new self who is being renewed to a true knowledge according to the image of the One who created him**" (Colossians 3:10). This new self "has been created in righteousness and holiness of the truth" (Ephesians 4:24). The new self also includes a new mind, a mind tuned to truth. You're able to appraise things to see if they're true because you "have the mind of Christ" (1 Corinthians 2:15–16).

Colossians tells us to "set your mind on the things above, not on the things that are on earth" (3:2). Why not make it your goal this year to study some portions of the Bible that you've never really studied before? Discover new insights, new precepts, new promises as you study book by book.[10] It will give you a new appreciation of what it means to be His and will keep you from being caught up in the world.

O Father, make this next year a time of unsurpassed hope and renewal as I seek the riches of Your truth.

December 27

As we think about our goals and dreams for the coming year, let's remember that someday everything on earth will be destroyed. Every record of human accomplishment, every impressive monument, everything made with human hands will be dissolved by fire:

> **But the day of the Lord will come like a thief, in which the heavens will pass away with a roar and the elements will be destroyed with intense heat, and the earth and its works will be burned up.** Since all these things are to be destroyed in this way, what sort of people ought you to be in holy conduct and godliness. (2 Peter 3:10–11)

Only that which was done by the Spirit of God will abide. These will become our treasures in heaven—the things we have done by the Spirit in accordance with the Word of God and for God's glory.

Oh, that the eyes of our understanding would be open so that we would not give our time and energies to accumulating earthly treasures!

What do you and I really treasure? Do we care more about the applause of the world or the approval of God? Are we in danger of becoming entangled with the affairs of this life? The more comfortable we become, the harder it is to remember that we're only sojourners and pilgrims upon this earth and our citizenship is in heaven (1 Peter 2:11, NKJV; Philippians 3:20).

I must ask you, my friend, where is your focus? Upon what have you set your heart and affections?

~

Take a few minutes to think about what distracts you from pure devotion to Jesus Christ. Then ask God what to do about it.

December 28

Deciding to lay up treasures in heaven rather than on earth is great preparation for the new year, but in the next few months, how will we handle the seductiveness of things that would consume our energies and draw us away from undistracted devotion to our God? We find Jesus' answer to this question in Matthew 6:22–23: "**The eye is the lamp of the body; so then if your eye is clear, your whole body will be full of light. But if your eye is bad, your whole body will be full of darkness.**"

The problem is our eyes; they're a path of seduction. It's a problem as old as the Garden of Eden. Eve's downfall came when she took her focus off God and put it on the fruit of the tree of the knowledge of good and evil: "When the woman saw that the tree was good for food, and that it was a delight to the eyes, and that the tree was desirable to make one wise, she took from its fruit and ate; and she gave also to her husband with her, and he ate" (Genesis 3:6).

Do you see the progression in this verse? Eve saw, desired, took, ate...and gave it to another.

Is it any wonder Jesus tells us that the lamp of the body is the eye? Our eyes are the windows that let light into our bodies. Clean windows let in more light. Dirty windows obscure the light. Our eyes, therefore, determine the amount of light that comes into our bodies.

How clean are the windows to your soul today?

Lord, I want to walk before You in integrity, keeping my eyes focused on You and Your holy way. With the psalmist David, I commit to "set no worthless thing before my eyes" (Psalm 101:3).

December 29

Beloved, as we seek to walk through this day—and the coming year—in faith, Jesus Christ, the Author and Perfecter of faith, serves as our glorious example (Hebrews 12:2). You and I must fix our eyes on Him, observing how He walked in total poverty of spirit. Remember, Jesus was God, the mighty Sovereign of the universe. And yet while He walked on earth as a man, He lived in total dependence on God.

It's interesting to note that before Jesus Christ ever began His public ministry, He was baptized because He wanted to "fulfill all righteousness."

> Then Jesus arrived from Galilee at the Jordan coming to John, to be baptized by him. But John tried to prevent Him, saying, "I have need to be baptized by You, and do You come to me?" But Jesus answering said to him, **"Permit it at this time; for in this way it is fitting for us to fulfill all righteousness."** (Matthew 3:13–15)

At Jesus' baptism the Spirit of God descended upon Him as a dove, and a voice spoke out of the heavens saying, "This is My beloved Son, in whom I am well-pleased" (Matthew 3:17).

If we want to please God, we are to walk as Jesus walked. As He was totally dependent upon the Spirit, so we must depend on Him as well. The words we speak are to be God's words. The works we do are to be His works. All our activities are to be directed by the Spirit of God.

Teach me to walk in the steps of Jesus my Savior, in full dependence on the power and guidance of the Holy Spirit. Fill me with Your wisdom so my works and words, attitudes and actions will be directed by You.

December 30

If you are following Jesus and walking in the light, what will your life look like? Jesus said, **"I am the Light of the world; he who follows Me will not walk in the darkness, but will have the Light of life"** (John 8:12). So if you're following Him, your life will shine with "the Light of life." Christ in you, the hope of glory, will be evident in your every word, your every action, your every attitude and response—especially in the midst of difficult circumstances.

As you face the year ahead, remember that you are the light of the world. And the world sees the difference when you...

walk in poverty of spirit,
mourn over sin,
bow in submission before His sovereignty,
walk in true meekness before God and man,
hunger and thirst for righteousness,
and count it all joy when you are persecuted for righteousness.

When you consistently live in this way, your life will truly reflect Jesus. The proof of your faith, even though tested by fire, will result in praise and glory and honor. Your light will help dispel the darkness that threatens to cover your corner of the world.

So seek Him with all your heart, soul, mind, and strength. In His love and by His power, you and I can light up this dark, despairing world!

Make me perfect even as You are perfect, dear Father in heaven. Guide my footsteps that I may closely follow the example of Jesus and bring His light to a world blinded by sin.

December 31

As you prepare your heart for a new year, won't you make it your goal to walk in poverty of spirit? To do so means that you abide in the Vine and allow the life of the Vine, by God's Spirit, to flow through you so that you might bear fruit. **"I am the vine, you are the branches; he who abides in Me and I in him, he bears much fruit, for apart from Me you can do nothing"** (John 15:5).

To walk in poverty of spirit is to live out the truth of Philippians 2:12–13: "So then, my beloved, just as you have always obeyed, not as in my presence only, but now much more in my absence, work out your salvation with fear and trembling; for it is God who is at work in you, both to will and to work for His good pleasure."

To "work out your salvation" means to carry out to completion that which God desires to accomplish in you. And He will not only give you the ability to do it; He will give you the will to do it. For this reason, walking in poverty of spirit means allowing God to have full rein within your life. To control you. It means going where He wants you to go. Saying all He wants you to say. Being all He wants you to be.

The bottom line? Those who are poor in spirit walk in total dependence upon God. Does that describe your life, as you read these words?

If your life does not reflect a poverty of spirit that leads you to walk in complete dependence on the Holy Spirit, confess to God that you have been walking apart from Him. Ask your Creator and Redeemer to transform your heart and your attitude. Then release the reins of your life into His hands.

Notes

1. Kay Arthur, *Beloved: From God's Heart to Yours* (Eugene, OR: Harvest House, 1995), 176.

2. J. Dwight Pentecost, *The Sermon on the Mount: Contemporary Insights for a Christian Lifestyle* (Portland, OR: Multnomah, 1982), 127.

3. Charles R. Erdman, *The Epistle of Paul to the Ephesians* (Philadelphia: Westminster Press), 53.

4. Paraphrased from Dorothy Gawne Coslet, *Madame Jeanne Guyon: Child of Another World* (Fort Washington, PA: Christian Literature Crusade, 1984). Used by permission.

5. Poem by Madame Guyon. Printed source unknown.

6. Pamela Rosewell, *The Five Silent Years of Corrie ten Boom* (Grand Rapids: Zondervan, 1986), 85.

7. W. E. Vine, *An Expository Dictionary of New Testament Words,* vol. 3 (Old Tappan, NJ: Revell, 1966), 207.

8. Robert A. Guelich, *Sermon on the Mount: A Foundation for Understanding* (Waco, TX: Word, 1982).

9. James Orr, ed., *The International Standard Bible Encyclopedia,* vol. 2 (1939; reprint, Grand Rapids: Eerdmans, 1976), 1291.

10. Precept Ministries International has wonderful tools to help you discover truth for yourself. Go online at precept.org, or call 1-800-763-8280.

Personal Pages

Personal Pages

Personal Pages

Personal Pages

Personal Pages

About Kay Arthur and Precept Ministries International

KAY ARTHUR, executive vice president and cofounder of Precept Ministries International, is known around the world as a Bible teacher, author, conference speaker, and host of national radio and television programs.

Kay and her husband, Jack, founded Precept Ministries in 1970 in Chattanooga, Tennessee. Started as a fledgling ministry for teens, Precept today is a worldwide outreach that establishes children, teens, and adults in God's Word so they can discover the Bible's truths for themselves. Precept's inductive Bible studies are taught in all fifty states. The studies have been translated into sixty-six languages, reaching 120 countries.

Kay is the author of more than 120 books and inductive Bible study courses, with a total of more than five million books in print. Four of her books have received the ECPA Gold Medallion book award. She is sought after by groups throughout the world as an inspiring Bible teacher and conference speaker. Kay is also well known globally through her daily and weekly television programs.

Contact Precept Ministries for more information about inductive Bible studies in your area.

Precept Ministries International
P.O. Box 182218
Chattanooga, TN 37422-7218
800-763-8280
www.precept.org